EGYPTIAN ARABIC

A ROUGH GUIDE DICTIONARY PHRASEBOOK

D1352394

Compiled by

LEXUS

Credits

Compiled by Lexus with Ahmed M.A. Abdel-Hady
Lexus Series Editor: Sally Davies
Rough Guides Phrasebook Editor: Jonathan Buckley
Rough Guides Series Editor: Mark Ellingham

First edition published in 1998 by Rough Guides Ltd,
5th Floor, 80 Strand, London WC2R 0RL.
Revised in November 2002.

Distributed by the Penguin Group.

Penguin Books Ltd, 80 Strand, London WC2R 0RL
Penguin Books USA Inc., 375 Hudson Street, New York 10014, USA
Penguin Books Australia Ltd, 487 Maroondah Highway,
PO Box 257, Ringwood, Victoria 3134, Australia
Penguin Books Canada Ltd, Alcorn Avenue,
Toronto, Ontario, Canada M4V 1E4
Penguin Books (NZ) Ltd, 182–190 Wairau Road,
Auckland 10, New Zealand

Typeset in Bembo and Helvetica to an original design by Henry Iles.
Printed in Spain by Graphy Cems.

British Library Cataloguing in Publication Data
A catalogue for this book is available from the British Library.

ISBN 1-84353-174-7

HELP US GET IT RIGHT

Lexus and Rough Guides have made great efforts to be accurate and
informative in this Rough Guide Egyptian Arabic phrasebook. However, if
you feel we have overlooked a useful word or phrase, or have any other
comments to make about the book, please let us know. All contributors
will be acknowledged and the best letters will be rewarded with a free
Rough Guide phrasebook of your choice. Please write to 'Egyptian Arabic
Phrasebook Update', at either Strand (London) or Hudson Street (New
York) – for full addresses see above. Alternatively you can email us at
mail@roughguides.co.uk

Online information about Rough Guides can be found at our website
www.roughguides.com

CONTENTS

Introduction

The Rough Guide Egyptian Arabic phrasebook is a highly practical introduction to the contemporary language. Laid out in clear A-Z style, it uses key-word referencing to lead you straight to the words and phrases you want – so if you need to book a room, just look up 'room'. The Rough Guide gets straight to the point in every situation, in bars and shops, on trains and buses, and in hotels and banks.

The first part of the Rough Guide is a section called **Basics**, which sets out the fundamental rules of the language and its pro-nunciation, with plenty of practical examples. You'll also find here other essentials like numbers, dates, telling the time and basic phrases.

Forming the heart of the guide, the **English-Arabic** section gives easy-to-use transliterations of the Arabic words plus the text in Arabic script, so that if the pronunciation proves too tricky, you can simply indicate what you want to say. To get you involved quickly in two-way communication, the Rough Guide also includes dialogues featuring typical responses on key topics – such as renting a room and asking directions. Feature boxes fill you in on cultural pitfalls as well as the simple mechanics of how to make a phone call, what to do in an emergency, where to change money, and more. Throughout this section, cross-references enable you to pinpoint key facts and phrases, while asterisked words indi-cate where further information can be found in Basics.

The **Arabic-English** section is in two parts: a dictionary, arranged phonetically, of all the words and phrases you're likely to hear (starting with a section of slang and colloquialisms); then a compilation, arranged by subject, of many of the signs, labels, instructions and other basic words you might come across in print or in public places.

Finally the Rough Guide rounds off with an extensive **Menu Reader**. Consisting of food and drink sections arranged by sub-ject (each starting with a list of essential terms), it's indispensable whether you're eating out, stopping for a quick drink, or brows-ing through a local food market.

رحلة سعيدة!
reHla saAeeda!
have a good trip!

5

Basics

Pronunciation

Throughout this book, Arabic words have been transliterated into romanized form so that they can be read as though they were English bearing in mind the notes on pronunciation given below:

Vowels

a	as in **a**t
ā	longer **a** as in c**a**r
ay	as in s**ay**
e	as in b**e**d
ee	as in s**ee**
i	as in b**i**t
ī	sounds like **eye** or like the **ai** in Th**ai**
o	as in h**o**t
ō	**oa** as in m**oa**n
ow	as in n**ow**

Consonants

h	is always pronounced, except in the following combinations: gh, kh and sh
j	as in **j**am
J	like the **s** in lei**s**ure
kh	like the **ch** in the Scottish word lo**ch**
r	strongly rolled **r**
s	as in mi**ss**

When double consonants such as **bb** or **mm** occur, both letters should be pronounced.

Capitals D, S, T and Z are like d, s, t and z only more heavily pronounced.

Special Sounds

A	**aargh** sound, said from the throat, a heavy forced **a**
gh	like a French **r**
H	an emphatic **h**, said from the back of the throat
Q	similar to an emphatic pronunciation of 'cu' as in **cu**t, said from the back of the throat

'   a glottal stop, similar to that heard in regional forms
     of English when the letter 't' is not pronounced; for
     example, 'wa'er' for 'water'.

Q and ' represent the same letter in Egyptian Arabic, known
as the 'qaf'; however, when represented by Q, it is more
strongly pronounced.

Letters given in bold type indicate the part of the word to
be stressed.

An asterisk next to a word in the English-Arabic section
means that you should refer to the Basics section for further
information.

Abbreviations

adj	adjective	m	masculine
f	feminine	pl	plural
lit	literally	sing	singular

Arabic and the Arabic alphabet

Classical Arabic, the universal written language of the entire
Arabic-speaking world, is rarely spoken. Colloquial Arabic is
the spoken language and its grammar, pronunciation and
vocabulary vary between countries. The colloquial Arabic
used in this book is Egyptian.

Arabic is written from right to left. Each letter of the alphabet has up to four different forms: one where it stands alone,
one at the beginning of a word, one in the middle of a word
and one when it is the final letter. The alphabet as listed
below consists almost entirely of consonants; Arabic words
do not contain written short vowels (although the long
vowels are written). Words consist of a string of consonants
and the Arabic speaker knows from experience how the
vowels must be added in speech to make sense. Sometimes,
therefore, the same written word can often be pronounced
in more than one way, but usually only one version makes
sense in a particular context.

Isolated	Initial	Medial	Final	Pronounced
أ	أ ـ	ا	ا	a
ب	بـ	ـبـ	ـب	b
ت	تـ	ـتـ	ـت	t
ث	ثـ	ـثـ	ـث	t or s
ج	جـ	ـجـ	ـج	g
ح	حـ	ـحـ	ـح	H
خ	خـ	ـخـ	ـخ	kh
د			ـد	d
ذ			ـذ	z or d
ر			ـر	r
ز			ـز	z
س	سـ	ـسـ	ـس	s
ش	شـ	ـشـ	ـش	sh
ص	صـ	ـصـ	ـص	S
ض	ضـ	ـضـ	ـض	D
ط	طـ	ـطـ	ـط	T
ظ	ظـ	ـظـ	ـظ	Z
ع	عـ	ـعـ	ـع	A
غ	غـ	ـغـ	ـغ	gh
ف	فـ	ـفـ	ـف	f
ق	قـ	ـقـ	ـق	Q or '
ك	كـ	ـكـ	ـك	k
ل	لـ	ـلـ	ـل	l
م	مـ	ـمـ	ـم	m
ن	نـ	ـنـ	ـن	n
ة ه	هـ	ـهـ	ة ـه	h
و			ـو	w
ى	يـ	ـيـ	ـى	y

Nouns

Gender

All Arabic nouns have one of two genders – masculine or feminine. Most nouns ending in **-a** are feminine:

maktaba	**ahwa**	**garsona**
library	coffee; café	waitress

Some nouns that do not end in **-a** are feminine:

bint	**omm**	**shams**	**floos**
girl	mother	sun	money

The names of many countries, cities and parts of the body are feminine:

maSr	**aswān**	**TanTa**
Egypt	Aswan	Tanta

rās	**rigl**	**eed**
head	leg	hand

Feminine nouns that do not end in **-a** and are not obviously feminine are marked (f) in the English–Arabic section of this book.

Some masculine nouns end in **-a**; these are also indicated in the English–Arabic section:

howa
air (m)

All other nouns that do not end in **-a** or fall into the above categories can be assumed to be masculine.

Construct Form

Some rules require the final **-a** of a feminine noun to be replaced by **-it** when two nouns are used together. This is known as the construct form:

taraba**yza**	**akl**	**tarab**a**yzit el akl**
table	food	the food table

tazkara	**Tīyāra**	**t**a**zkarit el Tīyāra**
ticket	plane	the plane ticket

The construct form is also used to form the plural of some words (see below); it is also used with possessive suffixes (see page 20).

Plurals of Nouns

There are three types of plural in Arabic: the dual, the standard and the collective plural.

Dual Plural

This is used when referring to two of anything. It is formed by adding a suffix to the singular form of the noun.

To form the dual plural of masculine nouns and feminine nouns that do not end in **-a**, add **-ayn** to the noun:

ma**t-Haf**	**m**a**t-Hafayn**
museum	two museums

aTr	**a**Trayn
train	two trains

To form the dual plural of feminine nouns ending in **-a**, remove the final **-a** and add **-tayn**:

eza**za**	**ez**a**ztayn**
bottle	two bottles

ma**drasa**	**m**a**drastayn**
school	two schools

Aarab**ayy**a	Aarab**ay**tayn
car	two cars

For some nouns, the dual plural is formed by adding **-ayn** to the construct form:

13

sha'a	**sha'itayn**
apartment	two apartments
gizma	**gizmitayn**
shoe	two shoes

Standard Plural

To form this, add **-een** to masculine nouns:

farrān	**farraneen**
baker	bakers

Add **-t** to feminine nouns and change the final **a** to **ā**:

magalla	**magallāt**
magazine	magazines

Collective Plural

This plural is used to describe a whole class or group of items and it mostly occurs with fruit and vegetables collectively and generally. The collective plural of fruit and vegetables is more widely used than the singular or standard plural. If you need to refer to a singular item, you can do so by adding **-a** to the collective form:

toffāH (pl)	**toffāHa** (sing)
apples	an apple
khayār	**khayāra**
cucumbers	a cucumber

The singular and standard plural forms of these types of noun are only used if it is necessary to specify the number of items:

collective plural	singular	standard plural
mishmish	**mishmisha**	**talat mishmishāt**
apricots	an apricot	three apricots

Further examples of the collective form are:

bayD	**samak**	**shaAr**	**shagar**
eggs	fish	hair	trees

14

Irregular Plurals

Many Arabic nouns have irregular plurals. Here is a list of the most common ones:

singular		plural	
shanTa	bag	shonaT	bags
'bank'	bank	bnook	banks
sireer	bed	sarāyer	beds
Hizām	belt	Hizima	belts
kitāb	book	kotob	books
walad	boy	welād	boys
akh	brother	ekhwāt	brothers
gamal	camel	gimāl	camels
korsee	chair	karāsee	chairs
sigāra	cigarette	sagāyer	cigarettes
sitāra	curtain	satāyer	curtains
yōm	day	īyām	days
sāHib	friend	SoHāb	friends
bint	girl	banāt	girls
fondo'	hotel	fanādi'	hotels
bayt	house	byoot	houses
moftāH	key	mafāteeH	keys
gowāb	letter	gowabāt	letters
rāgil	man	riggāla	men
de'ee'a	minute	da'āye'	minutes
shahr	month	shihoor	months
gāmiA	mosque	gawāmiA	mosques
mat-Haf	museum	matāHif	museums
ism	name	asāmee	names
maktab	office	makātib	offices
Taba'	plate	aTba'	plates
ōDa	room	ewaD	rooms
TābeA	stamp	TawābeA	stamps
shāriA	street	shawāriA	streets
Tālib	student	Talaba	students
tazkara	ticket	tazākir	tickets
madeena	town	modon	towns
aTr	train	'oTora	trains
isbooA	week	asābeeA	weeks

Articles

The definite article (the) is **el**:

magalla	**el magalla**
magazine	the magazine

When the noun begins with **d, D, n, r, s, S, sh, t, T, z** or **Z**, the **l** is omitted from **el** and the initial consonant of the noun is lengthened. This change is optional for the letters **g** and **k**.

Some examples of nouns where **el** is assimilated:

SobH	**eS-SobH**	**Taboor**	**eT-Taboor**
morning	the morning	queue	the queue

The form of **el** also changes when it is used with some prepositions:

bee (by) + **el** = **bil**		**lee** (to) + **el** = **lil**	
bil gow	by air	**lil maTār**	to the airport
		lil fondo'	to the hotel
fee (in; per) + **el** = **fil**		**lil o'Sor**	to Luxor
fil baHr	in the sea		
fil maya	per cent	**Aala** (on) + **el** = **Aalal**	
fil ezāza	per bottle	**Aalal blāj**	on the beach
		Aalal korsee	on the chair

There is no indefinite article in Arabic. For example:

fondo' can mean 'hotel' or 'a hotel'

magalla can mean 'magazine' or 'a magazine'

Adjectives

Adjectives come after the noun they describe and agree with the noun in gender and number. The masculine form of the adjective is given in the English-Arabic and Arabic-English sections of this book. The feminine of adjectives is formed by adding **-a** to the masculine:

masculine	feminine	
be**A**eed	be**A**eeda	far
ke**beer**	ke**beera**	big

el mat-Haf beA**eed**
the museum is far

el gamA**a be**A**eeda**
the university is far

bayt kebeer**
a big house

sha'a kebeera**
a big apartment

Adjectives ending in **-ee** (for example, adjectives of nationality) change as shown below for the feminine:

masculine	feminine	
amrek**ā**nee	amrekan**aya**	American
A**a**rabee	Aarab**aya**	Arab
ostr**ā**lee	ostral**aya**	Australian
kana**dee**	kanad**aya**	Canadian
ma**S**ree	ma**S**raya	Egyptian
ingl**ee**zee	ingleez**aya**	English

If you use **awee** (very) with an adjective then this always follows the adjective it refers to:

el aTr saree**A awee**
the train is very quick

If the definite article is used then it must be repeated in front of the adjective(s) that refer to the noun:

el maH**atta er-ra'ees**aya**
the main station

el mat-Haf el Qowmee**
the national museum

el gizma es-sō**da**
the black shoes

Plural Adjectives

If a plural noun refers to people then the plural form of the adjective must be used. To form this, add **-een** to the singular adjective:

sing	plural	
m**o**m**tāz**	m**o**m**tāzeen**	excellent
T**a**bb**ā**kheen mo**m**t**ā**z**een**		excellent chefs

If a plural noun refers to inanimate objects, the feminine singular form of the adjective must be used (irrespective of the gender of the noun):

feminine	b**y**oot keb**ee**ra	big houses
masculine	otobees**ā**t sar**ee**Aa	fast buses

A dual plural noun should always be followed by a plural adjective, for example:

a'lam**ay**n kob**ā**r   two large pens

Irregular Plural Adjectives

Many plural adjectives are irregular. Here is a list of the most common ones:

singular	plural	
gam**ee**l	gom**ā**l	beautiful
rekh**ee**S	rokh**ā**S	cheap
neD**ee**f	noD**ā**f	clean
al**ee**l	ol**ā**l	few
keb**ee**r	kob**ā**r	large
ad**ee**m	od**ā**m	old (objects, buildings etc)
aHmar	Homr	red
Sogh**ī**yar	Sogh**ā**r	small
shed**ee**d	shod**ā**d	strong

Comparatives and Superlatives

The comparative (more expensive, bigger etc) and superlative (best, biggest etc) forms of the adjective are the same in Arabic. They do not change according to either gender or number.

Some common comparatives and superlatives are as follows:

adjective		comparative/superlative	
weHesh	bad	**awHash**	worse/worst
gameel	beautiful	**agmal**	more/most beautiful
kebeer	big	**akbar**	bigger/biggest
rekheeS	cheap	**arkhaS**	cheaper/cheapest
ghālee	expensive	**aghla**	more/most expensive
beAeed	far	**abAad**	further/furthest
kwayis	good	**aHsan**	better/best
keteer	many	**aktar**	more/most
Helw	nice; pretty	**aHla**	nicer/nicest; prettier/prettiest
Soghīyar	small	**aSgHar**	smaller/smallest

shemmāma akbar	**el shemmāma el akbar**
a bigger melon	the bigger/biggest melon

To compare two things, use the comparative form of the adjective and **min** (than):

abAad min	**aswān abAad min asyooT**
further than	Aswan is further (away) than Asiut

Demonstratives

Demonstrative pronouns and adjectives are as follows:

- **da** this (one); that (one) (m sing)
- **dee** this (one); that (one) (f sing); these; those (referring to objects or animals)
- **dōl** these; those (referring to people)

Demonstratives agree in number and gender with the noun they refer to. The word order when using demonstratives is:

el + noun + demonstrative adjective

el gamal da	**el ezāza dee**
this/that camel	this/that bottle

es-sowā'een dōl
these/those drivers

es-settat dōl
these/those women

el Hīwanāt dee
these/those animals

When the gender of a demonstrative is uncertain, then either **dee** or **da** may be used:

dee/da aHsan
that's better

momkin akhod dee/da?
can I have that one?

Possessives

Possessive adjectives are not separate words in Arabic; they are in the form of suffixes that are added to the noun to indicate the possessive. They are added either to a masculine noun or to the construct form of a feminine noun (see page 12).

The possessive suffixes are:

-ee	my	**-ha**	her
-ak	your (m sing)	**-na**	our
-ik	your (f sing)	**-koo**	your (pl)
-oo	his	**-hom**	their

alamee
my pen

tazkartak
your ticket
(said to a man)

tazkartik
your ticket
(said to a woman)

Aarabayyitna
our car

bayt-hom
their house

Possession can also be expressed using **btāA** (of). There are different forms of **btāA**, depending on whether the object possessed is masculine or feminine. These forms are also used to express the possessive pronoun (mine, yours etc):

m object	f object	
btāAee	btaAtee	my; mine
btāAak	btaAtak	your; yours (to a man)
btāAik	btaAtik	your; yours (to a woman)
btāAoo	btaAtoo	his
btaAha	btaAit-ha	her; hers
btaAna	btaAitna	our; ours
btaakoo	btaAitkoo	your; yours (pl)
btaAhom	btaAit-hom	their; theirs

The word order is: definite article + noun + btāA

el gizma btaAtee
my shoe; the shoe is mine

el korsee btāAee
my chair; the chair is mine

dee btaAtee! (f)
that/this is mine!

el kitāb btāAee
my book; the book is mine

el bayt btāAee
my house; the house is mine

btāA should only be used for objects and animals, not when referring to people. For example, to say 'my father' you must use the suffix form of the possessive on page 20. **btāA** should always be used with any word that originates from a foreign language:

el forsha btaAtee
my toothbrush

Pronouns

Subject Pronouns

Subject pronouns are as follows:

ana	I	**hay**ya	she; it
inta	you (m sing)	**eH**na	we
inti	you (f sing)	**in**too	you (pl)
howa	he; it	**hom**ma	they

In Arabic, subject pronouns may be omitted when the form of the verb makes it obvious who the subject of the sentence is. **ana** (I) is most likely to be omitted:

> **katabt**   I wrote

Direct and Indirect Object Pronouns

Direct object (me, you etc) or indirect object (to me, to you etc) personal pronouns in Arabic are in the form of suffixes that are added to the verb:

direct object		indirect object	
-ee	me	**-nee**	to me
-ak	you (m sing)	**-lak**	to you (m sing)
-ik	you (f sing)	**-lik**	to you (f sing)
-oo	him; it	**-loo**	to him; to it
-ha	her; it	**-lha**	to her; to it
-na	us	**-lina**	to us
-koo	you (pl)	**-likoo**	to you (pl)
-hom	them	**-lihom**	to them

sallimt Aalayhom   **baHebboo/baHebbaha** (m/f)
I greeted them   I like it

Haddeelak/Haddeelik el waHda bekhamsa geneeh
(to man/woman)
I'll give it to you for five pounds

When a sentence contains both direct and indirect object pronouns, the word order is the same as in English:

verb + direct object + indirect object

eddeehanee!
give it to me!

Pronouns and Prepositions

Pronoun suffixes are often added to prepositions. The suffixes vary depending on whether the preposition ends in a consonant or a vowel:

Aalashān	for	**maAa**	with
Aalashānee	for me	**maAāya**	with me
Aalashānak	for you (m sing)	**maAāk**	with you (m sing)
Aalashānik	for you (f sing)	**maAāik**	with you (f sing)
Aalashānoo	for him	**maAāh**	with him
Aalashanha	for her	**maAāha**	with her
Aalashanna	for us	**maAāna**	with us
Aalashankoo	for you (pl)	**maAākoo**	with you (pl)
Aalashanhom	for them	**maAāhom**	with them

The same endings can be used with these words:

min	**zay**	**Aala**
from	like	on; against; for

da minnoo	**hayya Taweela zayik**	**da Aalashanhom?**
that's from him	she's tall like you	is that for them?

'Of'

Phrases such as 'the name of the street' are expressed as follows:

noun (possessed) + el + noun (possessor)

ism esh-shāriA
the name of the street

Ainwān el mat-Haf
the address of the museum

raQam el otobees
the number of the bus

Feminine nouns that are possessed are in the construct form (see page 12):

shanTit el bint
the girl's bag

To make the phrase indefinite, omit the definite article:

Hettit Aaysh
a piece of bread

maHaTTit otobees
a bus stop

Verbs

Basic Verb Forms

There is no infinitive (to do, to buy etc) in Arabic. Instead, the basic form of the verb (the root) is the perfect tense of the third person masculine singular. This form is shown in the first column in the table of Arabic verbs below.

Where in English sentences you would use an infinitive, in Arabic both verbs must agree with the subject of the sentence:

Aīzeen nakol
we want to eat

The table shows the basic form of the verb (third person masculine singular, perfect tense) and the first person singular of the two Arabic tenses (see pages 25–27):

third person sing, perfect	first person sing, imperfect	first person sing, perfect	
sa'al	**as'al**	**sa'alt**	ask
kan		**kont**	be*
edir	**a'dar**	**edirt**	be able to
bada'	**abda'**	**bada't**	begin
gab	**ageeb**	**gibt**	bring
ishtara	**ashteree**	**ishtarayt**	buy
ga	**'āgee**	**gayt**	come*
sharab	**ashrab**	**sharabt**	drink
kal	**'ākol**	**kalt**	eat
edda	**addee**	**iddayt**	give
rāH	**arooH**	**roHt**	go*
	Aandee		have*
Aaraf	**aAraf**	**Aaraft**	know
Hab	**aHebb**	**Habbayt**	like; love
boSS	**aboSS**	**baSSayt**	look

third person sing, perfect	first person sing, imperfect	first person sing, perfect	
Aamal	aAmil	Aamalt	make; do
HaT	aHoT	HaTayt	put
'āl	a'ool	olt	say; tell
shāf	ashoof	shoft	see
nām	anām	nimt	sleep
itkallim	atkallim	kallimt	speak
khad	ākhod	khat	take
fakkar	afakkar	fakkart	think
fehim	afham	fehimt	understand*
mishee	imshee	mishayt	walk; go away
Aāz	aAyiz	Aozt	want*
ishtaghal	ashtaghal	ishtaghalt	work

* see pages 28–30

Tenses

There are only two true tenses of the verb in Arabic: the imperfect (indicates incomplete action in the present or the future) and the perfect (indicates completed action in the past). Whether the present or future is meant, is indicated by the different prefixes added to the imperfect verb form.

Imperfect Tense

The imperfect tense is used to make general statements and is formed by adding prefixes and suffixes to the verb stem. To obtain the verb stem, remove the initial **a-** from the first person singular imperfect form in the table above:

ashrab (I drink) gives the stem **-shrab**

The basic conjugation is obtained by adding the following prefixes and suffixes to the stem.

verb stem -**shrab**

prefix/suffix

a-	**a**shrab	I drink
ti-	**ti**shrab	you drink (m sing)
ti-...-ee	**ti**shrab**ee**	you drink (f sing)
yi-	**yi**shrab	he drinks
ti-	**ti**shrab	she drinks
ni-	**ni**shrab	we drink
ti-...-oo	**ti**shrab**oo**	you drink (pl)
yi-...-oo	**yi**shrab**oo**	they drink

You will find that sometimes the first vowel of the verb is pronounced or transliterated as **e** or **i** in different verbs, depending on the actual sound of the word.

Present Usage

The imperfect conjugation is used for the equivalent of the present tense. The prefix **bi-** is added to the forms of the imperfect tense to indicate that the action is taking place in the present:

verb stem -**shrab**

biashrab	I am drinking
bitishrab	you are drinking (m sing)
bitishrab**ee**	you are drinking (f sing)
biyishrab	he is drinking
bitishrab	she is drinking
binishrab	we are drinking
bitishrab**oo**	you are drinking (pl)
biyishrab**oo**	they are drinking

Future Usage

To indicate that an action will take place in the future, use the imperfect conjugation as above and modify it as follows, adding the prefix **Ha-**:

verb stem **-shrab**

H**a**shrab	I will drink
Hat**i**shrab	you will drink (m sing)
Hat**i**shrabee	you will drink (f sing)
H**ī**shrab	he will drink
Hat**i**shrab	she will drink
Han**i**shrab	we will drink
Hat**i**shraboo	you will drink (pl)
H**ī**shraboo	they will drink

Perfect Tense

The perfect tense is used to indicate completed action in the past. It is the equivalent of the simple past and the perfect tense in English. Therefore, '**ana kallimtoo**' translates as 'I spoke to him' or 'I have spoken to him' depending on the context.

The perfect tense is formed by adding suffixes to the third person masculine singular form.

Most verbs follow the pattern of the perfect conjugation below:

verb stem **katab-**
suffix

suffix		
-t	kat**a**bt	I wrote, I have written
-t	kat**a**bt	you wrote, you have written (m sing)
-tee	kat**a**btee	you wrote, you have written (f sing)
	kat**a**b	he wrote, he has written
-it	kat**a**bit	she wrote, she has written
-na	kat**a**bna	we wrote, we have written
-too	kat**a**btoo	you wrote, you have written (pl)
-oo	kat**a**boo	they wrote, you have written

Exceptions are the verbs 'give', 'like' and 'put'. For these, remove **-ayt** from the forms in the perfect column on pages 24–25 to obtain the verb stem and then add the following suffixes:

verb stem **idd-**

suffix

-ayt	idd**ayt**	I gave, I have given
-ayt	idd**ayt**	you gave, you have given (m sing)
-aytee	idd**aytee**	you gave, you have given (f sing)
	idd**a**	he gave, he has given
-it	**i**ddit	she gave, she has given
-ayna	idd**ayna**	we gave, we have given
-aytoo	idd**aytoo**	you gave, you have given (pl)
-oo	**i**ddoo	they gave, they have given

'To Be'

There is no present tense of the verb 'to be' in Arabic:

ag**a**ztak **i**mta? (to man)
when is your vacation?
lit: vacation your (suffix) when

ana min iskinder**aya**
I'm from Alexandria
lit: I from Alexandria

el mat-Haf el ma**s**ree ke**beer**
the Egyptian Museum is big
lit: the museum the Egyptian big

ki**t**ābak da?
is this your book?
lit: book your (suffix) this

In the past tense the verb 'to be' is as follows:

ana kont	I was
inta kont	you were (m sing)
inti k**o**ntee	you were (f sing)
h**o**wa kan	he was; it was
h**ay**ya k**ā**nit	she was; it was
e**H**na k**o**nna	we were
intoo k**o**ntoo	you were (pl)
h**o**mma ka**noo**	they were

ka**noo** fayn h**o**mma?	where were they?
k**ā**nit fayn?	where was it?

Negatives are formed in the standard way (see page 31):

inti mak**o**nteesh	you weren't
h**o**mma maka**noo**sh	they weren't

Note the following:

fee	there is; there are
mafeesh	there isn't; there aren't
kan fee	there was; there were
makansh fee	there wasn't; there weren't

'To Have'

The preposition **Aand** is used with the possessive suffixes to form the present tense of 'to have':

Aandee	I have
Aandak	you have (m sing)
Aandik	you have (f sing)
Aandoo	he has
Aandaha	she has
Aandina	we have
Aandokoo	you have (pl)
Aandohom	they have

The future tense of 'to have' is formed by adding the word **Hīkoon** before the present tense forms:

Hīkoon Aandee	I will have
Hīkoon Aandak	you will have etc

The past tense of 'to have' is formed by adding the word **kan** before the present tense forms:

kan Aandee	I had
kan Aandak	you had etc

'To Want'

The equivalent of the present tense of 'to want' (for all singular conjugations) is **Aayiz** (if the subject is masculine) and **Aīza** (if the subject is feminine). **Aīzeen** is used for all plural forms.

Negatives are formed by adding **mish**:

mish Aayiz ahwa
I don't want coffee

The past tense of 'to want' is as follows:

kont Aayiz	I wanted (m)
kont Aīza	I wanted (f)
kont Aayiz	you wanted (m sing)
kontee Aīza	you wanted (f sing)
kan Aayiz	he wanted
kanit Aīza	she wanted
konna Aīzeen	we wanted
kontoo Aīzeen	you wanted (pl)
kanoo Aīzeen	they wanted

The negative is:

makontish Aayiz	I didn't want (m)
makontish Aīza	I didn't want (f)
makontish Aayiz	you didn't want (m sing)
makonteesh Aīza	you didn't want (f sing)
makanshee Aayiz	he didn't want
makanitshee Aīza	she didn't want
makonnash Aīzeen	we didn't want
makontoosh Aīzeen	you didn't want (pl)
makanoosh Aīzeen	they didn't want

'To Come', 'To Go', 'To Understand'

The following are often used as alternatives to the usual present tense:

	come	go	understand
all m sing forms	gī	rīeH	fāhim
all f sing forms	gīya	rīHa	fahma
all plural forms	gīyeen	rīHeen	fahmeen

For example:

ana rīeH	inti fahma?
I'm going	do you understand?

To make these negative, add the word **mish** before the verbal form:

ana mish rīeH
I'm not going

Negatives

To form the negative, add **ma-** to the beginning of the verb and **-sh** to the end:

bashrab	**mabashrabsh**
I drink	I don't drink
Aamalt	**maAamaltish**
I did	I haven't done

Another way of making a verb negative is to place the word **mish** before the verb:

ana māshee	**mish māshee**
I am going	I am not going

There are a few verbs which must take the **mish** form of the negative. For example, 'to want' and the alternatives of the present tense mentioned above (i.e. 'to go', 'to come' and 'to understand').

mish rīeH	**mish fāhim**	**mish gīya**
I am not going	I don't understand	I am not coming

Imperative

To form an imperative, take the second person singular or plural of the imperfect tense and remove the initial **t-**:

ishrab!
drink up!

Some other useful imperatives are:

o'Aod!	**warrehālee**	**estanna hena**
sit down!	show it to me	stay here
imshee!	**o'af!**	**taAala hena!**
go away!	stop!	come here!

To form the negative imperative take the second person singular or plural of the verb in the imperfect tense and add **ma-** at the beginning and **-sh** at the end:

matroHsh!	**matestannash**	**matboSsish**
don't go!	don't wait	don't look

Questions

To change a statement into a question, use the same intonation at the end as you would in English:

da toHfa	**da toHfa?**
it's an antique	it's an antique?

Interrogatives

fayn?	**lay?**	**imta?**	**izzay?**
where?	why?	when?	how?

Interrogatives usually come at the end of a question. They are sometimes used at the beginning of a sentence for special emphasis:

el mat-Haf fayn?
OR **fayn el mat-Haf?**
where is the museum?

Dates

In business, Egypt uses the Western calendar; for Islamic holidays and festivals, legal and state affairs the lunar calendar is used (see public holidays page 162).

Use the numbers on pages 35–36 to form dates. For the first of the month, the ordinal can also be used. The word order for dates is:

day + month + year

Thus:

8 February 1998

tamania fibrīyer alf we tisAomaya tamania we tisAeen
lit: eight February thousand and nine hundred eight and ninety

5 September

khamsa sebtambir

27 December 1998

sabAa we Aishreen disambir alf we tosAomaya tamania we
tisAeen

Days

Monday	yōm el itnayn	يوم لإثنين
Tuesday	yōm et-talāt	يوم الثلاث
Wednesday	yōm el arbaA	يوم الأربع
Thursday	yōm el khamees	يوم الخميس
Friday	yōm el gomAa	يوم الجمعة
Saturday	yōm es-sabt	يوم السبت
Sunday	yōm el Had	يوم الحدّ

Months

January	yanāyer	يناير
February	fibrīyer	فبراير
March	māris	مارس
April	ibreel	إبريل
May	māyo	مايو
June	yonyo	يونيو
July	yolyo	يوليو

33

August	aghosTos	أغسطس
September	sebtamber	سبتمبر
October	oktōbar	أكتوبر
November	novamber	نوفمبر
December	disamber	ديسمبر

Time

what time is it? es-sāAa kam?
(it's) one o'clock es-sāAa waHda
(it's) two o'clock es-sāAa itnayn
at one o'clock es-sāAa waHda
at two o'clock es-sāAa itnayn
five past one es-sāAa waHda we khamsa
ten past two es-sāAa itnayn we Aashara
quarter past one es-sāAa waHda we robA
quarter past two es-sāAa itnayn we robA
half past two es-sāAa itnayn we noS
half past ten es-sāAa Aashara we noS
twenty to one waHda illa tilt
twenty to ten Aashara illa tilt
quarter to one waHda illa robA
quarter to two itnayn illa robA
am eS-SobH
pm (in the afternoon) baAd eD-Dohr
  (in the evening) bil layl
2am es-sāAa itnayn eS-SobH
2pm es-sāAa itnayn
6am es-sāAa sitta eS-SobH
6pm es-sāAa sitta bil layl
10am es-sāAa Aashara eS-SobH
10pm es-sāAa Aashara bil layl
noon eD-Dohr
midnight noS el layl

hour sāAa
minute de'ee'a
second sanya
two minutes de'i'tayn
quarter of an hour robA sāAa
half an hour noS sāAa
three quarters of an hour talat erbaA sāAa

Numbers

For numbers above ten (except multiples of ten), **we** ('and') is used. Thus, 31 is **wāHid we talateen** (literally 'one and thirty'), 27 is **sabAa we Aishreen** (literally 'seven and twenty') and so on.

0	Sifr	٠	17	sabaAtāshar	١٧
1	wāHid (m), waHda (f)	١	18	tamantāshar	١٨
2	itnayn	٢	19	tisaAtāshar	١٩
3	talāta	٣	20	Aishreen	٢٠
4	arbaAa	٤	21	wāHid we Aishreen	٢١
5	khamsa	٥	22	itnayn we Aishreen	٢٢
6	sitta	٦	30	talateen	٣٠
7	sabAa	٧	31	wāHid we talateen	٣١
8	tamania	٨	32	itnayn we talateen	٣٢
9	tisAa	٩	40	arbiAeen	٤٠
10	Aashara	١٠	41	wāHid we arbiAeen	٤١
11	Hidāshar	١١	50	khamseen	٥٠
12	itnāshar	١٢	51	wāHid we khamseen	٥١
13	talattāshar	١٣	60	sitteen	٦٠
14	arbaAtāshar	١٤	70	sabAeen	٧٠
15	khamastāshar	١٥	80	tamaneen	٨٠
16	sittāshar	١٦	90	tisAeen	٩٠

100	maya	١٠٠	300	toltomaya	٣٠٠
101	maya we wāHid	١٠١	400	robAomaya	٤٠٠
102	maya witnayn	١٠٢	500	khomsomaya	٥٠٠
103	maya we talāta	١٠٣	600	sittoomaya	٦٠٠
104	maya we arbaAa	١٠٤	700	sobAomaya	٧٠٠
105	maya we khamsa	١٠٥	800	tomnomaya	٨٠٠
200	mitayn	٢٠٠	900	tisAomaya	٩٠٠

1,000	alf	١٠٠٠
2,000	alfayn	٢٠٠٠
3,000	talat talāf	٣٠٠٠
10,000	Aashar talāf	١٠٠٠٠
50,000	khamseen alf	٥٠٠٠٠
1,000,000	milyōn	١٠٠٠٠٠٠

Ordinals

	masculine	feminine	masculine	feminine
1st	el owil	el oola	الأوّل	الأُولى
2nd	et-tānee	et-tania	الثاني	الثانية
3rd	et-tālit	et-talta	الثالث	الثالثة
4th	er-rābiA	er-rabAa	الرابع	الرابعة
5th	el khāmis	el khamsa	الخامس	الخامسة
6th	es-sāddis	es-sadsa	السادس	السادسة
7th	es-sābiA	es-sabAa	السابع	السابعة
8th	et-tāmin	et-tamna	الثامن	الثامنة
9th	et-tāsiA	et-tassAa	التاسع	التاسعة
10th	el Aāshir	el Aashra	العاشر	العاشرة

36

Basic Phrases

yes īwa

أيوه

no la'

لأ

OK kwayis

كويس

hello ahlan

أهلاً

(answer on phone) aloo

ألو

good morning SabāH el khayr

صباح الخير

good evening masā' el khayr

مساء الخير

good night masā' el khayr

مساء الخير

goodbye maAassalāma

مع السلامة

see you! netlā'a baAdayn!

نتلاقى بعدين!

see you later ashoofak baAdayn

أشوفك بعدين

please (to man/woman) low samaHt/samaHtee

لو سمحت/سمحتى

yes, please īwa, low samaHt/samaHtee

لو سمحت/سمحتى أيوه

could you please ...? momkin ... low samaHt/samaHtee?

ممكن ...لو سمحت/ سمحتى؟

please don't ... ma ... low samaHt/samaHtee

ما ...لو سمحت/ سمحتى

thanks, thank you shokran

شكراً

thank you very much shokran giddan

شكراً جداً

no thanks la' motshakkir

لأُشكر

don't mention it el Aafw

العفو

how do you do? (to man/ woman) Aāmil/Aāmla ay?

عامل/عاملة إيه؟

how are you? (to man/woman) izzayak/izzayik?

إزّيك/ إزّيكِ؟

fine, thanks, and you? (to man/woman) bekhayr, shokran, winta/winti?

بخير، شكراً، وإنتَ/ وإنتِ؟

pleased to meet you tsharrafna

تشرفنا

excuse me (to get past: to man/woman) low samaHt/ samaHtee

لو سمحت/سمحتى

(to get attention) min faDlak

من فضلك

(to say sorry: said by man/ woman) ana āsif/āsfa

أنا آسف/أسفة

I'm sorry (said by man/woman) ana āsif/āsfa

أنا آسف/أسفة

sorry?/pardon (me)?

afanddim?

أفنّدم؟

I see (I understand) īwa

أيوه

I don't understand mish

fāhim

مش فاهم

speak: do you speak

English? (to man/woman)

betikkallim/betikkallimee

ingleezee?

بتتكلّم/بتتكلّمى
إنجليزى؟

I don't speak ... ana

mabakkallimsh ...

أنا مابتكلّمش ...

could you repeat that?

momkin teAeed/teAeedee

tanee?

تعيد/تعيدى ثانى؟
ممكن

Conversion Tables

1 centimetre = 0.39 inches   1 inch = 2.54 cm

1 metre = 39.37 inches = 1.09 yards   1 foot = 30.48 cm

1 kilometre = 0.62 miles = 5/8 mile   1 yard = 0.91 m

1 mile = 1.61 km

km	1	2	3	4	5	10	20	30	40	50	100
miles	0.6	1.2	1.9	2.5	3.1	6.2	12.4	18.6	24.8	31.0	62.1

miles	1	2	3	4	5	10	20	30	40	50	100
km	1.6	3.2	4.8	6.4	8.0	16.1	32.2	48.3	64.4	80.5	161

1 gram = 0.035 ounces   1 kilo = 1000 g = 2.2 pounds

g	100	250	500
oz	3.5	8.75	17.5

1 oz = 28.35 g

1 lb = 0.45 kg

kg	0.5	1	2	3	4	5	6	7	8	9	10
lb	1.1	2.2	4.4	6.6	8.8	11.0	13.2	15.4	17.6	19.8	22.0

kg	20	30	40	50	60	70	80	90	100
lb	44	66	88	110	132	154	176	198	220

lb	0.5	1	2	3	4	5	6	7	8	9	10	20
kg	0.2	0.5	0.9	1.4	1.8	2.3	2.7	3.2	3.6	4.1	4.5	9.0

1 litre = 1.75 UK pints / 2.13 US pints

1 UK pint = 0.57 l   1 UK gallon = 4.55 l
1 US pint = 0.47 l   1 US gallon = 3.79 l

centigrade / Celsius $°C = (°F - 32) \times 5/9$

°C	-5	0	5	10	15	18	20	25	30	36.8	38
°F	23	32	41	50	59	64	68	77	86	98.4	100.4

Fahrenheit $°F = (°C \times 9/5) + 32$

°F	23	32	40	50	60	65	70	80	85	98.4	101
°C	-5	0	4	10	16	18	21	27	29	36.8	38.3

English → Arabic

A

a, an*

about: about 20 Hawālee
Aishreen

حوالي ٢٠

it's about 5 o'clock Hawālee
es-saAa khamsa

حوالي الساعة ٥

a film about Egypt 'film'
Aan maSr

فيلم عن مصر

above foo'

فوق

abroad (go) lil khāreg

للخارج

(live) fil khāreg

في الخارج

absorbent cotton oTn
Tebbee

قطن طبي

accept mwāfi'

موافق

accident Hadsa

حادثة

there's been an accident
kan fee Hadsa

كان في حادثة

accommodation sakan

سكن

see room and hotel

accurate maZbooT

مضبوط

ache wagaA

وجع

my back aches Dahree
wageAni

ظهري واجعني

across: across the road Aabr
esh-shāriA

عبر الشارع

address Ainwān

عنوان

what's your address? (to man/
woman) Ainwānak/
Ainwānik ay?

عنوانك/عنوانِك ايه؟

 The words for street
(shāriA), road (Taree') and
square (medān) always
precede the name in Arabic addresses. Whole blocks may often share a
single number, which may be in
Arabic or English. The number also
precedes the words street, avenue
etc. Foreigners may write addresses
in romanized Arabic as follows:

Adil Ameen
8 Abedoos Street
Shobra
1121
Cairo – Egypt

address book kitāb

Aanaween

كتاب عناوين

admission charge rasm
eddokhool

رسم الدخول

adult (man/woman) bāligh/
balgha

بالغ/ بالغة

advance: in advance
mo'addam

مقدّم

aeroplane Tīyāra

طيارة

after baAd

بعد

after you (to man/woman)
baAdak/baAdik

بعدكَ/ بعدكِ

after lunch baAd el-ghada

بعد الغدا

afternoon baAd eD-Dohr

بعد الظهر

in the afternoon feD-
Dohraya

فى الظهرية

this afternoon eD-Dohraya

الظهرية

aftershave kolonya baAd el
Helā'a

كولونيا بعد الحلاقة

aftersun cream kraym shams

كريم شمس

afterwards baAdayn

بعدين

again marra tania

مرّة ثانية

against Did

ضد

age Aomr

عمر

ago: a week ago min isbooA

من اسبوع

an hour ago min sāAa

من ساعة

agree: I agree ana mwāfi'

انا موافق

AIDS eedz

ايدز

air howa

هوا

by air beT-Tīyāra

بالطيارة

air-conditioning takyeef howa

تكييف هوا

airmail: by airmail bil bareed
eg-gowee

بالبريد الجوّى

airmail envelope zarf bareed
gowee

ظرف بريد جوّى

airplane Tīyāra

طيارة

airport maTār

مطار

to the airport, please lil
maTār, low samaHt

للمطار، لو سمحت

airport bus otobees el maTār

اوتوبيس المطار

airport tax Dareebit el maTār

ضريبة المطار

aisle seat korsee Aala
elmamar

كرسى على الممر

alabaster rokhām

رخام

alarm clock minabbeh

منبه

alcohol koHol

كوحول

Alcohol can be obtained in
most parts of Egypt, but
the range of outlets is limited. In the Western Desert oases or
Middle Egypt, its sale is severely
restricted or entirely prohibited. As a
rule of thumb, hotels or Greek restaurants are the places to try. When you
do manage to locate a drink, bear in
mind that the hot dry climate makes
for dehydration, and agonising hang-
overs can easily result from
overindulgence. Public drunkenness
is totally unacceptable in Egypt.
see **beer**, **wine** and **café**

alcoholic koHolee

كوحولى

Alexandria iskinderaya

اسكندرية

Algeria eggazā'ir

الجزاير

Algerian gazīree

جزايرى

all kol

كل

all of it koloo

كله

all of them kolohom

كلهم

that's all, thanks bas keda,
shokran

بس كده، شكرا

Allah Allāh

الله

praise be to Allah el Hamdo
lillāh

الحمد لله

allergic: I'm allergic to ... ana
Aandee Hasasaya min ...

انا عندى حساسية من...

alligator timsāH

تمساح

allowed: is it allowed? da
masmooH?

دا مسموح؟

all right kwayis

كويس

I'm all right (said by man/
woman) ana kwayis/

kwayisa

انا كويس/كويسة

are you all right? (to man)

inta kwayis?

انت كويس؟

(to woman) inti kwayisa?

انتي كويسة؟

almond lōz

لوز

almost ta'reeban

تقريبا

alone waHeed

وحيد

already khalāS

خلاص

also kamān

كمان

although berrāghm min

بالرغم من

altogether kolohom

كلهم

always dīman

دايماً

am*

am: at 7am es-sāAa sabAa eS-SobH

الساعة سبعة الصبح

at 1am es-sāAa waHda eS-SobH

الساعة واحدة الصبح

amazing (surprising) mish

maA'ool

مش معقول

(very good) momtāz

ممتاز

ambulance isAāf

اسعاف

call an ambulance! eTlob el isAāf!

اطلب الاسعاف!

Dial 211 for the ambulance service

America amreeka

امريكا

American amrekānee

امريكاني

I'm American (said by man/woman) ana amrekānee/amrekanaya

أنا امريكاني
/امريكانية

among bayn

بين

amp: a 13-amp fuse talat-tashar ambeer 'fuse'

١٣ امبير فيوز

ancient adeem

قديم

and wa

و

angry zaAlān

زعلان

animal Hīyawān

حيوان

ankle kaAb

كعب

annoy: this man's annoying
me er-rāgil da
miDaye'nee

الراجل دا مضايقنى

annoying mozAig

مزعج

another tanee

ثانى

can we have another room?
momkin nākhod ōDa
tania?

ممكن ناخد اوضة ثانية؟

another beer, please (to man/
woman) momkin beera
tania, low samaHt/
samaHtee?

ممكن بيرة ثانية، لو
سمحت/سمحتى؟

antibiotics moDād Hīyowee

مضاد حيوى

antihistamine dowa
lelHasāsaya (m)

دوا للحساسية

antique: is it an antique? da
toHfa?

دا تحفة؟

antique shop maHal toHaf

محل تحف

antiquities toHaf

تحف

antiseptic bing lilgrooH

بنج للجروح

any: have you got any bread?
(to man/woman) Aandak/
Aandik Aaysh?

عندك/عندِك عيش؟

do you have any ...? (to man/
woman) fee Aandak/
Aandik ... khāliS?

فى عندك/عندِك ...
خالص؟

sorry, I don't have any (said
by man/woman) āsif/āsfa,
maAandeesh khāliS

آسف/أسفة ما عنديش
خالص

anybody aī Had

أىّ حد

does anybody speak
English? fee aī Had
bayetkallim inglayzi?

فى أىّ حد بيتكلم
إنجليزى؟

there wasn't anybody there
makansh fee aī Had
hināk

ماكانش فى أىّ حد هناك

anything aī Hāga
أيّ حاجة

dialogue

anything else? aī Hāga
tania?
nothing else, thanks
mafeesh aī Hāga tania,
shokran
would you like anything to
drink? (to man) teHīb
teshrab aī Hāga?
(to woman) teHīb-bee
teshrabee aī Hāga?
I don't want anything,
thanks (said by man/woman)
ana mish Aayiz/Aīza aī
Hāga, shokran

apart from monfaSil
منفصل
apartment sha'a
شقة
appetizer fateH lil shahaya
فاتح للشهية
apple toffāHa
تفاحة
appointment maAād
معاد

dialogue

good morning, how can I
help you? SabāH elkhayr,
momkin asaAdak?
I'd like to make an
appointment (said by
man/woman) ana Aayiz/Aīza
aHgiz maAād
what time would you like?
(to man) imta teHeb
teHgiz elmaAād?
(to woman) imta teHebbee
teHgizee elmaAād?
three o'clock es-sāAa talā
ta
I'm afraid that's not possible lil'asaf mish momkin
is four o'clock all right? (to
man) teHeb teHgiz es-
sāAa arbaAa?
(to woman) teHebbee
teHgizee es-sāAa arbaAa?
yes, that will be fine īwa,
da maAād kwayis
the name was ...? el
esmhowa ...?

apricot mishmish
مشمش
April ibreel
أبريل

Arab Aarabee

عربى

the Arabs el Aarab

العرب

Arabic (language) logha
Aarabaya

لغة عربية

archeology asār

آثار

are*

area manTe'a

منطقة

arm drāA

ذراع

**arrange: will you arrange it
for us?** (to man/woman)
momkin terattibha/
terattibiha lena?

ممكن ترتبها/ ترتيبها لنا؟

arrival weSool

وصول

arrive waSal

وصل

when do we arrive?
HanewSal imta?

حنوصل إمتى؟

has my fax arrived yet?
waSal faksi walla lessa?

وصل فاكسى وللا لسة؟

we arrived today waSalna
en-naharda

وصلنا النهار دا

art fann

فن

art gallery Sālit AarD el finoon

صالة عرض الفنون

as: as big as kebeer zaī

كبير زى

as soon as possible be'sraA
wa't

بأسرع وقت

ashore Aash-shaT

على الشط

ashtray Taffya

طفّاية

ask Talab

طلب

I didn't ask for this maTalabtish da

ما طلبتش دا

could you ask him to ...? (to
man) momkin tis'aloo
ye-...?

ممكن تسأله يـ ... ؟

(to woman) momkin tis'alha
te-...?

ممكن تسألها تـ ... ؟

asleep: she's asleep hayya
nīma

هىّ نايمة

aspirin asbreen

أسبرين

asthma rabw

ربو

Aswan aswān

أسوان

at: at the hotel Aand el fondo'

عند الفندق

at the station Aand el maHaTTa

عند المحطة

at six o'clock es-sāAa sitta

الساعة ستة

at Ahmed's Aand aHmad

عند أحمد

ATM el 'bank' esh-shakhSee

البنك الشخصي

August aghosTos

أغسطس

aunt (mother's sister) khāla

خالة

(father's sister) Aamma

عمّة

Australia ostralya

أستراليا

Australian ostrālee

أسترالي

I'm Australian (said by man/ woman) ana ostrālee/ ostralaya

أنا أسترالي/أسترالية

autumn khareef

خريف

in the autumn fil khareef

فى الخريف

avenue Taree'

طريق

awake: is he awake? howa SāHee?

هوّ صاحى؟

is she awake? hayya SaHīa?

هيّ صاحية؟

away: is it far away? howa da beAeed?

هوّ دا بعيد؟

awful faZeeA

فظيع

B

baby 'baby'

بيبى

baby food akl aTfāl

أكل أطفال

baby's bottle ezāzit reDāAa

قزازة رضاعة

baby-sitter dāda

دادة

back (of body) Dahr

ظهر

(back part) Teez

طيز

at the back fil ākher

فى الآخر

can I have my money back?

momkin araggaA floosee?

ممكن أرجّع فلوسى؟

come back ragaA

رجع

go back rāH

راح

backache wagaA feD-Dahr

وجع فى الظهر

bad weHesh, mish kwayis

وحش ،مش كويس

a bad headache SodāA
shedeed

صداع شديد

badly weHesh, mish kwayis

وحش ،مش كويس

bag shanTa

شنطة

(carrier bag) kees

كيس

baggage shonaT

شُنط

baggage checkroom maktab
amanāt

مكتب أمانات

baggage claim akhd el
HaQā'ib

أخذ الحقائب

bakery (for bread) forn

فرن

(for cakes) makhbaz

مخبز

balcony (of house) balakōna

بلكونة

a room with a balcony ōDa
bebalakōna

أوضة ببلكونة

ball kōra

كورة

ballpoint pen alam gāf

قلم جاف

banana mōza

موزة

band (musical) fer'a

فرقة

bandage robāT shāsh

رباط شاش

Bandaid® blastar

بلاستر

bank (money) 'bank'

بنك

Opening hours are generally Monday to Thursday 8.30am–2.30pm, plus an evening shift (5–8pm in winter, 6–9pm in summer); some banks also open similar hours on Saturday and from 10am to noon on Sunday. Most foreign banks open Mon–Thurs 8.30am–1pm, and sometimes on Sunday. For arriving visitors, the banks at Cairo airport and the border crossings from Israel are open 24 hours daily, and those at ports open whenever a ship docks. In addition, 5-star hotels have a

24-hour banking and money changing service.
Commission is not generally charged on straight exchanges, but there might be a small stamp duty. Rather than going through the hassle of re-exchanging Egyptian pounds, it's better to spend it all before leaving. Forex bureaux (the generic term for private exchanges) are largely confined to Cairo, Alexandria and the Canal Cities. As a rule of thumb, Forex offer the best rates for cash, but may not take traveller's cheques; the transaction is also faster than in banks. If you're carrying American Express or Thomas Cook traveller's cheques – or cash – it's often quicker to do business at their local branches.

bank account Hisāb fil 'bank'
حساب فى البنك
bar bār
بار
see beer and café
barber's Salōn Hilā'a
صالون حلاقة
bargaining mosowma
مساومة

dialogue

how much are they?
bekam da?
ten pounds each el wāHid

beAashara geneeh
that's too expensive da ghālee awee
how about five pounds? khalleena bekamsa geneeh?
I'll let you have it for eight pounds Haddihālak bita-manya geneeh
can you reduce it a bit more? (to man/woman) momkin tenazzil/tenaz-zilee es-seAr shwaya kamān?
OK, it's a deal Tayib, khalāS Hashtreeha

Bargaining is standard practice in markets, but it's not the custom to bargain in large Western-style shops or supermarkets.
When bargaining, start by offering half the suggested price; the seller might then suggest you pay two-thirds. If the seller won't reduce the price after being asked twice, then it's polite not to insist any further and you should accept the price or decide not to buy.

basket (for storage) afaS
قفص
(in shop) sabat
سبت

bath banyo
بانيو
  can I have a bath? momkin
  ākhod Hammām?
  ممكن آخذ حمام؟
bathroom Hammām
حمام
  with a private bathroom
  beHammām khāS
  بحمام خاص
bath towel fooTit
  Hammām
  فوطة حمام
bathtub HōD
حوض
battery baTTaraya
بطاريّة
bay khaleeg
خليج
bazaar soo'
سوق
be*
beach blāJ
بلاج
  on the beach Aalal blāJ
  على البلاج
  see dress and women
beach mat Haseerit blāJ
  حصيرة بلاج
beach umbrella shamsayit
  blāJ
  شمسية بلاج

beads kharaz
خرز
beans fool
فول
  (dried) lobyā
  لوبيا
  green beans fāSolya
  فاصوليا
beard da'n (f)
ذقن
beautiful gameel
جميل
because Aalashān
علشان
  because of ... bisabab
  e-...
  بسبب ال ...
bed sireer
سرير
  I'm going to bed now ana
  dākhil anam dilwa'tee
  أنا داخل أنام دلوقتى
bed and breakfast nōm
  wefTār
  نوم وفطار
  see hotel
Bedouin badawee
بدوى
bedroom Hogrit nōm
  حجرة نوم
beef betelloo
بتلو

beer beera

بيرة

two beers, please (to man/woman) ezaztayn beera, low samaHt/ samaHtee

قزازتين بيرة، لوسمحت/ سمحتى

Beer is the most widely available form of alcohol in Egypt. The main beer brewed under licence is Stella – a light lager in half-litre bottles. Stella Export, with a blue rather than yellow label, is pricier and comes in smaller bottles. Marzen, a dark bock beer, appears briefly in the spring; Aswali is a dark beer produced in Aswan. Imported beer, which is the most expensive, only appears in bars, expensive hotels and restaurants. There is also Birrel, a non-alcoholic beer.

before abl

قبل

beggar shaHāt

شحات

begin bada'

بدأ

when does it begin? biteb-da' imta?

بتبدأ إمتى؟

beginner (man/woman) mobta-di'/mobtadi'a

مبتدئ/ مبتدئة

beginning: at the beginning fil bedāya

فى البداية

behind wara

ورا

behind me warāya

ورايا

belly-dancer ra'āSa

رقاصة

belly-dancing ra'S shar'ee

رقص شرقى

below taHt

تحت

belt Hizām

حزام

bend (in road) malaf

ملف

berth (on ship) sireer

سرير

beside: beside the ... gamb e-...

جنب ال ...

best aHsan

أحسن

better aHsan

أحسن

are you feeling better? (to man) inta kwayis?

إنت كويس؟

(to woman) inti kwayisa?

إنتى كويسة؟

between bayn

بين

beyond abAad min

أبعد من

bicycle Aagala

عجلة

big kebeer

كبير

too big kebeer awee

كبير قوى

it's not big enough Soghīyar awee

صغير قوى

bikini bikeenee

بيكينى

bill fatoora

فاتورة

(US: banknote) wara'

ورق

could I have the bill, please?

(to man/woman) momkin el fatoora, low samaHt/ samaHtee?

ممكن الفاتورة، لو سمحت/سمحتى؟

see tipping

bin zibāla

زبالة

bird Tayr

طير

birthday Aeed milād

عيد ميلاد

happy birthday! Aeed milād saAeed!

عيد ميلاد سعيد!

biscuit baskōt

بسكوت

bit: a little bit Hetta Soghīyara

حتة صغيرة

a big bit Hetta kebeera

حتة كبيرة

a bit of ... Hetta min el ...

حتة من ال ...

a bit expensive ghāliya shwaya

غالية شوية

bite (by insect) arSa

قرصة

(by animal) AaDDa

عضّة

bitter (taste etc) mor

مر

black eswid

أسود

blanket baTTanaya

بطانية

bless you! rabbina yebarek lak!

ربنا يبارك لك!

blind aAma

أعمى

blinds satāyer

ستاير

blocked mazdood

مسدود

blond (adj) ash'ar

أشقر

blood damm

دم

high blood pressure DaghT damm mortafiA

ضغط دم مرتفع

blouse blooza

بلوزة

blow-dry seshwār

سيشوار

blue azra'

أزرق

blue eyes Aoyoon zar'a

عيون زرقة

boarding house bansyōn

بنسيون

boarding pass biTa'it SoAood

بطاقة صعود

boat markib

مركب

(for passengers) 'launch'

لنش

(Egyptian sailboat) falooka

فلوكة

body gism

جسم

boiled egg bayD masloo'

بيض مسلوق

bone AaDm

عضم

bonnet (of car) kabboot

كبّوت

book (noun) kitāb

كتاب

(verb) Hagaz

حجز

can I book a seat? momkin aHgiz korsee?

ممكن أحجز كرسى؟

dialogue

I'd like to book a table for two momkin aHgiz Tarabayza litnayn
what time would you like it booked for? (to man) el sāAa kām teHeb teHgezhā?
(to woman) el sāAa kām teHebee teHgezeeha?
half past seven sabaAa wenoS
that's fine kwayis
and your name? wel esm eeh?

bookshop, bookstore
maktaba
مكتبة

boot (footwear) gizma 'boot'
جزمة بوت
(of car) shanTa
شنطة

border (of country) Hedood
حدود

bored: I'm bored (said by man/
woman) ana zah'ān/zah'āna
أنا زهقان/زهقانة

boring momil
مُمِل

born: I was born in Manchester
ana etwaladt fi 'Manchester'
انا إتولدت فى
مانشستر

borrow (money) istalaf
إستلف
(other items) istaAār
إستعار
may I borrow ...? (item)
momkin astaAeer ...?
ممكن استعير...؟

both litnayn
الإثنين

bother: sorry to bother you
(said by man/woman) ana
āsif/āsfa Aalāl izAāg
أنا آسف/أسفة على
الإزعاج

bottle ezāza
قزازة
a bottle of beer ezāzit
beera
قزازة بيرة

bottle-opener fattāHa
فتاحة

bottom (of person) Teez
طيز
at the bottom of the ... (hill,
street etc) Aand ākhir el ...
عند آخر ال...

box Sandoo'
صندوق

box office shebbāk tazākir
تذاكر

boy walad
ولد

boyfriend SāHib
صاحب

bra sotyāna
سوتيانا

bracelet iswera
إسورة

brains mokh
مخ

brakes farāmil
فرامل

brandy 'cognac'
كونياك

brass neHās aSfar
نحاس أصفر

made of brass min en-neHās

من النحاس

bread Aaysh

عيش

white bread Aaysh feeno

عيش فينو

brown bread Aaysh beradda

عيش بردّة

wholemeal bread Aaysh baladee

عيش بلدى

white pitta bread Aaysh shāmee

عيش شامى

break (verb) kasar

كسر

I've broken the ... kasart el ...

كسرت ال ...

I think I've broken my wrist aZon innee kasart resghee

أظن إنّى كسرت رسغى

break down AaTal

عطل

I've broken down el Aarabaya AaTalit

العربية عطلت

breakdown (mechanical) AoTl

عطل

breakdown service khidma lelAarabayyāt

خدمة للعربيات

breakfast feTār

فطار

The typical breakfast in Egypt consists of dried broad beans (fool medammis) cooked in a variety of ways (for example with oil, tahini or tomatoes), falāfel (mashed then fried broad beans), cheese, boiled eggs, bread (baguette or flat bread), jams and omelettes. Most Egyptians prefer to have fool medammis and falāfel for breakfast, but younger people tend to have cornflakes or other cereals.

break-in: I've had a break-in ana baytee itsara'

أنا بيتى إتسرق

breast bezz

بز

breeze nisma

نسمة

bridge (over river) kobree

كوبرى

brief mokhtaSar

مختصر

briefcase shanTa

شنطة

bright (light etc) zāhee

زاهى

bright red aHmar zāhee

أحمر زاهى

brilliant (idea, person)
momtāz

ممتاز

bring gāb

جاب

I'll bring it back later ana
Hageebo tāni baAdayn

أنا حاجيبه تاني بعدين

Britain ingiltera

إنجلترا

British ingleezee

إنجليزى

brochure nashra

نشره

broken maksoor

مكسور

brooch brōJ

بروج

broom moknisa

مكنسه

brother akh

أخ

brother-in-law neseeb

نسيب

brown bonnay

بنّى

bruise waram

ورم

brush (noun) forsha

فرشة

buffet car Aarabayyit el akl

عربية الأكل

buggy (for child) Aarabayyit
aTfāl

عربية أطفال

building mabna

مبنى

bunk sireer

سرير

bureau de change maktab
Sarf

مكتب صرف

see bank

burglary Hādis sir'a

حادث سرقة

burn (noun) Haree'a

حريقة

(verb) Hara'

حرق

burnt: this is burnt da
maHroo'

دا محروق

burst: a burst pipe masoora
maksoora

ماسورة مكسورة

bus otobees

أوتوبيس

what number bus is it to ...?
otobees nimra kam yerooH
li ...?

أوتوبيس نمرة كام يروح
ل ....؟

when is the next bus to ...?
(when at stop) el otobees

ellay bayrooH le ... gī imta?

الأوتوبيس اللى بيروح
لـ ... جاى إمتى؟

(when booking) imta el
otobees el-lee bayrooH
le ... baAdo?

إمتى الأوتوبيس اللى
بيروح بعده؟

what time is the last bus?
imta ākhir otobees?

إمتى آخر أوتوبيس؟

dialogue

does this bus go to ...?
howa el otobees da bay-
rooH le ...?
no, you need a number ...
(to man) la', inta Aayiz
otobees nimra ...
(to woman) la', inti Aīza
otobees nimra ...

 Inter-city buses are an inexpensive way to travel, and are often preferable to trains. Besides being quicker for short trips along the Nile Valley, buses serve areas beyond the rail network, such as Sinai, the oases, Abu Simbel and Hurghada. On most routes there's a choice between air-conditioned (A/C) buses – which are usually new(ish) and fast – and non-A/C ones, generally old and uncomfortable. The former are invariably more expensive, but whether their A/C actually works depends on the bus company and the route.

Though most towns have a single bus depot for all destinations, cities such as Cairo, Alexandria, Port Said and Ismailiya have several terminals. English- or French-speaking staff are fairly common at the larger ones, but rare in the provinces. Timetables (usually posted in Arabic only) change frequently so check the times in person. Hotels in Sinai and the oases, and the tourist offices in Luxor and Aswan can also supply information.

At city terminals, tickets are normally sold from kiosks, up to 24 hours in advance for A/C or long-haul services. In the provinces, tickets may only be available an hour or so before departure, or on the bus itself in the case of through services, which are often standing room only when they arrive. Passengers on A/C services are usually assigned a seat (the number is written in Arabic on your ticket).

business shoghl

شغل

bus station mow'af otobees

موقف أوتوبيس

bus stop maHaTTit otobees

محطة أوتوبيس

busy maJghool

مشغول

I'm busy tomorrow (said by man/woman) ana maJghool/maJghoola bokra

أنا مشغول/مشغولة بكرة

but lākin

لكن

butcher's gazzār

جزّار

butter zebda

زبدة

button zorār

زرار

buy ishtara

إشترى

where can I buy ...? fayn a'adar ashteree ...?

فين أقدر أشترى ....؟

by: by bus bil otobees

بالأوتوبيس

by car bil Aarabayya

بالعربيّة

by the window gamb esh-shebbāk

جنب الشبّاك

by the sea gamb el baHr

جنب البحر

by Thursday yōm el khamees

يوم الخميس

bye maAssalāma

مع السلامة

C

cabin (on ship) kabeena

كبينة

café ahwa

قهوة

The most popular Egyptian drinks are tea, coffee, fruit juices and familiar brands of soft drinks. Invitations to drink tea ('teshrab shi?') are as much a part of Egyptian life as they are in Britain. All these beverages are widely consumed in traditional coffee houses or tearooms (ahwa), which are predominantly male territory. Foreign women won't be turned away but may feel uneasy, especially if unaccompanied by a man. For a more relaxed tea or coffee, go to one of the middle-class places (in larger towns), which are often joined to patisseries, and where Egyptian women may be found.

Cairo el Qahira

القاهرة

Old Cairo maSr el adeema

مصر القديمة

cake shop Halawanee

حلوانى

call (verb) nadah

نده

(to phone) ettaSal

إتّصل

what's it called? ismaha ay?

إسمها ايه؟

he/she is called ...

ismoh/ismaha ...

إسمه/إسمها ...

please call the doctor

momkin teTlob el doktōr?

ممكن تطلب الدكتور؟

please give me a call at
7.30am tomorrow (to man)

low samaHt ittaSil bayya
bokra el saAa sabAa wenoS

لو سمحت إتصل بى بكرة
الساعة ٧,٣٠ الصبح

(to woman) low samaHtee
ittaSilee bayya bokra el
saAa sabAa wenoS

لو سمحتى إتصلى بى
بكرة الساعة ٧,٣٠
الصبح

please ask him to call me (to
man/woman) low samaHt/
samaHtee ool/oolee loh

yettaSil baya

لوسمحت/سمحتى قول/
قولى له يتصل بى

call back: I'll call back later
(come back) ana HargaA
tānee baAdayn

أنا حارجع تانى بعدين

(phone back) ana HateSil
tānee

أنا حاتّصل تانى

call round: I'll call round
tomorrow Hāgee bokra

حاجى بكرة

camcorder kamirit tasgeel

كاميرة تسجيل

camel gamal

جمل

camel driver raAee gemāl

راعى جمل

camel racing sibā' gimāl

سباق جمال

camel ride rokoob eg-gimāl

ركوب جمال

how much is a camel ride
to ...? bekam rokoob eg-
gimāl le ...?

بكم ركوب الجمال ل...؟

camel trip reHla beg-gimāl

رحلة بالجمال

camera kamira

كاميرة

camera shop maHal kamirāt

محل كاميرات

camp (verb) Aaskar

عسكر

can we camp here?
momkin neAaskar hena?

ممكن نعسكر هنا؟

camping gas gaz el-moAaskar

جاز المعسكر

campsite mowQiA
el-moAaskar

موقع المعسكر

Most campsites are located on the coast, lack shade and often have few facilities. Rather better are the occasional campsites attached to hotels, which may offer ready-pitched tents with camp beds, plus use of the hotel shower and toilet. As for camping rough, you should always check with the authorities about any coastal site – some beaches are mined, others patrolled by the military. In the oases it's less of a problem, though any land near water will belong to someone, so ask permission.

can (tin) SafeeHa

صفيحة

a can of beer Aelbit beera

علبة بيرة

can*: can you ...? (to

man/woman) momkin
inta/inti ...?

ممكن إنت/إنتى ...؟

can I have ...? momkin
ana ...?

ممكن أنا ...؟

I can't ... ma'adartish ...

ماقدرش ...

Canada 'Canada'

كندا

Canadian kanadee

كندى

I'm Canadian (said by
man/woman) ana
kanadee/kanadaya

أنا كندى/كنديّة

canal Qanāl

قناة

cancel lagha

لغى

candies Halawayāt

حلويّات

candle shamAa

شمعة

can-opener fattāHa

فتّاحة

cap (of bottle) ghaTā

غطا

captain (of ship) QobTān

قبطان

car Aarabayya

عربيّة

by car bil Aarabayya

بالعربيّة

card (birthday etc) kart

كارت

here's my (business) card da el kart betaAee

دا الكارت بتاعى

careful HareeS

حريص

be careful! khallee balak!

خلّى بالك!

caretaker (man/woman) far-rāsh/farrāsha

فرّاش/فرّاشة

car ferry maAadayya

معديّة

car park mow'af Aarabayyāt

موقف عربيّات

carpet siggāda

سجّادة

car rental ta'geer Aarabayyāt

تأجير عربيّات

Renting a car pays obvious dividends if you are pushed for time or plan to visit remote sites, but whether you'd want to drive yourself is another matter – it's not much more expensive to hire a car with a driver. Any branch of Misr Travel, and numerous local tour agencies, can fix you up with a car and driver. An alternative is simply to negotiate with local taxi drivers.

carriage (of train) Aarabayyit aTr

عربيّة قطر

carrier bag kees

كيس

carry shāl

شال

carry-cot Hammālit aTfāl

حمّالة أطفال

carton kartōn

كرتون

carving naHt

نحت

carwash ghaseel Aarabayya

غسيل عربيّة

cash (noun) floos

فلوس

(verb) Saraf

صرف

will you cash this for me? momkin teSriflee da?

ممكن تصرف لى دا؟

cash desk kays

كيس

cash dispenser el 'bank' esh-shakhSee

البنك الشخصى

cassette 'cassette'

كاسيت

cassette recorder tazgeel

تسجيل

castle alAa

قلعة

casualty department Qism el
Tawāri'

قسم الطوارئ

cat otta

قطة

catacombs sarādeeb

سراديب

catch (ball, animal) masak

مسك

where do we catch the bus
to ...? minayn nākhod el
otobees le ...?

منين ناخذ الأُوتوبيس
ل...؟

Catholic kasoleeki

كاثوليكى

cave maghāra

مغارة

ceiling sa'f

سقف

cemetery Torab

طرب

(historic, Islamic) madfan

مدفن

centigrade daraga
me'awaya

درجة مئويّة

centimetre 'santimetre'

سنتيمتر

central ra'eesee

رئيسى

centre wesT

وسط

how do we get to the city
centre? izzay newSal li
wesT el balad?

إزّاى نوصل لوسط البلد؟

ceramics khazaf

خزف

cereal Hoboob

حبوب

certainly TabAan

طبعاً

certainly not la' TabAan

لأ طبعاً

chair korsee

كرسى

change (noun: money) Sarf

صرف

(verb: money) Saraf

صرف

can I change this for ...?
momkin aghīyar da
be ...?

ممكن أغيّر دا ب...؟

I don't have any change
maAayeesh aī fakka

ماعييش فكة

can you give me change for

65

a five-pound note? momkin
teddeeni fakkit khamsa
geneeh?

ممكن تدينى فكّة خمسة
جنيه؟

dialogue

do we have to change
(trains)? eHna lāzim
nighīyar?
yes, change at Luxor/no,
it's a direct train naAam,
Hanghīyar fi lo'sor/la', da
aTr sareeA

changed: to get changed
Ha'aghīyar

حاغيّر

charge (noun) taman

ثمن

(verb) Hāsib

حاسب

cheap rekheeS

رخيص

do you have anything
cheaper? (to man/woman)
Aandak/Aandik aī Hāga
arkhaS?

عندك/عندك أيّ
حاجة أرخص؟

check (verb) kashaf

كشف

check (US: noun) sheek

شيك

(bill) fatoora

فاتورة

could you check the ...,
please (to man/woman)
momkin tekshif/tekshifee
Aala ..., low samaHt/
samaHtee

ممكن تكشف/تكشفى
على ... لو سمحت/
سمحتى؟

check book daftar sheekāt

دفتر شيكات

check card kart sheekāt

كارت شيكات

check in: where do we have to
check in? fayn iHna
lāzim nesallim esh-
shonaT?

فين إحنا لازم نسلّم
الشنط؟

check-in moragaAīt el kown-
tar

مراجعة الكاونتر

cheek (on face) khad

خد

cheerio! 'bye-bye'!

باى باى!

cheers! (toast) fee SeHHetak!

فى صحّتك!

cheese gibna

جبنة

chemist's agzakhana

اجزاخانة

see pharmacy

cheque sheek

شيك

do you take cheques? (to
man/woman) bitākhod/
bitakhdee sheekāt?

بتاخذ/بتاخذى شيكات؟

see traveller's cheque

cheque book daftar sheekāt

دفتر شيكات

cheque card kart sheekāt

كارت شيكات

chess shaTarang

شطرنج

chest Sedr

صدر

chewing gum lebān

لبان

chicken frākh

فراخ

child Tefl

طفل

children aTfāl

أطفال

child minder dāda

دادة

children's pool Hammām
sibāHa lil aTfāl

حمّام سباحة للأطفال

children's portion naSeeb
aTfāl

نصيب أطفال

chilled sa'Aa

سقعة

chin da'n (f)

ذقن

Chinese Seenee

صينى

chips baTāTis maHammara (f)

بطاطس محمّرة

(US) shebsee®

شيبسى

chocolate shokalāta

شوكولاتة

milk chocolate shokalāta bil
laban

شوكولاتة باللبن

plain chocolate shokalāta
sāda

شوكولاتة سادة

a hot chocolate kakow

كاكاو

cholera 'cholera'

كوليرا

choose ikhtār

إختار

Christian meseeHee

مسيحى

Christmas Aeed milād el meseeH

عيد ميلاد المسيح

Christmas Eve wa'fit Aeed milād el meseeH

وقفة عيد ميلاد المسيح

merry Christmas! Aeed milād saAeed!

عيد ميلاد سعيد!

church kineesa

كنيسة

cigar sigār

سيجار

cigarette sigāra

سيجارة

Almost the entire adult male population of Egypt smokes, and offering cigarettes around is common practice. The most popular brand is Cleopatra. Locally produced versions of Marlboro, Rothmans and Camel have a much higher tar content than their equivalents at home; the genuine article can be found in duty-free shops.

cigarette lighter wallāAet sagāyer

ولّاعة سجاير

cinema 'cinema'

سينما

cinnamon erfa

قرفة

circle Hala'a

حلقة

citadel alAa

قلعة

city madeena

مدينة

city centre wesT el balad

وسط البلد

clean (adj) neDeef

نظيف

can you clean these clothes for me? momkin tenaD-Daf el hedoom dee Aalashā-nee?

ممكن تنظيف الهدوم دى علشانى؟

cleaning solution (for contact lenses) maHlool tanDeef

محلول تنظيف

cleansing lotion marham tanDeef

مرهم تنظيف

clear wāDiH

واضح

clever shāTer

شاطر

cliff Hāfit el gabal

حافة الجبل

climbing TolooA

طلوع

clinic Aayāda
عيادة

clock saAet HayT
ساعة حيط

close (verb) āfāl
قفل

dialogue

what time do you close?
imta beti'filo?
we close at 8pm on week-
days and 6pm on
Saturdays beni'fil es-sāaa
tamanya ayyām el esbooa
wes-sāaa sitta ayyām es-
sabt
do you close for lunch?
beti'fil saAt el ghada?
yes, between 1 and
3.30pm naAam, min es-
sāAa waHda les-sāAa
talāta wenoS

closed āfil
قافل

cloth (fabric) omāsh
قماش
(for cleaning etc) Hettit omāsh
حتة قماش

clothes hedoom
هدوم

clothes line Habl ghaseel
حبل غسيل

clothes peg maJbak ghaseel
مشبك غسيل

cloud seHāb
سحاب

cloudy meghīyem
مغيّم

clutch debrayāJ
دبرياج

coach (on train) Aarabayyit
aTr
عربيّة قطر

coach trip reHla syaHayya bil
otobees
رحلة سياحية بالأوتوبيس

coast sāHil
ساحل

on the coast ala es-sāHil
على الساحل

coat (long coat) balTo
بالطو
(jacket) Jākit
جاكت

coathanger shammāAa
شمّاعة

cobra teAbān kobra
تعبان كوبرا

cockroach SorSār
صرصار

code (for phoning) kōd
كود

what's the (dialling) code for Alexandria? ay raQam el kōd betāA iskinderaya?

إيه رقم الكود بتاع إسكندريّة؟

coffee ahwa

قهوة

two coffees, please (to man/woman) itneen ahwa, low samaHt/samaHtee

إتنين قهوة، لو سمحت/ سمحتى

 Coffee is traditionally of the Turkish kind, served in tiny cups or glasses and pre-sugared as customers specify. Most middle-class or tourist establishments also serve European-style instant coffee, made from Nescafé or Misrcafe rather than Turkish coffee, with the option of having it with milk.

Some useful terms:
ahwa sāda coffee without sugar
ahwa Aar-reeHa slightly sweetened coffee
ahwa mazbooTa medium-sweet coffee
ahwa zayāda very sweet coffee
ahwa meHowega coffee spiced with cardomom seeds
ahwa bel-laban coffee with milk

coffee house ahwa

قهوة

coin Aomla

عملة

Coke® kakoola®

كاكولا

cold bard

برد

I'm cold (said by man/woman) ana bardān/bardāna

انا بردان/بردانة

I have a cold ana Aandee zokām

أنا عندى زكام

collapse: he's collapsed oghma Aalayh

أغمى عليه

collar yā'a

ياقة

collect akhad

أخذ

I've come to collect ... ana gī akhod ...

أنا جاى آخذ ...

college kollaya

كليّة

colour lōn

لون

do you have this in other colours? (to man/woman) Aandak/Aandik alwān ghayr dee?

عندك/عندِك ألوان غير دى؟

colour film 'film' milowwin

فيلم ملون

comb mishT

مشط

come waSal

وصل

dialogue

where do you come from?
(to man/woman) inta/inti
minayn?
I come from Edinburgh
ana min 'Edinburgh'

come back ragaA

رجع

I'll come back tomorrow ana
HargaA bokra

أنا حارجع بكرة

come in ga

جا

comfortable moreeH

مريح

compact disc 'CD'

سي دى

company (business) shirka

شركة

compartment (on train) Salōn

صالون

compass boSla

بوصلة

complaint shakwa

شكوى

I have a complaint Aandee
shakwa

عندى شكوى

completely tamām

تمام

computer 'computer'

كومبيوتر

concert Hafla moseeQayya

حفلة موسيقيّة

conditioner (for hair) monaAim
lil shaAr

منعم للشعر

condom Aāzil Tibbee

عازل طبّى

conference mo'tamar

مؤتمر

confirm akkid

أكِّد

congratulations! mabrook!

مبروك!

connection waSla

وصلة

constipation imsāk

إمساك

consulate QonSolaya

قنصليّة

contact lenses Aadasāt
lasQa

عدسات لاصقة

contraceptive mãneA lil Haml

مانع للحمل

convenient molã'im

ملائم

that's not convenient da mish molã'im

دا مش ملائم

cook (verb) Tabakh

طبّاخ

not cooked nĩ

نى

cooker botagãz

بوتاجاز

cookie baskõt

بسكوت

cool raTeb

رطب

Coptic ebTee

قبطى

Coptic monastery dayr ebTee

دير قبطى

coriander kozbara

كزبرة

cork fĩlla

فلّة

corkscrew bareema lifatH el azaïz

برّيمة لفتح القزايز

corner: on the corner Aalal naSya

على الناصية

in the corner fil rokn

فى الركن

cornflakes 'cornflakes'

كورن فلايكس

correct (right) SaH

صح

corridor Tor'a

طرقة

cosmetics mawãd tagmeel

مواد تجميل

cost (verb) kallif

كلف

how much does it cost? bekam?

بكام؟

cot sireer aTfãl

سرير أطفال

cotton oTn

قطن

cotton wool oTn Tebbee

قطن طبّى

couch (sofa) kanaba

كنبة

couchette sireer

سرير

cough koHHa

كحة

cough medicine dowa koHHa

دوا كحة

could: could you ...? (to
  man/woman) momkin
  inta/inti ...?
ممكن إنت/إنتى ...؟
could I have ...? momkin
  ana ākhod ...?
ممكن أنا آخد ...؟
I couldn't ...
  ma'adartish ...
ماقدرتش ...
country (nation) balad
بلد
(countryside) reef
ريف
couple (two people) itnayn
إثنين
a couple of ... gōz ...
جوز ...
courier morāfiQ sayāHee
مرافق سياحى
course: of course TabAan
طبعا
of course not la' TabAan
لأ طبعاً
cousin (on mother's side: aunt's
  daughter) bint khala
بنت خالة
(aunt's son) ibn khala
إبن خالة
(uncle's daughter) bint khāl
بنت خال

(uncle's son) ibn khāl
إبن خال
(on father's side: aunt's daughter)
  bint Aamma
بنت عمة
(aunt's son) ibn Aamma
إبن عمة
(uncle's daughter) bint
  Aamm
بنت عم
(uncle's son) ibn Aamm
إبن عم
cow ba'ara
بقرة
crab kāborya
كابوريا
craft shop maHal kherdawā
  tee
محل خضرواتى
crash (noun) Hādsa
حادثة
I've had a crash HaSalit lee
  Hādsa
حصلت لى حادثة
crazy magnoon
مجنون
cream (in cake, lotion) 'cream'
كريم
(colour) kraymi
كريمى
creche HaDāna
حضانة

credit card 'credit card'

كريديت كارد

do you take credit cards? (to man/woman)

bit**a**khod/bit**a**khdee 'credit card'?

بتاخد/بتاخدى
كريديت كارد؟

dialogue

can I pay by credit card?
m**o**mkin adfaA bil 'credit card'?

which card do you want to use? (to man) aī 'card'
teHebb testakhdim?
(to woman) aī 'card'
teHebbee testakhdimee?

Access/Visa

yes, sir naAam ya ost**a**z

what's the number? ay el-raQam?

and the expiry date? we ay **a**khir miAad intihā'ō?

Credit cards are accepted at major hotels, top-flight restaurants, some shops and airline offices, but virtually nowhere else. American Express, Mastercard and Visa are the likeliest to be accepted. In Cairo, Alexandria, Luxor, Hurghada and a few other main tourist resorts, branches of the Banque Misr have cash machines/ATMs that allow you to withdraw cash using Visa, Mastercard or Cirrus cards.

crime
Pickpockets can be a problem in Cairo, notably in queues and on the crowded buses to the pyramids. To play safe, keep your valuables in a money belt or a pouch under your shirt. Generally, though, casual theft is more of a problem. Campsites, hostels and cheap hotels often have poor security, making it unwise to leave valuables there. At most places, you can deposit them at the reception (always get a receipt for cash).

crisps shebsee®

شيبسى

crockery fokhār

فخار

crossing (by sea) Aoboor

عبور

crossroads taQ**a**ToA Toro'

تقاطع طرق

crowd n**a**s ket**ee**r

ناس كثير

(at sporting event) motafar-regeen

متفرجين

crowded zaHma

زحمة

crown (on tooth) tāg

تاج

cruise Aoboor

عبور

If you're looking for a cruise once in Egypt, shop around and don't necessarily go for the cheapest deal: some boats leave a lot to be desired in terms of hygiene and living conditions, so always try to look round the vessel first. The best deals are available from local agents (or directly from the boats) in Luxor or Aswan.

Feluccas, the lateen-sailed boats used on the Nile since antiquity, still serve as transport along many stretches of the river and are favoured by tourists for sunset cruises.

crutches Aokkāz

عكاز

cry (verb) Sarakh

صرخ

cucumber (small) khayār

خيار

(large) fa'oos

فاقوس

cumin kammoon

كمون

cup fongān

فنجان

a cup of ..., please (to man/woman) fongān ..., low samaHt/samaHtee

فنجان ....، لو سمحت/ سمحتى

cupboard dolāb

دولاب

cure (verb) shafa

شفى

curly akrat

أكرت

current (in water, electric) tīyār

تيّار

curtains satāyer

ستاير

cushion makhadda

مخده

custom gomrok

جمرك

Customs gamārek

جمارك

Egyptian Customs allows you to bring in 200 cigarettes (or 250g of tobacco) and one litre of alcohol. Though personal effects and cameras are exempt from duty, items such as electronic equipment and video cameras should be declared and listed on the form provided. If you lose them, they will be assumed 'sold' when you come to leave and you will have to pay 100 per cent duty unless you have police documentation of theft. On items with a high resale value (for example laptop computers or video cameras) you may be required to pay a deposit against possible duty charges, which is refundable on departure. If Customs officers insist on impounding goods, get a receipt and contact your consulate.

cut (noun) 'iTAa

قطعة

(verb) aTaA

قطع

I've cut myself ana Aowart nafsee

أنا عوّرت نفسي

cutlery faD-Dayāt

فضّيات

Cyprus obroS

قبرص

D

dad abb, baba

أب، بابا

daily yowmayan

يوميا

damage (verb) kharrab

خرب

damaged kharrabt

خربت

I'm sorry, I've damaged this (said by man/woman) ana āsif/āsfa, ana kharrabtahā

أنا آسف/آسفة، أنا خرّبتها

damn! ellaAna!

اللعنة!

damp (adj) raTeb

رطب

dance (noun) ra'S

رقص

(verb) ra'aS

رقص

would you like to dance? (to woman) teHebee tor'oSee?

تحبي ترقصي؟

dangerous khaTar

خطر

Danish denmarkee

دنماركي

dark (adj: colour) Dalma

ظلمة

(hair) asmar

أسمر

it's getting dark HatDallim

حتضلم

date*: what's the date today? et-tareekh ay en-naharda?

التاريخ إيه النهارده؟

let's make a date for next

Monday khalleena nerattib maAād layōm letnayn eg-gī

خلّينا نرتب معاد ليوم الاثنين الجاى

dates (fruit) balaH

بلح

daughter bint

بنت

daughter-in-law mrāt ibn

مراة إبن

dawn fagr

فجر

at dawn Aand el fagr

عند الفجر

day yōm

يوم

the day after el yōm el-lee baAdo

اليوم اللى بعده

the day after tomorrow baAd bokra

بعد بكرة

the day before el yōm el-lee ablo

اليوم اللى قبله

the day before yesterday owil embāriH

أول إمبارح

every day kol yōm

كل يوم

all day Tool el yōm

طول اليوم

in two days' time khilāl yōmayn

خلال يومين

have a nice day! yōm saAeed!

يوم سعيد !

day trip reHla yōmaya

رحلة يومية

dead mīyit

ميت

deaf aTrash

أطرش

deal (business) SafQa

صفقة

it's a deal ettafa'na

إتفقنا

death mōt

موت

decaffeinated coffee ahwa bedoon kafayn

قهوة بدون كافيين

December disamber

ديسمبر

decide Qar-rar

قرّر

we haven't decided yet lessa maQar-rarnāsh

ماقرّرناش

deck (on ship) Dahr el markib

ظهر المركب

deckchair korsee blāj

كرسى بلاج

deep ghoweeT

غويط

definitely TabAan

طبعا

definitely not la' TabAan

لا طبعا

degree (qualification) shahāda gamiAayya

شهادة جامعية

dehydrated (person) mīyit min el AaTash

ميت من العطش

dehydration gafāf

جفاف

delay (noun) ye'khar

يأخر

deliberately bil'aSd

بالقصد

delicacy nak-ha

نكهة

delicatessen ba'āl

بقال

delicious lazeez

لذيذ

deliver waSSal

وصّل

delivery (of mail) towSeel

توصيل

Denmark ed-denmark

الدنمارك

dental floss khayT

lelasnān

خيط للسنان

dentist garrāH asnān

جرّاح أسنان

dialogue

> it's this one here dee el-
> lee hena
> this one? dee?
> no, that one la' dee
> here? hena?
> yes īwa

dentures Ta'm asnān

طقم أسنان

deodorant mozeel lereeHt el Aara'

مزيل لريحة العرق

department Qism

قسم

department store maHal kebeer

محل كبير

departure safar

سفر

departure lounge Sālit es-safar

صالة السفر

depend: it depends yimkin

يمكن

it depends on ... yeAtemid

Aala ...

يعتمد على ...

deposit Aarboon

عربون

desert SaHara

صحرا

in the desert fee eS-
SaHara

فى الصحرا

dessert Helw

حلو

destination maHaTTa

محطّة

develop HammaD

خمّض

dialogue

could you develop these
films? momkin
teHammaD el aflām dee?
yes, certainly īwa, TabAan
when will they be ready?
imta yekhalaSoo?
tomorrow afternoon bokra
baAd eD-Dohr
how much is the four-hour
service? bekam khidmet
arbaA saAāt?

diabetic (noun) mareeD

bes-sokkar

مريض بالسكّر

dial (verb) Darab telefōn

ضرب تليفون

dialling code nimrit el
kōd

نمرة الكود

To dial direct, dial 00 for
an international line, then
dial the country code
(below), followed by the number,
leaving out the initial digit of the
local code:

Australia 61   Canada 1
Ireland 353   New Zealand 64
UK 44   USA 1

diamond mās

ماس

diaper kafoola

كافولة

diarrhoea es-hāl

إسهال

do you have something for
diarrhoea? (to man/woman)
Aandak/Aandik Haga lil
es-hāl?

عندك/عندك حاجة
للإسهال؟

diary mofakkera

مفكّرة

Di

79

didn't* ma Aamaltish

ما عملتش

die māt

مات

diesel deezil

ديزل

diet rayJeem

ريجيم

I'm on a diet ana baAmil
rayJeem

أنا باعمل ريجيم

I have to follow a
special diet lāzim
attabiA rayJeem
moAayan

لازم أتبع ريجيم معيّن

difference ekhtelāf

إختلاف

what's the difference? ay el
far'?

إيه الفرق؟

different mokhtalif

مختلف

this one is different da
mokhtalif

دا مختلف

a different table Tarabayza
tania

طرابيزة ثانية

difficult SaAb

صعب

difficulty SoAooba

صعوبة

dinghy markib SoghIyar

مركب صغيّر

dining room ōDit es-sofra

أوضة السفرة

(in hotel) Sālit el akl

صالة الأكل

dinner (evening meal) Aasha

عشا

to have dinner yetAash-sha

يتعشا

direct (adj) mobāshir

مباشر

is there a direct train? fee
aTr mobāshir?

في قطر مباشر؟

direction ettigāh

إتجاه

which direction is it? fee ay
ettigāh?

في أيّ إتجاه؟

is it in this direction? fil
ettigāh da?

في الإتجاه دا؟

directory enquiries daleel
telefonāt

دليل تليفونات

 The number for directory
enquiries is 140;
international directory
enquiries is 125.

dirt was**ā**kha

وساخة

dirty mish neDeef

مش نظيف

disabled moAowaQ

معوّق

is there access for the disabled? fee bab lil moAowaQeen?

فى باب للمعوّقين؟

disappear ekhtafa

إختفى

it's disappeared ekhtafit

إختفت

disappointed: I was disappointed ana kh**ā**b amalee

أنا خاب أملى

disappointing mokhayib lil am**ā**l

مخيّب للآمال

disaster karsa

كارثة

disco 'disco'

ديسكو

discount takhfeeD

تخفيض

is there a discount? fee takhfeeD?

فى تخفيض؟

disease maraD

مرض

disgusting mo'rif

مقرف

dish (meal) wagba

وجبة

(bowl) Tab'a

طبق

disk (for computer) desk

ديسك

disposable diapers/nappies n**ā**bee

نابى

distance mas**ā**fa

مسافة

in the distance beAeed

بعيد

district manTe'a

منطقة

disturb ezA**ā**g

إزعاج

diving board manaT

منط

divorced (man/woman) meTala'/meTala'a

مطلق/مطلقة

dizzy: I feel dizzy (said by man/woman) ana d**ā**yekh/d**ī**kha

أنا دايخ/دايخة

do (verb) Aamal

عمل

what shall we do? HaneAmel ay?

حنعمل إيه؟

how do you do it? (to man/woman) beteAmelhā/beteAmelayhā ezzāī?

بتعملها/بتعمليها إزاى؟

will you do it for me? (to man/woman) momkin teAmeloo/teAmelayhā Aalashānee?

ممكن تعمله/تعمليها علشانى؟

dialogues

how do you do? (to man/woman) izzayak/izzayik?

nice to meet you forSa saAeeda

what do you do? (work: to man/woman) betishtaghal/ betishtaghalee ay?

I'm a teacher (said by man/woman) ana modariss/modarissa

and you? (to man/woman) we inta/inti?

I'm a student (said by man/woman) ana Tālib/Tāliba

what are you doing this evening? (to man/woman) HateAmil/HateAmilee ay el-leelādee?

we're going out for a drink Hanokhrog neshrab

do you want to join us? (to man/woman) teHebb/ teHebbee teegee maAāna?

do you want coffee? (to man) teHebb teshrab ahwa?

(to woman) teHebbee teshrabee ahwa?

I do, but she doesn't (said by man/woman) ana Aayiz/ Aīza, bas hayya mish Aīza

doctor (man/woman) doktōr/ doktōra

دكتور/دكتورة

we need a doctor eHna meHtageen doktōr

إحنا محتاجين دكتور

please call a doctor momkin teTlob doktōr?

ممكن تطلب دكتور؟

dialogue

where does it hurt? (to man/woman) fayn byew-gaAak/byewgaAik?

right here hena beZZabT

does that hurt now? (to man/woman)
byewgaAak/byewgaAik delwa'tee?

yes īwa

take this to the pharmacy
khod dee lil agzakhāna

Private doctors are common; expect to pay about 50 Egyptian pounds a session, excluding the price of any drugs you are prescribed. If you get seriously ill, private hospitals are generally preferable to public sector ones. Those attached to universities are usually well equipped and competent, but small town hospitals are often inadequate. Many hospitals (mostashfa) require a deposit of around 200 Egyptian pounds. Normally you must pay this on admission and a delayed payment by your insurance company is not acceptable. Obviously, it's advisable to take out health insurance before you travel.

document mostanad

مستند

dog kalb

كلب

doll Aaroosa leAba

لعبة

domestic flight reHla dākhilaya

رحلة داخلية

donkey Homār

حمار

donkey-drawn cart HanToor

حنطور

don't!* la'!

لا!

don't do that! mateAmelsh keda!

ماتعملش كده!

door bab

باب

doorman bowwāb

بواب

double gōz

جوز

double bed sireer litnayn

سرير لثنين

double room ōDa litnayn

أوضة لثنين

down taHt

تحت

down here hena taHt

هنا تحت

put it down over there
HoTTaha henāk

حُطها هناك

it's down there on the right
hayya henāk Aala elyemeen

هيّ هناك على اليمين

Do

it's further down the road
hayya oddām shwīya

هيّ قدّام شويّة

downmarket (restaurant etc)
maA'ool

معقول

downstairs ed-dōr et-taHtā
nee

الدور التحتاني

dozen dasta

دستة

half a dozen noS dasta

نص دستة

drawer dorg

درج

drawing rasm

رسم

dreadful mo'rif

مقرف

dream (noun) Helm

حلم

dress (noun) fostān

فستان

Be aware of the importance of dress: shorts are acceptable only at beach resorts (and for women only in private resorts or along the Aqaba coast). In the oases, where attractions include open-air springs and hot pools, it's OK to bathe – but do so in at least a T-shirt and leggings: oasis people are among the

most conservative in the country. Shirts (for both sexes) should cover your shoulders. For women particularly, the more modest your dress, the less hassle you will attract: loose opaque clothes that cover all 'immodest' areas (thighs, upper arms, chest), and hide your contours are a big help, and essential if you are travelling alone in rural areas, where long hair should also be covered.

Bear in mind that northern Egypt can be cold and damp in winter, while the desert gets freezing at night, even in the spring and autumn. A warm sweater is invaluable. So, too, are a solid pair of shoes: burst pipes are commonplace, and wandering around muddy streets in sodden sandals is a miserable experience.

dressed: to get dressed labas

لبس

dressing gown rōb deshamb-
bar

روب ديشامبر

drink (noun: alcoholic) shorb

شرب

(non-alcoholic) mashroob

مشروب

(verb) sharab

شرب

a cold drink Haga sa'Aa

حاجة ساقعة

can I get you a drink? (to

man/woman)

teshrab/teshrabee Hāga?

تشرب/تشربى حاجة؟

what would you like (to drink)? (to man) teHebb teshrab ay?

تحب تشرب إيه؟

(to woman) teHebbee teshrabee ay?

تحبى تشربى إيه؟

no thanks, I don't drink la' shokran, ana mabashrabsh

لأ شكراً، أنا مابشربش

I'll just have a drink of water ana Hākhod kobbāyit mīya bas

أنا حاخذ كوبّاية ميّة بس

drinking water mīyit shorb

ميّة شرب

is this drinking water? el mīya SalHa lesh-shorb?

الميّة صالحة للشرب

drive (verb) sā'

ساق

we drove here gayna bil Aarabayya

جينا بالعربية

I'll drive you home HawaSalak lil bayt bil Aarabayya

حوصلك بالعربية

driver (man/woman)

sowā'/sowā'a

سوّاق/سوّاقة

driving

Driving in Egypt is not for the faint-hearted or inexperienced motorist. Although driving on the right is pretty much universal, other rules of the road vary. Traffic in cities is relentless and anarchic, with vehicles weaving between lanes, signalling by horn. Two beeps means 'I'm alongside and about to overtake.' A single long blast means 'I can't (won't) stop and I'm coming through!'. Extending your hand, fingers raised and tips together, is the signal for 'watch out, don't pass now'; spreading your fingers and flipping them forwards indicates 'go ahead'. Although the car in front usually has right of way, buses and trams always take precedence.

On country roads – including the two-lane east and west bank highways along the Nile Valley – trucks and cars routinely overtake in the face of oncoming traffic. The passing car usually flashes its lights as a warning, but not always. Most roads are bumpy, with deep potholes and all manner of traffic, including donkey carts and camels. Avoid driving after dark, when Egyptians drive without lights, only flashing them to high beam when they see

85

another car approaching. The official speed limit is 90km per hour (100km on the Cairo-Alexandria desert road), but on certain stretches it can be as low as 30km per hour. The minimum age for driving in Egypt is 25 years, the maximum age is 70 years.

driving licence rokhSit sewā'a

رخصة سواقة

drop: just a drop, please (of drink: to man/woman) shwīya Soghīyareen, low samaHt/samaHtee

شويّة صغيّرين،
لو سمحت/سمحتى

drug dowa (m)

دوا

drugs (narcotics) mokhaddarāt

مخدّرات

Egypt has strict anti-drugs laws that make hanging or life imprisonment mandatory for convicted smugglers and dealers (which could be interpreted to mean someone caught with a few sachets of the stuff). Mere possession or use merits a severe prison sentence and a heavy fine (plus legal costs). Despite this, bango (marijuana) is still consumed by Egyptians who can afford it, and by tourists in Dahab, Luxor, Aswan, Hurghada and Cairo.

drunk (adj) sakrān

سكران

dry (adj) nāshif

ناشف

(wine) 'dry'

دراى

dry-cleaner tanDeef Aala en-nāshif

تنظيف على الناشف

due: he was due to arrive yesterday howa kan mafrooD yewsal en-naharda

هوّ كان مفروض يوصل النهار ده

when is the train due? el aTr gī imta?

القطر جاى إمتى؟

dull (pain) mo'lim

مؤلم

(boring) momil

ممل

dummy (baby's) bazzāza

بزّازة

during fee nafs elwa't

فى نفس الوقت

dust torāb

تراب

dusty metarrab

متّرب

Dutch holāndee

هولاندى

duty-free (goods) beDāAa
Horra

بضاعة حرّة

duty-free shop maHal
beDāAa Horra

محل بضاعة حرّة

duvet leHāf

لحاف

dynasty osra malakaya

أسرة ملكية

dysentery dosentārya

دوسنتاريا

E

each (every) kol

كل

how much are they each?
bekam el waHda?

بكام الواحدة؟

ear widān

ودان

earache: I have earache
widānee wagaAānee

ودانى وجعانى

early badree

بدرى

early in the morning eS-
SobH badree

الصبح بدرى

I called by earlier ana

Aaddayt badree

أنا عدّيت بدرى

earrings Hel'ān

حلقان

earthenware fokhar

فخار

east shar'

شرق

in the east fesh-shar

فى الشرق

Easter Aeed sham el neseem

عيد شم النسيم

eastern shar'ee

شرقى

Eastern Desert eS-SaHara'
esh-shar'aya

الصحراء الشرقيّة

easy sahl

سهل

eat kol

كل

we've already eaten, thanks
eHna kalna khalāS,
shokran

إحنا أكلنا خلاص، شكرا

eau de toilette kolonia

كولونيا

economy class daraga tania

درجة ثانية

egg bayDa

بيضة

Egypt maSr

مصر

Ancient Egypt maSr el farAoonaya

مصر الفرعونيّة

Egyptian maSree

مصرى

either: either ... or ...
ay ... ow ...

أى ... أو ...

either of them ay wāHid feehom

أىّ واحد فيهم

elbow kooA

كوع

electric bil kahraba

بالكهربا

electrical appliances adawāt kahrabā'ayya

أدوات كهربائيّة

electrician kahrabā'ee

كهربائى

electricity kahraba

كهرباء

elevator asansayr

أسانسير

The current in Egypt is 220V, 50Hz. North American travellers with appliances designed for 110V should bring a converter. Most sockets are for round-pronged plugs, so you'll

need an adaptor. Brief power cuts are quite common.

else: something else Hāga tania

حاجة ثانية

somewhere else Hetta tania

حتة ثانية

dialogue

would you like anything else? (to man/woman) teHeb/teHebbee aī shay' tānee?
no, nothing else, thanks la', bas keda, shokran

e-mail 'e-mail'

إيميل

embassy safāra

سفارة

emergency Tawāri'

طوارئ

this is an emergency! dee Hālit Tawāri'!

دى حالة طوارئ!

emergency exit bab eT-Tawāri'

باب الطوارئ

empty fāDee

فاضى

end (noun) nehāya

نهاية

at the end of the street fee

ākhr eT-Taree'

فى آخر الطريق

when does it end? betekhlaS

imta?

بتخلص إمتى؟

engaged (toilet, telephone)

maJghool

مشغول

(to be married: man/woman)

khāTeb/makhTooba

خاطب/مخطوبة

engine (car) motōr

موتور

England ingiltera

إنجلترا

English ingleezee

إنجليزى

I'm English (said by

man/woman) ana

ingleezee/ingleezaya

أنا إنجليزى/إنجليزية

do you speak English? (to

man/woman)

betitkallim/betitkallimee

ingleezee?

بتتكلّم/ بتتكلمى

إنجليزى؟

enjoy: enjoy oneself istamtaA

إستمتع

dialogue

how did you like the film?
(to man/woman) Aagabak/
Aagabik el 'film'?
I enjoyed it very much, did
you enjoy it? Aagabnee
geddan, istamtaAt beeh?

enjoyable momteA

ممتع

enlargement (of photo)

takbeer

تكبير

enormous Dakhm

ضخم

enough kifāya

كفاية

there's not enough mish

kifāya

مش كفاية

it's not big enough mish

kebeer kifāya

مش كبير كفاية

that's enough da kifāya

دا كفاية

entrance madkhal

مدخل

envelope Zarf

ظرف

epileptic moSāb bil SaraA

مصاب بالصرع

equipment moAiddāt

معدّات

error ghalaT

غلط

especially khoSooSan

خصوصاً

essential asāsee

أساسي

it is essential that ... da Darooree en ...

دا ضروري ان ...

Eurocheque esh sheek el orobbee

الشيك الأوروبي

Eurocheque card kart esh sheek el orobbee

كارت الشيك الأوروبي

Europe orobba

أوروبا

European orobbee

أوروبي

even Hatta

حتّى

even if ... Hatta low ...

حتّى لو...

evening mesa

مساء

this evening ellaylādee

الليلة دى

in the evening bil layl

بالليل

evening meal Aasha

عشا

eventually akheeran

آخيرا

ever abadan

أبداً

dialogue

have you ever been to the Egyptian Museum? (to man) Aomrak roHt lil mat-Haf el-maSree? (to woman) Aomrik roHtee lil mat-Haf el-maSree?

yes, I was there two years ago īwa, roHt henāk min sanatayn

every kol

كل

every day kol yōm

كل يوم

everyone kol wāHid

كل واحد

everything kol Hāga

كل حاجة

everywhere kol Hetta

كل حتة

exactly! beZZabT!

بالضبط!

exam imtaHān

إمتحان

example mesāl

مثال

for example masalan

مثلا

excellent momtāz

ممتاز

except maAada

ماعدا

excess baggage Aafsh zayid

عفش زايد

exchange rate seAr et-taH-weel

سعر التحويل

exciting (day, holiday) gameel

جميل

(film) moseer

مثير

excursion reHla oSīyara

رحلة قصيرة

excuse me (to get past: to man/woman) low samaHt/samaHtee

لو سمحت/سمحتى

(to get attention) min faDlak

من فضلك

(to say sorry: said by man/woman) ana āsif/āsfa

أنا آسف/آسفة

exhaust (pipe) eJ-Jakmān

الجاكمان

exhausted (tired) mayit min et-taAab

ميّت من التعب

exhibition maAraD

معرض

exit khoroog

خروج

where's the nearest exit?

fayn a'rab bab?

فين أقرب باب؟

expect towaQQaA

توقع

expensive ghālee

غالى

experienced khabeer

خبير

explain waDDaH

وضّح

can you explain that? (to man/woman) momkin tewaDDaH/tewaDDaHee da?

ممكن توضّح/توضّحى دا؟

express (mail) mestaAgil

مستعجل

(train) magaree

مجرى

extension (telephone) taHweela

تحويلة

extension 221, please (to man/woman) taHweela may-tayn wāHid weAeshreen, low samaHt/samaHtee

تحويلة ٢٢١ لو سمحت/
سمحتى

extension lead meHowil

محول

extra: can we have an extra
one? momkin nākhod
wāHid zayāda?

ممكن ناخذ واحد زيادة؟

do you charge extra for
that? Had-daffaAnee aktar
Aashān da?

حتدفعنا أكتر علشان
دا؟

extraordinary ghayr Aādee

غير عادى

extremely giddan

جدا

eye Aayn (f)

عين

will you keep an eye on my
suitcase for me? (to man/
woman) momkin tekhallee
bālak/balik min shanTe-
tee?

ممكن تخلى بالك/
بالك من شنطتى؟

eye drops aTra lil Aayn

قطرة للعين

eyeglasses naDDāra

بظّارة

F

face wish

وش

factory maSnaA

مصنع

Fahrenheit Fahrenhayt

فهرنهايت

faint (verb) oghma Aalayh

أغمى عليه

she's fainted oghma Aalay-
ha

أغمى عليها

I feel faint (said by man/woman)
ana Hasis/Has-sa ennee
Hayoghma Aalaya

أنا حاسس/حاسّة
إنّى حايُغمى على

fair (funfair) moolid

مولد

(trade) maAraD

معرض

(adj) AarD

عرض

fairly belHa'

بالحق

fake (noun) ta'leed

تقليد

fall (verb) we'eA

وقع

she's had a fall hayya
we'Ait

هيّ وقعت

fall khareef

خريف

in the fall fil khareef

في الخريف

false mozayaf

مزيّف

family Aayla

عيلة

famous mash-hoor

مشهور

fan (electrical, hand-held)
marwaHa

مروحة

(sports: man/woman)
moshaggeA/moshaggeAa

مشجع / مشجعة

fantastic modhish

مدهش

far beAeed

بعيد

dialogue

is it far from here? howa
beAeed min hena?
no, not very far la', mish
beAeed awee
well how far? Hawālee ad
ay?

it's about 20 kilometres
Hawālee Aeshreen
kelomitr

fare ogra

أجرة

farm mazraAa

مزرعة

fashionable ākher mōDa

آخر موضة

fast sareeA

سريع

fat (person) tekheen

تخين

(on meat) simeen

سمين

father abb

أب

father-in-law Hama

حما

faucet Hanafaya

حنفيّة

fault zamb

ذنب

sorry, it was my fault (said by
man/woman) āsif/āsfa, da kan
zambee ana

آسف/أسفة، دا كان ذنبي
أنا

it's not my fault mosh zambee ana

مش ذنبي أنا

93

faulty fee Aayb

فى عيب

favourite mofaDDal

مفضّل

fax (noun) 'fax'

فاكس

(verb) fakas

فكس

 Most hotels with three or more stars have fax machines, making fax the best way to reserve a room from abroad. Faxes can be sent from (and received at) certain telephone offices in the main cities; you can also have them sent to American Express offices, who'll hold them like client mail but won't notify the recipient.

fax machine gihāz 'fax'

جهاز فاكس

February fibrīyer

فبراير

feel: I feel hot (said by man/woman) ana Harrān/Harrāna

أنا حرّان/حرّانة

I feel unwell (said by man/woman) ana taAbān/taAbāna

أنا تعبان/تعبانة

I feel like going for a walk (said by man/woman) ana

Aayiz/Aīza atmasha

أنا عايز/عايزة أتمشّى

how are you feeling? (to man/woman) izzay SeHetak/SeHetik?

إزّاى صحّتك/صحّتك؟

I'm feeling much better (said by man/woman) ana Hāsis/Has-sa bitaHasson

أنا حاسس/حاسّة بتحسّن

fence soor

سور

fender (US) ekseDām

إكسضام

ferry meAaddaya

معدّية

Local ferries cross the Nile and the Suez Canal at various points. They are generally cheap, battered and crowded. There are also smarter tourist ferries between Luxor and the West Bank, but it's more fun to use the ordinary boats.
Long-distance services are confined to the Red Sea and the Gulf of Aqaba, where the old slow boats have largely been superseded by the Flying Cat, a deluxe high-speed catamaran that zips over from Hurghada to Sharm el-Sheik once a day in under two hours. The fare isn't much more than that charged by the last of the old boats (which take over

five hours), and is worth it to avoid the long overland journey via Suez. The Flying Cat also runs to the Jordanian port of Aqaba, and takes diving groups to various destinations.

festival mahragān

مهرجان

Moolids are the equivalent of medieval European saints' fairs: their ostensible aim is to obtain blessing (baraka) from the saint, but the social and cultural dimensions are equally important. Moolids are an opportunity for people to escape their hard-working lives in several days of festivities, and for friends and families from different villages to meet.

The largest events draw crowds of over a million, with people running stalls and rides, and music blaring into the small hours. Smaller, rural moolids tend to be heavier on the practical devotion, with people bringing their children or livestock for blessing, or the sick to be cured.

fetch gāb

جاب

I'll fetch him Hageeboh

حاجيبه

will you come and fetch me

later? momkin tegee takhodnee baAdayn?

ممكن تيجى تاخدني بعدين؟

feverish maHmoom

محموم

few: (a) few shwīya

شويّة

a few days baAd shwīyet ayyām

بعد شويّة أيّام

fiancé khaTeeb

خطيب

fiancée khaTeeba

خطيبة

field magāl

مجال

fight (noun) khinā'a

خناقة

figs teen

تين

fill in mala

ملى

do I have to fill this in? howa ana lāzim amla dee?

هوّ أنا لازم أملى دى؟

fill up mala

ملى

fill it up, please imlāha, low samaHt

إملاها، لو سمحت

filling (in sandwich, in tooth)

Hashw

حشو

film 'film'

فيلم

dialogue

do you have this kind of
film? (to man/woman) Aan-
dak/Aandik 'film' min
en-nooA da?
yes, how many expo-
sures? (to man/woman) Īwa,
Aayiz/Aīza kām?
36 sitta wetalateen

film processing taHmeeD

aflām

تحميض أفلام

filthy wesikh

وسخ

find (verb) la'a

لأ

I can't find it mosh
la'eeh

مش لقيه

I've found it la'aytoh

لقيته

find out iktashaf

إكتشف

could you find out for me?
(to man/woman) momkin

teshoof/ teshoofee le?

ممكن تشوف/تشوفى لى؟

fine (weather) kwayis

كويّس

(punishment) gharāma

غرامة

dialogues

how are you? (to
man/woman) izzayak/izza-
yik?
I'm fine, thanks (said by
man/woman) ana
kwayis/kwayisa, shokran

is that OK? da kwayis?
that's fine, thanks da
kwayis, shokran

finger SobaA

صبع

finish (verb) khalaS

خلاص

I haven't finished yet lessa
makhal-laStish

لسة ماخلصتش

when does it finish?
betekhal-laS imta?

بتخلص إمتى؟

fire (in hearth) nār (f)

نار

(campfire) nār el mokhayam

نار المخيّم

(blaze) lahab

لهب

fire! Haree'a!

حريقة

can we light a fire here?

momkin newallaA nār

hena?

ممكن نولّع نار هنا؟

it's on fire mewallaAa

مولعة

fire alarm garas inzār

جرس إنذار

fire brigade el maTāfee

المطافئ

The number for the fire
brigade is 125.

fire escape makhrag Haree'

مخرج حريق

fire extinguisher Taffīyet

Haree'

طفّاية حريق

first awwil (m)/olā (f)

أوّل/أولى

I was first (said by man/woman)

ana kont el awwil/olā

أنا كنت الأوّل/الأولى

at first awwalan

أوّلا

the first time el marra el olā

المرة الأولى

first on the left el awwal

Aala eedak esh-shemāl

الأوّل على إيدك الشمال

first aid isAāf awwalee

إسعاف أوّلي

first-aid kit shanTit isAāf

awwalee

شنطة إسعاف أوّلي

first-class (travel etc) daraga

olā

درجة أولى

first floor ed-dōr el awwil

الدور الأوّل

(US) ed-dōr el arDee

الدور الأرضى

first name esm

إسم

fish (noun) samak

سمك

fishing Sayd samak

صيد سمك

fishing boat markib Sayd

مركب صيد

fishing village Qaryit Sayd

samak

قرية صيد سمك

fishmonger's bayyāA samak

بيّاع سمك

fit (attack) azma

أزمة

fit: it doesn't fit me mish
monāsib laya

مش مناسب لى

fitting room ōDit taghyeer
malābis

أوضة تغيير ملابس

fix (arrange) rattib

رتّب

can you fix this? (repair)
momkin teSSallaH da?

ممكن تصلح دا؟

fizzy fowwār

فوّار

flag Aalam

علم

flannel fooTit wish

فوطة وش

flash (for camera) 'flash'

فلاش

flat (noun: apartment) sha'-a

شقّة

(adj) mosaTTaH

مسطح

I've got a flat tyre el
kowetsh nayim

الكاوتش نايم

flavour TaAm

طعم

flea barghoot

برغوت

flight reHla gowaya

رحلة جوّية

flight number raQam er-riHla

رقم الرحلة

flippers zaAānif

زعانف

flood fīaDān

فيضان

floor (of room) arD (f)

أرض

(storey) dōr

دور

on the floor Aalal arD

على الأرض

florist maHal zohoor

محل زهور

flour de'ee'

دقيق

flower warda

وردة

flu infelwanza

إنفلونزا

fluent: he speaks fluent Arabic
howa bayetkallim Aarabee
kwayis awee

هوّ بيتكلّم عربى كويّس
قوى

fly (noun) dibbāna

دبّانة

(verb) Tar

طار

fly spray bakhākhit dibbān

بخّاخة دبّان

fog shaboora

شابّورة

foggy: it's foggy eg-gow shaboora

الجوّ شابّورة

folk dancing ra'S shaAbee

رقص شعبى

folk music moseeQa shaAbaya

موسيقى شعبيّة

(in Upper Egypt) moseeQa
SeAeedee

موسيقى صعيدى

follow tebeA

تبع

follow me emshee waraya

إمشى ورايا

food akl

اكل

food poisoning tasammom

تسمم

food shop/store maHal be'ala

محل بقالة

foot (of person) rigl

رجل

(measurement) adam

قدم

on foot Aala er-riglayn

على الرجلين

football (game) korit Qadam

كورة قدم

(ball) kora

كورة

football match motsh kora

ماتش كورة

for: do you have something
for ...? (headache/diarrhoea etc:
to man/woman)
Aandak/Aandik Haga
le ...?

عندك/عندِك حاجة
ل...؟

dialogues

who's the molokhayya for?
lemeen el molokhayya?
that's for me dee Aalasha
nee
and this one? wedee?
that's for her dee Alashān-
ha

where do I get the bus for
Giza? minayn akhod el
otobees el-lee bayrooh
eg-geeza?
the bus for Giza leaves
from Rameses Street
otobees eg-geeza
bayeTlaA min shāriA
ramsees

how long have you been
here? kam ba'alak hena?

I've been here for two days, how about you? (to man/woman) ba'ālee hena yōmayn, winta/winti?

I've been here for a week ba'ālee hena esbooA

forehead oora
قورة

foreign agnabee
أجنبى

foreigner (man/woman) agnabee/agnabaya
أجنبى/أجنبية

forest ghāba
غابة

forget nasa
نسى

I forget, I've forgotten nasayt
نسيت

fork shōka
شوكة

(in road) tafreeAa
تفريعة

form (document) namoozag
نموذج

formal rasmee
رسمى

fortnight isboAayn
إسبوعين

fortress alAa
قلعة

fortunately leHosn el HaZ
لحسن الحظ

forward: could you forward my mail? momkin tebaAt/tebaAtee gowabātee Aalal Ainwān eg-gedeed?
ممكن تبعت/تبعتى جواباتى على العنوان الجديد؟

forwarding address el Ainwān eg-gedeed
العنوان الجديد

fountain (ornamental) nafoora
نافورة

(for drinking) Hanafaya
حنفيّة

foyer Sāla
صالة

fracture (noun) sha'
شق

France faransa
فرنسا

free (no charge) bebalāsh
ببلاش

is it free (of charge)? da bebalāsh?
دا ببلاش؟

freeway eT-Taree' es-sareeA
الطريق السريع

freezer frayzar
فريزر

French faransāwee

فرنساوى

French fries baTaTes

meHammara

بطاطس محمّرة

frequent AalaTool

على طول

how frequent is the bus

to Ma'adee? kam

otobees bayrooH el

maAādee?

كم أوتوبيس بيروح

المعادى؟

fresh Tāza

طازة

fresh orange juice AaSeer

borto'an Tāza

عصير برتقان طازة

Friday el gomAa

الجمعة

fridge tallāga

تلاجة

fried ma'lee

مقلى

fried egg bayDa ma'laya

بيضة مقليّة

friend (male/female)

SaHib/SaHba

صاحب/صاحبة

friendly Hebbee

حبّى

from min

من

when does the next train

from Alexandria arrive? imta

yewSal el aTr el gī min

iskinderaya?

امتى يوصل القطر

الجاى من إسكندريّة؟

from Monday to Friday min

el etnayn lil gomAa

من الإثنين للجمعة

from next Thursday min el

khamees el gī

من الخميس الجاى

dialogue

where are you from? (to
man) inta minayn?
(to woman) inti minayn?
I'm from Slough ana min
'Slough'

front wag-ha

واجهة

in front oddām

قدّام

in front of the hotel oddām

el fondo'

قدّام الفندق

at the front fil mo'addima

فى المقدّمة

fruit fawākih

فواكه

fruit juice AaSeer fawākih

عصير فواكه

full malyān

مليان

it's full of ... malyana ...

مليانة ...

I'm full (said by man/woman)

ana shabAān/shabAāna

أنا شبعان/ شبعانة

full board iQāma kamla

إقامة كاملة

funeral ganāza

جنازة

funny (strange) ghareeb

غريب

(amusing) mosallee

مسلّى

furniture asās

أساس

further abAad

أبعد

it's further down the road

hayya oddām shwīya

هيّ قدّام شويّة

dialogue

how much further is it to
Shubra? fāDil kam keelo

Aala shobra?

about five kilometres

Hawālee khamsa keelo

future mosta'bal

مستقبل

in future fil most'abal

فى المستقبل

G

gallon gālōn

جالون

game (cards etc) kotshayna

كوتشينة

(match) 'match'

ماتش

(meat) Sayd

صيد

garage (for fuel) maHaTTit
banzeen

محطّة بنزين

(for repairs) warshit
Aarabayyāt

ورشة عربيّات

(for parking) mow'af
Aarabayyāt

موقف عربيّات

garden gonayna

جنينة

garlic tōm

توم

gas gāz

جاز

(US) banzeen

بنزين

gas can SafeeHet banzeen

صفيحة بنزين

gas cylinder amboobit

botagāz

أنبوبة بوتاجاز

gas station maHaTTit

banzeen

محطّة بنزين

gate bawwāba

بوّابة

gearbox el feteess

الفتيس

gear lever Aamood el feteess

عمود

gears troos

تروس

general (adj) Aām

عام

gents (toilet) tawalet rigālee,

Hammām er-rigāl

تواليت رجالي، حمّام الرجال

genuine (antique etc)

Ha'ee'ee

حقيقى

German almānee

ألمانى

Germany almānya

ألمانيّة

get (fetch) gāb

جاب

could you get me another
one, please? (to man)
momkin tegeeb le waHda
tania, low samaHt?

ممكن تجيب لى
واحدة ثانية، لوسمحت؟

(to woman) momkin tegee-
bee le waHda tania, low
samaHtee?

ممكن تجيبى لى
واحدة ثانية، لوسمحتى؟

how do I get to ...? izzay
arooH le ...?

إزاى أروح لـ...؟

do you know where I can
get them? teAraf minayn
a'dar ageebhom?

تعرف منين أقدر أجيبهم؟

dialogue

can I get you a drink? (to
man/woman) teshrab/
teshrabee ay?

no, I'll get this one la', ana
el-lee HaTlob el mar-
rādee

what would you like? (to

man/woman) teHeb/
teHebbee teshrab/
teshrabee ay?
a glass of red wine kās
nebeet aHmar

get back (return) ragaA

رجع

get in (arrive) waSal

وصل

get off nazal

نزل

where do I get off? anzil
fayn?

أنزل فين؟

get on (to train etc) rakab

ركب

get out (of car etc) nazal

نزل

get up (in the morning) SaHā

صحى

gift hedaya

هديّة

gift shop maHal hadāya

محل هدايا

gin Jin

جن

a gin and tonic, please (to
man/woman) Jin we tonik,
low samaHt/samaHtee

جن وتونيك، لو سمحت/
سمحتى

girl bint

بنت

girlfriend Sahba

صاحبة

give ed-da

إدّى

can you give me some
change? momkin
teddeenee shwīyet
fakka?

ممكن تدّينى شويّة فكّة؟

I gave it to him ana eddit-
haloo

إدّيتها له

will you give this to ...?
momkin teddee da le ...?

ممكن تدّى دا ل ...؟

dialogue

how much do you want for
this? (to man) Aayiz tebeeA
el waHda bekām?
(to woman) Aīza tebeAee el
waHda bekām?
I'll give it to you for five
pounds (to man/woman)
Haddeelak/ Haddeelik
elwaHda bekhamsa
geneeh

give back ragaA

رجّع

glass (material) ezāz

قزاز

(tumbler) kobbāya

كوبّايا

(wine glass) kās

كاس

a glass of water kās mīya

كاس ميّة

glasses naDDāra

نظّارة

go raH

راح

we'd like to go to the Opera House Aīzeen nerooH le dār elobra

عايزين نروح لدار الأوبرا

where are you going? (to man) inta rīeH fayn?

إنت رايح فين؟

(to woman) inti rīHa fayn?

إنتى رايحة فين؟

where does this bus go? fayn rīeH el otobees da?

فين رايح الأوتوبيس دا؟

let's go! yalla nimshee!

يللا نمشى!

she's gone (left) hayya meshet

هيّ مشت

where has he gone? fayn

raH howa?

فين راح هوّ؟

I went there last week ana roHt hināk el esbōA el-lee fāt

أنا رحت هناك الأسبوع اللى فات

go away emshee min hena

إمشى من هنا

go away! emshee!

إمشى!

go back (return) ragaA

رجع

go down (the stairs etc) nazal

نزل

go in dakhal

دخل

go out: do you want to go out tonight? (to man) Aayiz tokhrog e-laylade?

عايز تخرج الليلة دى؟

(to woman) Aīza tokhrogee e-laylade?

عايزة تخرجى الليلة دى؟

go through mar

مر

go up (the stairs etc) TalaA

طلع

goat meAza

معزة

god rab

رب

105

God allāh

الله

God willing inshā'llāh

إن شاء الله

goddess ilāha

إلاهة

goggles naDDara Tibbaya

نظّارة طبِّية

gold dahab

ذهب

good kwayis

كويس

good! kwayis!

كويس!

it's no good mish kwayis

مش كويس

goodbye maAssalāma

مع السلامة

good evening masā' el khayr

مساء الخير

Good Friday el gomAa el Hazeena

الجمعة الحزينة

good morning SabāH el khayr

صباح الخير

good night masā' el khayr

مساء الخير

got: we've got to leave iHna lāzim nemshee

إحنا لازم نمشى

have you got any ...? (to man/woman) Aandak/Aandik aī ...?

عندك/ عندِك أى ...؟

government Hokooma

حكومة

gradually shwīya shwīya

شويّة شويّة

gram(me) grām

جرام

granddaughter Hafeeda

حفيدة

grandfather gid

جد

grandmother gidda

جدة

grandson Hafeed

حفيد

grapefruit graybfroot

جريب فروت

grapefruit juice AaSeer graybfroot

عصير جريب فروت

grapes Aenab

عنب

(small, seedless) Aenab banā-tee

عنب بناتى

(large) Aenab fayyoomee

عنب فيّومى

grass Hasheesh

حشيش

grateful motshakkir

متشكّر

gravy Tāgin

طاجن

great (excellent) AaZeem

عظيم

that's great! da AaZeem!

دا عظيم!

a great success nagāH kebeer

نجاح كبير

Great Britain beriTanya el AoZma

بريطانيا العظمى

Greece el yonān

اليونان

greedy TamaA

طمع

Greek yonānee

يونانى

green akhDar

أخضر

green card (car insurance) 'green card'

جرين كارد

greengrocer's (vegetable shop) khoDaree

خضرى

(fruit shop) fakahānee

فكهانى

grey romādee

رمادى

grilled mashwee

مشوى

grocer's ba'āl

بقّال

ground arD (f)

أرض

on the ground Aalal arD

على الأرض

ground floor ed-dōr el arDee

الدور الأرضى

group magmooAa

مجموعة

guest (man/woman) Dayf/Dayfa

ضيف/ضيفة

When invited into someone's home, it's the custom to take your shoes off before entering the reception rooms. It's also customary to take a gift: sweet pastries (or tea and sugar in rural areas) are always acceptable. At a communal meal, it is important to use the right hand and not the left – Muslims use that hand for washing after going to the toilet.

guesthouse bansayōn

بنسيون

see hotel

guide (man/woman)

morshid/morshida

مرشد/مرشدة

 Official guides can be engaged through branches of Misr Travel, American Express and Thomas Cook, local tourist offices and large hotels. You can also hire them on the spot at the Antiquities Museum in Cairo and the Pyramids of Giza. They normally charge a fixed hourly rate, which can be shared among a group of people, though obviously a group would be expected to make some sort of additional tip. Such professional guides can be useful at major sites, like the Valley of the Kings, where they will be able to ease your way through queues at the tombs.
Far more common are local, self-appointed guides, who fall into two main categories. At ancient sites there are often plenty of loungers-around, who will offer to show you 'secret tombs' or 'special reliefs', or just present themselves in tombs or temples, with palms outstretched. They don't have a lot to offer and you can usually get rid of them by reading aloud from a guide book. The other kind – most often encountered in a small town or village – are people who genuinely want to help out foreigners, and maybe practise their English at the same time. They are often teenagers. Services offered could be escorting you from one taxi depot to another,

or showing you the route to the market or a local site. The majority of people you meet in this way don't expect money and you could risk offence by offering. If people want money from you for such activities, they won't be shy about asking. An official version of this kind of guiding is offered by members of the Tourist Friends Association, who often approach lost-looking foreigners at bus and train stations, and will swiftly produce their identity cards. They are generally students, very friendly and helpful, and not on the make. Be courteous, even if you don't want their help.

guidebook daleel sayāHee

دليل سياحى

guided tour gowla mowwa-gaha

جولة موجّهة

guitar gitār

جيتار

Gulf: the Gulf States diwal el khaleeg el Aarabee

دول الخليج العربى

gum (in mouth) lessa

لسّة

gun (rifle) bondo'aya

بندقيّة

(pistol) mosaddas

مسدس

H

hair shaAr
شعر

hairbrush forshit shaAr
فرشة شعر

haircut Hilā'a
حلاقة

hairdresser's (men's) Hallā'
حلاق

(women's) kowafayr
كوافير

hairdryer seshwār
سشوار

hair spray mossabbit shaAr
مثبت شعر

half noS
نص

half an hour noS sāAa
نص ساعة

half a litre noS litr
نص لتر

about half that Hawālee noS da
حوالى نص دا

half board noS eQāma
نص إقامة

half-bottle noS ezāza
نص قزازة

half fare noS tazkara
نص تذكرة

half-price noS et-taman
نص الثمن

ham werk khanzeer
ورك خنزير

hamburger 'hamburger'
هامبورجر

hand eed
إيد

handbag shanTit eed
شنطة إيد

handbrake farāmil yad
فرامل يد

handkerchief mandeel
منديل

handle (on door) okra
أُكرة

(on suitcase etc) eed
إيد

hand luggage shanTa
شنطة

hangover āsār esh-shorb
آثار الشرب

I've got a hangover (said by man/woman) ana mosāb/mosāba biāsār esh-shorb
أنا مصاب/مصابة بآثار الشرب

happen HaSal
حصل

what's happening? ayh

el-lee momkin yeHsal?

إيه اللى ممكن يحصل؟

what has happened? ayh
el-lee HaSal?

إيه اللى حصل؟

happy mabsooT

مبسوط

I'm not happy about this
(said by man/woman) ana
mish mabsooT/mabSooTA
beda

أنا مش مبسوط /مبسوطة

harbour meena

ميناء

hard gāmid

جامد

(difficult) SaAb

صعب

hard-boiled egg bayDa
masloo'a awee

بيضة مسلوقة قوى

hard lenses Aadasa lāSQa

عدسة لاصقة

hardly: hardly ever nādir

نادر

hardware shop maHal adawāt
manzilaya

محل أدوات منزلية

hat Ta'aya

طاقية

hate (verb) karah

كره

have* akhad

أخذ

can I have a ...? momkin
ākhod ...?

ممكن آخذ ... ؟

do you have ...? (to man/
woman) fee Aandak/
Aandik ...?

فى عندك/عندِك ... ؟

what'll you have? (to man/
woman) Hateshrab/
Hateshrabee ay?

حتشرب/حتشربى إيه؟

I have to leave now ana
lāzim amshee delwa'tee

أنا لازم أمشى دلوقتى

do I have to ...? lāzim
ana ...?

لازم أنا ... ؟

can we have some ...?
momkin nākhod
shwīyet ...?

ممكن ناخد شويّة ... ؟

hayfever Homma el-'ash

حمّى القش

he* howa

هوا

head rās (f)

راس

headache SodāA

صداع

headlights en-noor el

oddamānee

النور القدّمانى

healthy SeHHee

صحّى

health

Despite the potential
health hazards of travel in
Egypt, the majority of visitors
experience nothing worse than a
bout of diarrhoea. If symptoms
persist more than a few days, seek
medical help.
The main things to guard against are
heatstroke and food poisoning, with
rare meat and raw shellfish topping
the danger list. Just use common
sense, and accustom your stomach
gradually to Egyptian cooking.
Asking for dishes very hot ('sokhna
awee') will reduce the risk of
catching anything. Take prompt care
of cuts and skin irritations, since flies
can quickly spread infection.
Many visitors experience problems
with Egypt's intense heat; you can
easily become dehydrated without
realising it. Dehydration is
exacerbated by alcohol, coffee and
tea. Drink plenty of other fluids (at
least three litres per day; twice as
much if you're exerting yourself) and
take a bit of extra salt with your
food. Wear a hat and loose-fitting
clothes (not synthetic fabrics), and a
high factor sunscreen to protect
against sunburn. Avoid going out in
the middle of the day and wear a T-
shirt when snorkelling, as the sun
burns you even quicker in the water.

hear simeA

سمع

dialogue

can you hear me? (to man)
te'dar tismaAnee?
(to woman) te'daree
tismaAeenee?
**I can't hear you, could you
repeat that?** (to man/woman)
ana mish samAak/
samAik, momkin teAeed/
teAeedee tānee?

heart alb

قلب

heart attack zabHa Sadrayya

ذبحة صدريّة

heat Harāra

حرارة

heatstroke Darbit shams

ضربة شمس

heavy ti'eel

ثقيل

heel (of foot, of shoe) kaAb

كعب

could you heel these?
momkin terakkib lee kaAb
fee dōl?

ممكن تركّب
لى كعب فى دول؟

heelbar taSleeH gezam

تصليح جزم

height (of person) Tool

طول

(mountain) Aolow

علو

helicopter 'helicopter'

هليكوبتر

hello ahlan

أهلاً

(answer on phone) aloo

ألو

helmet (for motorcycle) khōza

خوذة

help (noun) mosaAda

مساعدة

(verb) sāAid

ساعد

help! el Ha'oonay!

الحقوني!

can you help me? momkin tesaAednee?

ممكن تساعدني؟

thank you very much for your help (to man/woman) shokran giddan Aala mosaAdetak/mosaAdetik laya

شكراً جداً على مساعدتك/مساعدتك ليّا

helpful khadoom

خدوم

hepatitis eltihāb fil kibd

إلتهاب في الكبد

her*: I haven't seen her mashoftahāsh

ماشوفتهاش

to her leha

ليها

with her maAāha

معاها

for her Aalashanha

علشانها

that's her da btaAha

دا بتاعها

that's her towel dee fooTit-ha

دى فوطتها

herbal tea shī aAshāb

شاى أعشاب

herbs aAshāb

أعشاب

here hena

هنا

here is/are ... hena el ...

هنا ال ...

here you are (to man/woman) etfaDDal/etfaD-Dalee

إتفضّل/إتفضّلى

hers* btaAha

بتاعها

that's hers da btaAha

دا بتاعها

hey! (to man/woman) inta!/inti!

إنت!/إنتى!

hi! (hello) ahlan!

أهلا!

hide (verb) istakhabba

إستخبّى

hieroglyphics hayroghleefee

هيروغليفى

high Aālee

عالى

highchair korsee Aālee

كرسى عالى

highway eT-Taree' es-sareeA

الطريق السريع

hill maTlaA

مطلع

him*: I haven't seen him
mashoft-hoosh

ماشوفتهوش

to him leh

له

with him maAāh

معاه

for him Aalashānoo

علشانه

that's him howa da

هوّ دا

hip hansh

هنش

hire aggar

أجّر

for hire lil egār

للإيجار

where can I hire a car? fayn
a'dar a'aggar Aarabaya?

فين أقدر الأجر عربيّة؟

see rent

his*: it's his car Aarabeeto

عربيته

that's his da btāAo

بتاعه

hit (verb) Darab

ضرب

hitch-hike oto-stob

أوتوستوب

In the countryside and desert, where buses may be sporadic or non-existent, it is standard practice for lorries (Aarabayyāt na'l) and pick-up trucks (beejō) to carry and charge passengers. You may be asked to pay a little more than the locals, or have to bargain over a price, but it's straightforward enough. Getting rides in tractors is another possibility in rural areas.

hobby hewāya

هواية

hold (verb) masak

مسك

Ho

hole khorm

خرم

holiday agāza

أجازة

on holiday fi agāza

فى أجازة

Holland holanda

هولندا

home bayt

بيت

at home (in my house etc) fil bayt

فى البيت

(in my country) baladee

بلدى

we go home tomorrow Han-rowwaH bokra le baladna

حنروّح بكرة لبلدنا

honest ameen

أمين

honey Aasal naHl

عسل نحل

honeymoon shahr el Aasal

شهر العسل

hood (US: of car) kabboot

كبّوت

hope itmanna

إتمنّى

I hope so atmanna kida

أتمنّى كده

I hope not matmannāsh

ماتمنّاش

hopefully inshā'allāh

إن شاء اللّه

horn (of car) kalaks

كلاكس

horrible morAeb

مرعب

horse HoSān

حصان

horse-drawn buggy HanToor

حنطور

horse riding rikoob el khayl

ركوب الخيل

hospital mostashfa

مستشفى

hospitality karam

كرم

thank you for your hospitality shokran Aala alkaram

شكراً على الكرم

hot (water etc) sokhn

سخن

(spicy) Hāmee

حامى

I'm hot (said by man/woman) ana Harrān/Harrāna

أنا حرّان/حرّانة

it's hot eg-gow Harr

الجوّ حر

hotel fondo'

فندق

Egyptian hotels are loosely categorized by star ratings, ranging from five-star deluxe class down to one-star. Below this range there are also unclassified hotels and guesthouses, some of them tailored to foreign backpackers, others mostly used by Egyptians. The categorizations tend to have more meaning in the higher bands; once you're down to one or two stars the differences are often hard to detect.

Deluxe hotels are almost exclusively modern and chain-owned with swimming pools, bars, restaurants, air-conditioning and all the usual international facilities. Four-star hotels can be more characterful, including some famous (and reconditioned) names from the old tradition of Egyptian tourism. There is the odd gem amongst three-star hotels, though most of them are 1970s towers, often becoming a little shabby. Facilities like air-conditioning and plumbing can be unreliable.

At two- and one-star level, you rarely get air-conditioning, though better places will supply fans, and old-style buildings with balconies, high ceilings and louvred windows are well designed to cope with the heat. However, they can be distinctly chilly in winter, as they rarely have any form of heating.

Some of the cheaper hotels are classified as guesthouses (bansyōn) which makes little difference in terms of the facilities, but tends to signify family ownership and a friendlier ambience.

At the cheap end of the scale, in the most popular tourist towns, like Luxor and Hurghada, you also get 'student hostels', specifically aimed at backpackers. They are often quite well run and equipped, if a bit cramped.

Bookings for the four- and five- star hotels are best made through the central reservation office of the chain owning the hotel. At mid-range hotels, it is worth trying to book ahead if you want to stay in a particular place in Cairo, Alex, Aswan or Luxor. Elsewhere, – and at all the cheaper hotels – most people just turn up.

Most hotels levy a service charge (12 per cent) plus local taxes (2-15 per cent) on top of their quoted rates. Breakfast is generally provided and may or may not be included in the room rate. Extra charges most commonly turn up at mid-range hotels, which may add on a few pounds for a fan or air-conditioning, or a TV.

hotel room Hogrit fondo'
حجرة فندق

hour sāAa
ساعة

house bayt
بيت

 HO

115

how izzay

إزّاى

how many? ad ay?

قد إيه؟

how do you do? (to man/
woman) Aāmil/Aāmla ay?

عامل/عاملة إيه؟

dialogues

how are you? (to man/
woman) izzayak/izzayik?

fine, thanks, and you? (to
man/woman) bekhayr,
shokran, winta/winti?

how much are they?
bekām?

five pounds each elwaHda
be khamsa geneeh

I'll take it iddeenee
waHda

humid roTooba

رطوبة

hungry gooA

جوع

are you hungry? (to man) inta
gaAān?

إنت جعان؟

(to woman) inti gaAāna?

إنتى جعانة؟

hurry (verb) istaAgil

إستعجل

I'm in a hurry (said by man/
woman) ana mistaAgil/
mistaAgila

أنا مستعجل/مستعجلة

there's no hurry Aala
mehlak

على مهلك

hurry up! yalla besorAa!

يللا بسرعة!

hurt (verb) wagaA

وجع

it really hurts Ha'ee'ee
bitowgaA

حقيقى بتوجع

husband gōz

جوز

hydrofoil 'launch'
maTTāT

لنش مطّاط

I

I ana

أنا

ice talg

ثلج

with ice bee talg

بالثلج

no ice, thanks min ghayr

talg, shokran

من غير ثلج، شكرا

ice cream Jelātee

جيلاتى

ice-cream cone Jelātee bee
baskōt

جيلاتى بيسكوت

iced coffee ahwa
metalliga

قهوة متلّجة

ice lolly loleeta

لوليتا

idea fikra

فكرة

idiot ghabee

غبى

if low

لو

ignition tadweer

تدوير

ill Aīyān

عيّان

I feel ill (said by man/woman)
ana Aīyān/Aīyāna

أنا عيّان/عيّانة

illness maraD

مرض

imitation (leather etc) ta'leed

تقليد

immediately Hālan

حالاً

important mohim

مهم

it's very important da
mohim awee

دا مهم قوى

it's not important da mish
mohim

دا مش مهم

impossible mostaHeel

مستحيل

impressive mo'assir

مؤثّر

improve taHseen

تحسين

I want to improve my
Arabic (said by man/
woman) ana Aayiz/Aīza
aHassin el Aarabee
betāAee

أنا عايز/عايزة
أحسّن العربى بتاعى

in: it's in the centre fee el
wesT

فى الوسط

in my car fee Aarabeetee

فى عربيتى

in Cairo fil Qāhira

فى القاهرة

in two days from now khilāl
yomayn

خلال يومين

in five minutes khilāl

khamas da'āye'

خلال خمس دقايق

in May fee mayoo

فى مايو

in English bil ingleezee

بالإنجليزى

in Arabic bil Aarabee

بالعربى

is he in? howa mowgood?

هوّ موجود؟

inch booSa

بوصة

include yeshmal

يشمل

does that include meals? da shāmel el wagabāt?

دا شامل الوجبات؟

is that included? da maHsoob fes seAr?

دا محسوب فى السعر؟

inconvenient mish molā'im

مش ملائم

incredible mod-hish

مدهش

Indian hindee

هندى

indicator eshārit noor

إشارة نور

indigestion soo' haDm

سوء هضم

indoor pool Hammām sibāHa

dākhelee

حمّام سباحة داخلى

indoors dākhelee

داخلى

inexpensive rekheeS

رخيص

infection Aadwa

عدوى

infectious moAdee

معدى

inflammation eltihāb

إلتهاب

informal mish rasmee

مش رسمى

information maAlomāt

معلومات

do you have any information about ...? (to man/woman) Aandak/Aandik maAlomāt Aan ...?

عندك/عندِك معلومات عن ...؟

information desk esteAlamāt

إستعلامات

injection Ho'na

حقنة

injured etgaraH

إتجرح

she's been injured hayya etgaraHet

هىّ إتجرحت

innocent baree'a
بريئة

insect Hashara
حشرةٌ

insect bite arSit Hashara
قرصة حشرةٌ

do you have anything for insect bites? (to man/woman)
Aandak/Aandik aī Hāga
Did arS el Hasharāt?
عندكَ/عندك أيحاجة
ضدقرصَ الحشرات؟

insecticide spray mobeed
Hasharee SiH-Hee
مبيد حشرى صحّى

insect repellent Tārid lil
Hasharāt
طارد للحشرات

inside gowa
جوّه

inside the hotel gowa el
fondo'
جوّه الفندق

let's sit inside yalla no'Aod
gowa
يللا نقعد جوّه

insist: I insist ana moSir
أنا مصر

instant coffee naskafee
نسكافيه

instead badal
بدل

give me that one instead
eddeenee wāHid tānee
badal da
إدّينى واحد تانى بدل دا

instead of ... badal min ...
بدل من ...

insulin ansooleen
أنسولين

insurance ta'meen
تأمين

intelligent zakee
ذكى

interested: I'm interested in ...
ana mohtam be ...
أنا مهتم ب...

interesting momteA
مُتع

that's very interesting da
momteA awee
دا مُتع قوى

international Aālamee
عالمى

Internet 'Internet'
إنترنت

interpreter (man) motargim
fowree
مترجم فورى

(woman) motargima
fowraya
مترجم فورية

intersection taQāToA Toro'
تقاطع طرق

119

interval (at theatre) estirāHa

إستراحة

into le

ل

I'm not into that ana
mabaHebbish da

أنا ماباحبّش دا

introduce Aarraf

عرّف

may I introduce ...? momkin
aAarrafak bee ...?

ممكن أعرّفك ب...

invitation (general) daAwa

دعوة

(for meal) Aezooma

عزومة

invite daAa

دعى

Iran irān

إيران

Iraq el Arā'

العراق

Ireland īrlanda

أيرلندا

Irish īrlandee

أيرلندى

I'm Irish (said by man/woman)
ana īrlandee/īrlandaya

أنا أيرلندى/أيرلندية

iron (for ironing) makwa

مكوى

can you iron these for me?
momkin tekwee dool
Aalashanee?

ممكن تكوى دول علشانى؟

is*

island gezeera

جزيرة

Israel isra'eel

إسرائيل

Israeli isra'eelee

إسرائيلى

it* howa/hayya (m/f)

هوّ/هيّ

it is ... da/dee ... (m/f)

دا/دى ...

is it ...? ... da/dee?

دا/دى ...؟

where is it? fayn da/dee?

فين دا/دى

it's him howa da

هوّ دا

it's her hayya dee

هيّ دى

it was ... kan/kānit ...
(m/f)

كان/كانت ...

I like it baHebbo/
baHebbaha (m/f)

بحبه/بحبها

Italian eTālee

إيطالى

Italy eTālya

إيطاليا

itch: it itches

bitakolnee

بتاكلني

J

jacket Jākit

جاكت

jam mirabba

مربّى

jammed: it's jammed

maHshoor

محشور

January yanāyer

يناير

jar (noun) barTamān

برطمان

jaw fakk

فك

jazz moseeQa el Jāz

موسيقى الجاز

jealous ghīrān

غيران

jeans Jeenz

جينز

jeep jeb

جيب

jellyfish andeel baHr

قنديل بحر

Jerusalem el Qods

القدس

jetty raSeef

رصيف

jeweller's megowharātee

مجوهراتى

(also repairs) Sāyegh

صايغ

jewellery megowharāt

مجوهرات

Jewish yahoodee

يهودى

job shoghl

شغل

joke nokta

نكتة

Jordan el ordon

الأردن

journey reHla

رحلة

have a good journey! reHla

saAeeda!

رحلة سعيدة!

jug ebree'

إبريق

a jug of water shafsha'

mīya

شفشق ميّة

July yolyo

يوليو

jump (verb) noT

نط

junction taQāToA Toro'

تقاطع طرق

June yonyo

يونيو

just (only) bas

بس

just two itneen bas

إثنين بس

just for me laya ana bas

لىّ أنا بس

just here bas hena

بس هنا

not just now mish
delwa'tee

مش دلوقتى

we've just arrived eHna lessa
wāSleen delwa'tee

إحنا لسّة واصلين دلوقتى

K

keep: keep the change
khallee el bā'ee

خلّى الباقى

can I keep it? momkin
akhdo?

ممكن أخذه؟

please keep it momkin
tekhalleeh maAāk?

ممكن تخليه معاك؟

ketchup 'ketchup'

كيتش أب

kettle barrād

برّاد

key moftāH

مفتاح

the key for room 201,
please (to man/woman)
momkin moftāH ōDa
maytayn we wāHid,
low samaHt/
samaHtee?

ممكن مفتاح أوضة ٢٠١،
لو سمحت/سمحتى؟

keyring Hala'it mafateeH

حلقة مفاتيح

kidneys (in body) kelā

كلى

(food) kalāwee

كلاوى

kill atal

قتل

kilo keelo

كيلو

kilometre kelomitr

كيلومتر

how many kilometres is it
to ...? kam kelomitr
takhod liHad ...?

كم كيلومتر تاخذ لحد ...؟

kind (generous) kareem

كريم

that's very kind da zoo'
minnak

دا ذوق منّك

dialogue

which kind do you want?
(to man/woman) Aayiz/Aīza
aī nōA?
I want this kind (said by
man/woman) ana Aayiz/Aīza
en-nōA da

king malik

ملك

kiosk koshk

كشك

kiss (noun) bōsa

بوسة

(verb) bās

بس

 kissing
Kissing and/or embracing
in public should be
avoided in Egypt; it is considered as
a criminal offence and could lead to
a civil court case.

kitchen maTbakh

مطبخ

Kleenex® kleniks

كلينكس

knee rokba

ركبة

knickers libās Hareemee

لباس حريمّ

knife sikkeena

سكّينة

knock (verb) da'

دق

knock over (object) wa'aA

وقع

(pedestrian) khabaT

خبط

he's been knocked over
howa etkhabaT

هوّ إتخبط

know Aaraf

عرف

I don't know maArafsh

ماعرفش

I didn't know that ana
maAraftish da

أنا ماعرفتش دا

do you know where I can
find ...? te'dar te'ollee fayn
alā'ee ...?

تقدر تقول لى فين
الآقى ....؟

Koran Qor'ān

قرآن

Kuwait al kowayt

الكويت

L

label tekit

تيكت

ladies' room, ladies' (toilets)
tawalet Hareemee

تواليت حريمى

ladies' wear malābis
Hareemee

ملابس حريمى

lady madām

مدام

lager stella®

ستيللا

see beer

lake birka

بركة

Lake Nasser boHayrit nāSSer

بحيرة ناصر

lamb (meat) Dānee

ضانى

lamp lambba

لمبة

lane (small road) Hāra

حارة

language logha

لغة

language course kors logha

كورس لغة

large kebeer

كبير

last akheer

أخير

last week el isbooA el-lee
fāt

الإسبوع اللى فات

last Friday el gomAa el-lee
fāttit

الجمعة اللى فاتت

last night laylit imbbāreH

ليلة إمبارح

what time is the last train to
Alexandria? imta āakhir aTr
liskinderaya?

إمتى آخرقطرلسكندرية؟

late mit'kh-khar

متأخّر

sorry I'm late (said by
man/woman) āsif/asfa Aala
et-ta'kheer

آسف/أسفة على التأخير

the train was late el-'aTr
kan mit'akh-khar

القطر كان متأخّر

we must go – we'll be late
eHna lāzim nemshee –
Hanit'akh-khar

إحنا لازم نمشى، حنتأخر

it's getting late el wa't
etakh-khar

الوقت إتأخّر

later baAdayn

بعدين

I'll come back later ana
HargaA tanee

أنا خارجع ثانى

see you later ashoofak baA-
dayn

أشوفك بعدين

later on baAdayn

بعدين

latest akheer

آخر

by Wednesday at the latest
Aala ela'all yōm elarbaA

على الأقل يوم الأربع

laugh (verb) DaHak

ضحك

launderette, laundromat
maghsala afrangee

مغسلة أفرنجى

laundry (clothes) ghaseel

غسيل

(place) maghsala

مغسلة

In Egypt no one goes to the laundry: if they don't do their own, they send it out to a makwagee (a person who washes clothes and irons them). Wherever you are staying, there will either be an in-house makwagee, or one close by to call on. Some low-budget hotels in Luxor, Aswan and Hurghada allow guests to use their washing machine for free or for a

small charge. You can buy washing powder at most pharmacies. Dry cleaners are confined to Cairo, Aswan and Hurghada.

lavatory tawalet

تواليت

law Qânoon

قانون

lawyer (man/woman)
moHâmee/mohamaya

محامى/محاميّة

laxative molayin

مليّن

lazy kaslân

كسلان

lead (electrical) silk kahraba

سلك كهربا

(verb) Qâd

قاد

where does this lead to? da
yewaddee Aala fayn?

دا يودّى على فين؟

leaf wara'it shagar

ورقة شجر

leaflet manshoor

منشور

leak (noun) rashH

رشح

(verb) rashaH

رشح

the roof leaks essa'af bayer-shaH

السقف بيرشحّ

learn daras

درس

least: not in the least

eTlāQan

إطلاقا

at least 50 khamseen Aalal a'all

٥٠ على الأقل

leather gild

جلد

leave (verb) mashā

مشى

I am leaving tomorrow ana māshee bokra

أنا ماشى بكرة

he left yesterday howa mesha embbāriH

هوّ مشى إمّبارح

may I leave this here? momkin aseeb da hena?

ممكن أسيب دا هنا؟

I left my jacket in the bar nasayt eJākit btāAee fil bār

نسيت الجاكت بتاعى فى البار

when does the bus for the airport leave? el otobees el-lee bayrooH elmaTār

bayTlaA imta?

الأوتوبيس اللى بيروح المطار بيطلع إمتى؟

Lebanon libnān

لبنان

left shimāl

شمال

on the left Aala esh-shimāl

على الشمال

to the left lesh-shimāl

للشمال

turn left Howid shimāl

حوِّد شمال

there's none left mafDelshee Haga

مافضّلش حاجة

left-handed ashwal

أشول

left luggage (office) maktab amanāt

مكتب أمانات

leg rigl (f)

رجل

lemon lamoon

لمون

lemonade espatis®

إسباتس

lemon juice lamonāta

لموناتة

lemon tea shī be lamoon

شاى باللمون

lend sallif

سلّف

will you lend me your ...? (to man/woman) momkin tesal-lifnee/tesallifnee ... betāAak/betāAik?

ممكن تسلّفني/تسلّفيني ... بتاعُك/بتاعِك؟

lens (of camera) Aadasa

عدسة

less a'all

أقل

less than a'all min

أقل من

less expensive arkhaS

أرخص

lesson dars

درس

let (allow) yesmaH

يسمح

will you let me know? momkin teAarrafnee?

ممكن تعرّفني؟

I'll let you know Hab'a a'ool-lak

حبقى أقول لك

let's go for something to eat yalla nerooH nākol Haga

يللا نروح ناكل حاجة

let off nazzil

نزّل

will you let me off at ...? momkin tenazzilnee Aand ...?

ممكن تنزّلني عند ...؟

letter gowāb

جواب

do you have any letters for me? fee aī gowabāt laya?

في أي جوابات ليّ؟

letterbox Sandoo' el bosTa

صندوق البوسطة

see post office

lettuce khas

خس

lever (noun) Aatala

عتلة

library maktaba

مكتبة

Libya libya

ليبيا

licence rokhSa

رخصة

lid ghaTa

غطا

lie (verb: tell untruth) kazab

كذب

lie down yeSSaTTaH

يسّطّح

life Aomr

عمر

lifebelt Too' nagāh

طوق نجاه

lifeguard Hāris esh-shaT

حارس الشط

life jacket sotrit inQāz

سترة إنقاذ

lift (in building) asansayr

أسانسير

could you give me a lift?
momkin tewaSSalnee
belAarabayya?

ممكن توصّلنى بالعربيّة؟

would you like a lift? (to man)
Aayiznee awaSSalak?

عايزنى أوّصلك؟

(to woman) Aīzanee awaSSa-
lik?

عايزانى أوصّلك؟

light (noun) noor

نور

(not heavy) khafeef

خفيف

do you have a light? (for cigarette) maAak kabreet?

معاك كبريت؟

light green akhDar fāteH

أخضر فاتح

light bulb lamba

لمبة

I need a new light bulb (said

by man/woman) ana
Aayiz/Aīza lamba gedeeda

أنا عايز/عايزة لمبة
جديدة

lighter (cigarette) wallāAa

ولاّعة

lightning bar'

برق

like (verb) Hab

حب

I like it baHebbo/baHebba-
ha (m/f)

بحبّه/بحبّها

I like going for walks baHeb
atmashā

بحب أتمشّى

I like you (to man/woman) ana
baHebbak/baHebbik

أنا بحبّك/بحبِّك

I don't like it mabaHebboosh

مابحبّوش

do you like ...? (to man) inta
betHeb ...?

إنت بتحب ...؟

(to woman) inti
betHebbee ...?

إنتى بتحبّى ...؟

I'd like a beer (said by man/
woman) ana Aayiz/Aīza beera

أنا عايز/عايزة بيرة

Li

I'd like to go swimming (said by man/woman) ana Aayiz/Aīza aAoom

أنا عايز/عايزة أعوم

would you like a drink? (to man) inta Aayiz teshrab Haga?

إنت عايز تشرب حاجة؟

(to woman) inti Aīza teshrabee Haga?

إنتى عايزة تشربي حاجة؟

would you like to go for a walk? (to man) teHeb tetmasha?

تحب تتمشّى؟

(to woman) teHebbee tetmashee?

تحبّى تتمشّى؟

what's it like? hayya zay ay?

هىّ زى إيه؟

I want one like this (said by man/woman) ana Aayiz/Aīza waHda zay dee

أناعايز/عايزة واحدة زى دى

lime lamoon

لمون

line (on paper) SaTr

سطر

(phone) khaT

خط

could you give me an outside line? (to man/woman) momkin teftaHlee/teftaHelee khaT khāregee?

ممكن تفتح/تفتحي لى خط خارجى؟

lips shafāyef

شفايف

lip salve zebdit kakow

زبدة كاكاو

lipstick alam rōJ

قلم روج

liqueur sharāb mo'aTTar

شراب مقطّر

listen ismaA

إسمع

litre litr

لتر

little Soghīar

صغيّر

just a little, thanks shwīya Soghīareen, shokran

شويّة صغيّرين، شكراً

a little milk shwīyet laban

شويّة لبن

a little bit more shwīya kamān

شويّة كمان

live (verb) sakan

سكن

we live together eHna

sakneen maAa baAD

إحنا ساكنين مع بعض

dialogue

where do you live? (to man)
inta sākin fayn?
(to woman) inti sakna
fayn?
I live in London (said by
man/woman) ana sākin/
sakna fee 'London'

lively nasheeT

نشيط

liver (in body) kibd

كبد

(food) kibda

كبدة

loaf Aaysh

عيش

lobby (in hotel) madkhal

مدخل

lobster gambaree kebeer

جمبرى كبير

local maHallee

محلّى

can you recommend a local
restaurant? (to man/woman)
momkin te'ollee/te'olelee
fayn aHsan maTAam

maHallee?

ممكن تقوللي/تقوليلي
فين أحسن مطعم محلى؟

lock (noun) efl

قُفْل

(verb) afal

قفل

it's locked ma'fool

مقفول

lock in afal Aala

قفل على

lock out afal Aala

قفل على

I've locked myself out (of
room) el bab et'afāl Aalaya

الباب إتقفل علىّ

locker (for luggage etc) amanāt

أمانات

lollipop maSSāSa

مصّاصة

London 'London'

لندن

long Taweel

طويل

how long will it take to fix it?
betākhod ad ay wa't
Aalashan teSallaH dee?

بتاخذ قد إيه وقت
علشان تصلح دى؟

how long does it take?
betākhod ad ay?

بتاخذ قد إيه؟

a long time wa't Taweel

وقت طويل

one day/two days longer
yōm/yōmayn aTwal

يوم/يومين أطول

long-distance call mokalma
khārigaya

مكالمة خارجيّة

look: I'm just looking, thanks
ana batfarag bas, shokran

أنا باتفرج بس، شكرا

you don't look well (to man)
inta shaklak taAbān

إنت شكلك تعبان

(to woman) inti shaklik
taAbāna

إنتى شكلك تعبانة

look out! Hāsib!

حاسب

can I have a look? momkin
aboS?

ممكن أبص؟

look after khalla bāloh

خلّى باله

look at boS Aala

بص على

look for dowar Aala

دوّر على

I'm looking for ... ana
badowar Aala ...

أنا بدوّر على ...

look forward to anTaZir

أنتظر

I'm looking forward to it ana
monTaZir ashofoh

أنا منتظر أشوفه

loose (handle etc) sāyib

سايب

lorry loree

لورى

lose khesir

خسر

I'm lost, I want to get to ...
(said by man/woman) ana toht,
ana Aayiz/Aīza arooH le ...

أنا تهت، أنا عايز/عايزة
أروح ل...

I've lost my bag DaAet
shanTetee

ضاعت شنطتى

lost property (office) maktab
mafQodāt

مكتب مفقودات

lot: a lot, lots keteer

كثير

not a lot mish keteer

مش كثير

a lot of people nās keteer

ناس كثير

a lot bigger akbar bekteer

أكبر بكثير

I like it a lot baHebbo/

baHebbaha keteer (m/f)
باحبّه/باحبّها كثير

lotion marham
مرهم

loud Aālee
عالى

lounge Sāla
صالة

love (noun) Hob
حُب

(verb) Hab
حَب

I love Egypt ana baHeb maSr
أنا باحبّ مصر

lovely gameel
جميل

low (prices) rekheeS
رخيص

(bridge) wāTee
واطى

luck HaZ
حظ

good luck! HaZ saAeed!
حظ سعيد!

luggage shonaT
شنط

luggage trolley Aarabayyit shonaT
عربية شنط

lunch ghadā
غذاء

lungs ri'atayn
رئتين

Luxor lo'Sor
الأقصر

luxurious fakhm
فخم

luxury fakhāma
فخمه

M

machine makana
مكنه

magazine magalla
مجله

maid (in hotel) khaddāmit el ghoraf
خدامة الغرف

mail (noun) bosTa
بوسطه

(verb) baAat
بعث

is there any mail for me? fee aī bosTa laya?
في اي بوسطه ليه؟

mailbox Sandoo' el bosTa
صندوق البوسطه

see post office

main ra'eesee
رئيسي

main course elwagba
elra'eesaya

الوجبه الرئيسيه

main post office maktab
elbareed elra'eesee

مكتب البوسطه الرئيسي

main road eT-Taree' er-
ra'eesee

الطريق الرئيسي

make (brand name) marka

ماركه

(verb) Aemil

إعمل

what is it made of?
maAmoola min ay?

معموله من إيه؟

make-up mikyaJ

مكياج

malaria malaria

ملاريا

man ragil

راجل

manager (man/woman) mod-
eer/modeera

مدير/مديره

can I see the manager?
momkin ashoof el modeer?

ممكن اشوف المدير؟

mango manga

منجه

many keteer

كثير

not many mish keteer

مش كثير

map khareeTa

خريطه

General maps of Egypt are
on sale in Cairo, Luxor and
Aswan. City plans of Cairo
are also available. Elsewhere,
however, aside from fairly crude
maps of Alexandria, Luxor, Aswan
and Port Said, and photocopied
handouts in Mersa Matrouh and
Siwa Oasis, there are no town plans
to be found.

March maris

مارس

margarine zibda SinaAaya

زبده صناعيه

market soo'

سوق

marmalade nareng

نارنج

married: I'm married (said by
man/woman) ana
mitgowiz/mitgowiza

أنا متزوج/متزوجه

are you married? (to man)
inta mitgowiz?

إنت متزوج؟

(to woman) inti mitgowiza?

إنتي متزوجه؟

match (football etc) 'match'
ماتش

matches kabreet
كبريت

material (fabric) omāsh
قماش

matter: it doesn't matter maAlaysh
معلش

what's the matter? fee ay?
فى إيه؟

mattress martaba
مرتبه

May māyo
مايو

may: may I have another one? momkin ākhud wāHid tanee/waHda tania? (m/f)
ممكن اخد واحد تانى/واحده تانيه؟

may I come in? momkin adkhol?
ممكن ادخل؟

may I see it? momkin ashoofo/ashoofha? (m/f)
ممكن اشوفه/اشوفها؟

may I sit here? momkin aAod hena?
ممكن اقعد هنا؟

maybe yimkin
يمكن

mayonnaise mayonayz
مايونيز

me* ana
أنا

that's for me da/dee Aalashānee (m/f)
دا/دى علشانى

send it to me ibAat-hālee
إبعتها لى

me too wana kamān
وانا كمان

meal wagba
وجبه

dialogue

did you enjoy your meal?
(to man/woman)
Aagabak/Aagabik el akl?
it was excellent, thank you
kan momtāz, shokran

mean (verb) aSad
قصد

what do you mean? (to man/woman) aSdak/aSdik ay?
قصدك/قصدِك إيه؟

dialogue

what does this word mean? ek-kelma dee

maAnāha ay?

it means ... in English

maAnāha ... bil
ingleezee

meat laHma

لحمه

Mecca makka

مكه

mechanic makaneekee

ميكانيكى

medicine dowa (m)

دواء

Mediterranean el baHr el

metowaSSiT

البحر المتوسط

medium (adj: size)

metowaSSiT

متوسط

medium-dry noS gaffa

نصف جافة

medium-rare noS sewa

نصف سوا

medium-sized metowaSSiT

متوسط

meet ābil

قابل

nice to meet you forSa

saAeeda

فرصه سعيده

where shall I meet you? (to

man/woman) fayn momkin

a'ablak/a'ablik?

فين ممكن أقابلَك/أقابلِك؟

meeting egtimāA

إجتماع

meeting place makān

egtimāA

مكان إجتماع

melon shemmām

شمام

men reggāla

رجاله

mend SallaH

صلح

could you mend this for me?

(to man/woman) momkin

teSallaH/teSallaHee dee

layа?

ممكن تصلح/تصلحى

دى لى؟

men's room Hammām er-

rigāl

حمام الرجال

menswear malābis regālee

ملابس رجالى

mention: don't mention it el

Aafw

العفو

menu elmenew

المنيو

may I see the menu, please?

(to man/woman) momkin

ashoof elmenew, low
samaHt/samaHtee

ممكن أشوف المنيو لو
سمحت/سمحتى؟

see menu reader page 263

message resāla

رساله

are there any messages for
me? fee rasā'il
Aalashānee?

فى رسائل علشانى؟

I want to leave a message
for ... (said by man/woman)
ana Aayiz/Aīza aseeb resāla
le ...

أنا عايز/عايزه أسيب
رساله ل ...

metal (noun) maAdan

معدن

metre mitr

متر

midday eD-Dohr

الظهر

at midday eD-Dohr

الظهر

middle: in the middle fen-noS

فى النصف

in the middle of the night
fee noS ellayl

فى نصف الليل

the middle one elwasTānee

الوسطانى

Middle Egypt wesT maSr

وسط مصر

midnight noS ellayl

نصف الليل

at midnight fi noS ellayl

فى نصف الليل

might: I might ana momkin

أنا ممكن

I might not ana momkin
ma

أنا ممكن ما

I might want to stay another
day ana momkin a'Aud
yōm zayāda

أنا ممكن اقعد يوم زياده

mild (taste) mosh Hāmee

مش حامى

(weather) gameel

جميل

mile meel

ميل

milk laban

لبن

millimetre millimetr

ميليمتر

minaret ma'zana

مأذنه

mind: never mind maAlaysh

معلش

I've changed my mind ana
ghīyart ra'yee

أنا غيرت رأيى

dialogue

do you mind if I open
the window? (to man/
woman) Aandak/Aandik
māneA low fataHt esheb-
bāk?
no, I don't mind la',
maAandeesh māneA

mine*: it's mine da btāAee/
dee btaAtee (m/f)

دا بتاعى/دى بتاعتى

mineral water mīya
maAdanaya

ماء معدنيه

Bottled mineral water is
widely available,
particularly Baraka
('Blessing'); the Siwa brand is less
common. If tourists request water, it
is assumed they mean mineral water
unless they specifically ask for tap
water (mīya min elHanafaya), which
is safe to drink in major towns and
cities, but too chlorinated for the
average visitor's palate. When buying
bottled water, it is wise to check that
the seal is intact.
see water

minibus menīboS

مينى باص

minute de'ee'a

دقيقه

in a minute kamān shwīya

كمان شويه

just a minute de'ee'a
waHda

دقيقه واحده

mirror mrāya

مرايا

Miss ānisa

آنسه

miss: I missed the bus rāH
Aalaya el otobees

راح علىَّ الأوتوبيس

missing DāyiA

ضائع

one of my ... is missing
waHid min ... betooAee
DayiA

واحد من ... بتوعى
ضائع

there's a suitcase missing
fee shanTa DayiAa

فى شنطه ضائعه

mist shabboora

شبوره

mistake (noun) ghalTa

غلطه

I think there's a mistake
aZon en fee ghalTa
hena

أظن إن فى غلطة هنا

sorry, I've made a mistake (said by man/woman) āsif/āsfa, ana gheleᵀt

آسف/آسفة، أنا غلطت

mobile phone 'mobile phone'

موبايل فون

modern modayrn

مودرن

moisturizer kraym

كريم

moment: I won't be a moment mish Haᵗ'akhar

مش حاتأخر

monastery dayr

دير

Monday yōm el itnayn

يوم الإثنين

money floos (f)

فلوس

 Egypt's basic unit of currency is the Egyptian pound (geneeh), written as £E or LE. Notes are colour-coded as follows: £E1 (brown), £E5 (blue), £E10 (red), £E20 (green), £E50 (red), £E100 (green). The Egyptian pound is divided into 100 piastres (irsh), abbreviated by Westerners to pt. There are 25pt and 50pt notes, and variously-sized coins to the value of 5pt, 10pt, 20pt, 25pt, and 50pt; some 25pt coins have a hole in the middle. Formerly each piastre was divided into ten miliemes, making 1,000 miliemes to the pound. Though no longer in circulation, this denomination is still often expressed in prices (which follow the custom of using a comma instead of a decimal point: for example £E1,30).

Aside from ordinary spending, hard cash (usually US dollars) may be required for visas, border taxes etc. Do not bring New Zealand dollars, Irish punts, Scottish or Northern Irish pounds as these are not accepted by banks.

money belt shanTit wesT

شنطة وسط

month shahr

شهر

monument(s) asār

آثار

moon amar

قمر

more* tanee

ثاني

can I have some more water, please? (to man/woman) momkin ākhod shwīyit mīya kamān, low samaHt/samaHtee?

ممكن آخذ شوية ميه كمان، لو سمحت/سمحتي؟

more interesting momtiA

aktar

أكثر ممتع

more expensive aghla

أغلى

more than 50 aktar min khamseen

أكثر من خمسين

more than that aktar min keda

أكثر من كده

a lot more aktar bekteer

اكثر بكثير

dialogue

would you like some more? (to man) teHebb tākhod tānee?
(to woman) teHebbee takhdee tānee?
no, no more for me, thanks la, la' da kifāya, shokran
how about you? (to man/woman) winta/winti?
I don't want any more, thanks (said by man/woman) ana mish Aayiz/Aīza tanee, shokran

morning eS-SobH

الصبح

this morning ennaharda

eS-SobH

النهارده الصبح

in the morning eS-SobH

صبح

Morocco el maghrib

المغرب

mosque gāmiA

جامع

 Most of the mosques and their attached Islamic colleges (madrasas) that you'll want to visit are in Cairo, and are mostly classified as historic monuments. They are open routinely to non-Muslim visitors, although anyone not worshipping should avoid prayer times. Elsewhere in the country, mosques are not used to tourists and locals may object to your presence.
At all mosques, dress is important. Shorts (or short skirts) and exposed shoulders are out, and in some places women may be asked to cover their heads (a scarf might be provided). Above all, remember to remove your shoes upon entering the precinct. They will either be held by a shoe custodian (small ba'sheesh (tip) expected) or you can just leave them outside the door, or carry them in by hand (if you do this, place the soles together, as they are considered unclean).
see tip

mosquito namoosa

ناموسة

🏃 **mosquitoes and bugs**
Currently resurgent
throughout Africa, malaria
could become a problem in Egypt in
the future. Consult your doctor who
may recommend a prophylactic
course of Chloroquine, starting two
weeks before you leave home.
Beside the risk of malaria,
mosquitoes can make your life a
misery. Horribly ubiquitous over the
summer, these blood-sucking pests
are never entirely absent – even in
Cairo. The only solution is total war,
using fans, mosquito coils, rub-on
repellent and a plug-in device, sold
at pharmacies. The best guarantee of
a bite-less night's sleep is to bring a
mosquito net with long tapes, to pin
above your bed. Mosquitoes favour
shady, damp areas, and anywhere
around dusk.
Equally loathsome – and widespread
– are flies, which transmit various
diseases. Only insecticide spray or
air-conditioning offer any protection.

mosquito net shabakit
namosaya

شبكة ناموس

mosquito repellent kraym
Did en-nāmoos

كريم ضد الناموس

most: I like this one most of
all ana bafaDDal da Aala aī
shay' tanee

انا بافضل دا على
أى شئ تانى

most of the time mōAZam
el wa't

معظم الوقت

most tourists mōAZam
elsowwāH

معظم السواح

mostly mōAZam

معظم

mother omm

أم

mother-in-law Hamāt

حمات

motorbike motosikl

موتوسكل

motorboat 'launch'

لنش

motorway eT-Taree' es-
sareeA

الطريق السريع

mountain gabal

جبل

in the mountains fil gebāl

فى الجبال

mouse far

فار

moustache shanab

شنب

mouth bo'

بق

move (verb) itHarrak

إتحرك

he's moved to another room
howa na'al leōDa tania

هو نقل لأوضه تانيه

could you move your car?
(to man) momkin tin'il
Aarabeetak?

ممكن تنقل عربيتَك؟

(to woman) momkin tin'ilee
Aarabeetik?

ممكن تنقلى عربيتِك؟

could you move up a little?
(to man/woman) momkin teT-
laA/teTlaAee oddām
shwīya?

ممكن تطلع/تطلعى قدام شويه؟

movie 'film'

فيلم

movie theater 'cinema'

سينما

Mr ostāz

أستاذ

Mrs madām

مدام

much keteer

كثير

much worse mo'rif aktar

مقرف أكثر

much better aHsan bekteer

أحسن بكثير

much hotter askhan bekteer

أسخن بكثير

not much mish keteer

مش كثير

not very much mish keteer
awee

مش كثير قوى

I don't want very much (said
by man/woman) mish
Aayiz/Aīza keteer awee

مش عايز/عايزه كثير قوى

mud Teen

طين

mug (for drinking) kobbāya

كبايه

I've been mugged ana
etsar'at

أنا إتسرقت

mum omm

أم

mummy (in tomb) momya

مومياء

mural wara' Ha'iT

ورق حائط

museum mat-Haf

متحف

Museums are generally open daily 9am–5pm, except Friday when they close at 4pm.

mushrooms Aesh elghorāb

عش الغراب

music moseeQa

موسيقى

Muslim (adj) moslim

مسلم

mussels om el kholool

أم الخلول

must* : I must ... ana lāzim ...

أنا لازم

I mustn't drink alcohol ana mamnooA min shorb elkohol

أنا ممنوع من شرب الكحول

mustard maSTarda

مسطرده

my*: my ... ... btāAee/btaAtee (m/f)

بتاعى / بتاعتى

myself: I'll do it myself HaAmiloo benafsee

هاعملو بنفسى

by myself benafsee

بنفسى

N

nail (finger) Dofar

ظفر

name esm

إسم

my name's John esmee 'john'

إسمى جون

what's your name? (to man/woman) esmak/esmik ay?

إسمَك / إسمِك إيه؟

what is the name of this street? ay esm esh-shāriA da?

إيه إسم الشارع هذ دا؟

Literally 'father of' and 'mother of', aboo and omm are used both as honorific titles and also figuratively as a nickname. For example, if speaking to the father of someone called Magdi, you would address him as 'aboo Magdi' and his mother would be 'omm Magdi'; you would not use the surname and there is no direct equivalent of 'Mr' or 'Mrs'. Sometimes Egyptians prefer to be called by their nicknames. Some names have fixed nicknames: for example, the nickname for Muhammad or Ahmed is Hamada

whereas for Mustafa the nickname is
Darsh.
see you

napkin fooTa

فوطه

nappy kafoola

كافوله

narrow (street) dīya'

ضيق

nasty faZeeA

فظيع

national dowlee

دولى

nationality ginsaya

جنسيه

natural TabeeAee

طبيعى

navy (blue) azra'

أزرق

near gamb

جنب

is it near the city centre?
howa orīyib min wesT
elbalad?

هو قريب من وسط البلد؟

do you go near the beach?
inta bitAadee Aalal blāj?

إنت بتعدى على البلاج؟

where is the nearest ...?
fayn a'rab ...?

فين أقرب...؟

nearby orīyib awee

قريب قوى

nearly ta'reeban

تقريباً

necessary Darooree

ضرورى

neck (of body) ra'aba

رقبه

necklace Ao'd

عقد

necktie garafatta

جرافته

need: I need ... ana
meHtāg ...

أنا محتاج...

do I need to pay? howa ana
lāzim adfaA?

هو أنا لازم أدفع؟

needle ibra

إبره

neither: neither (one) of them
wala wāHid/wāHda min-
hom

ولا واحد/واحده منهم

neither ... nor ... la ...
wala ...

لا...ولا...

nephew (brother's son) ibn
akh

إبن أخ

(sister's son) ibn okht

إبن أخت

Netherlands Holandda
هولندا
never abadan
أبداً

dialogue

have you ever been to
Alexandria? (to man/woman)
maroHtish/maroHteesh
liskinderaya abadan?
no, never, I've never been
there la', maroHtish
henāk abadan

new gedeed
جديد
news (radio, TV etc) akhbār (f)
أخبار
newsagent's bayyāA garayid
بياع جرائد
newspaper gornāl
جرنال
newspaper kiosk koshk
garayid
كشك جرائد
New Year essana eggedeeda
السنه الجديده
Happy New Year! Aam
gedeed saAeed!
عام جديد سعيد!

Many Egyptians celebrate
the New Year with a party,
especially in hotels and
clubs. It is not advisable to park your
car in the street on New Year's Eve,
as Egyptians have a custom of
throwing all their unwanted glass
and china into the street to mark the
end of the year.

New Year's Eve laylit rās
es-sana
ليلة رأس السنه
New Zealand nyoozeelanda
نيوزيلاندا
New Zealander: I'm a New
Zealander (said by man/woman)
ana nyoozeelanddee/
nyoozeelanddaya
أنا نيوزيلاندي /
نيوزيلانديه
next ellay baAd
اللى بعد
the next street on the left
esh-shāriA eggīa Aala eshi-
māl
الشارع الجاى على
الشمال
at the next stop el-
maHaTTa eggīa
المحطه الجايه
next week el isbooA eggī
الإسبوع الجاى

next to gamb

جنب

nice (food) TeAem

طعم

(looks, person) kwayis

كويس

(view) gameel

جميل

niece (brother's daughter) bint akh

بنت أخ

(sister's daughter) bint okht

بنت أخت

night layl

ليل

at night bil layl

بالليل

good night tiSbaH Aala khayr

تصبح على خير

dialogue

do you have a single room for one night? (to man/woman) Aandak/Aandik ōDa lemoddit layla waHda

yes, madam īwa, ya hānim

how much is it per night?

bekām ellayla?

it's sixty pounds for one night besetteen geneeh fellayla

thank you, I'll take it shokran, Hakhodha

nightclub kabarayh

كباريه

nightdress ameeS nōm

قميص نوم

night porter ghafeer

غفير

Nile nahr en-neel

نهر النيل

Nile Valley wadee en-neel

وادى النيل

no la'

لا

I've no change maAandeesh fakka

معنديش فكه

there's no ... left mafeesh ... ba'ee

مفيش.... باقى

no way! abadan!

أبدا!

oh no! (upset) akh!

أخ!

nobody mafeesh Had

مفيش حد

there's nobody there

No

145

mafeesh Had henāk

مفيش حد هناك

noise dowsha

دوشه

noisy: it's too noisy da dow-sha awee

دا دوشه قوى

non-alcoholic min ghayr koHol

من غير كحول

none mafeesh

مفيش

nonsmoking compartment mamnooA et-tadkheen

ممنوع التدخين

noon Dohr

ظهر

at noon feD-Dohr

فى الظهر

no-one mafeesh Had

مفيش حد

nor: nor do I walana

ولا انا

normal Aādee

عادى

north shamāl

شمال

in the north fesh-shamāl

فى الشمال

to the north lesh-shamāl

للشمال

north of Cairo shamāl

el-Qāhira

شمال القاهره

northeast shamāl shar'

شمال شرق

Northern Ireland īrlanda esh-shamalāya

أيرلنده الشماليه

northwest shamāl gharb

شمال غرب

Norway en-norwayg

النرويج

Norwegian norwaygee

نرويجى

nose manakheer

مناخير

not* mish

مش

no, I'm not hungry la', ana mish gaAān

لا، أنا مش جعان

I don't want any, thank you la' mish Aayiz khāliS, shokran

لا مش عايز خالص، شكراً

it's not necessary mish lāzim

مش لازم

I didn't know that makon-tish aAraf keda

ما كنتش أعرف كده

not that one – this one mish

da – da

مش دا - دا

note (banknote) wara'

ورق

notebook (paper) noota

نوته

nothing mafeesh Hāga

مافيش حاجه

nothing for me, thanks
mafeesh Hāga laya,
shokran

مافيش حاجه لى، شكراً

nothing else mafeesh Haga
tania

مافيش حاجه تانيه

November novamber

نوفمبر

now delwa'tee

دلوقتى

number raQam

رقم

(figure) nimra

نمره

I've got the wrong number
maAaya raQam ghalaT

معايا رقم غلط

what is your phone number?
(to man/woman) ay raQam
telefōnak/telefōnik?

إيه رقم تليفونَك/
تليفونِك؟

number plate nimar
elAarabaya

نمر العربيه

nurse (man/woman)
momarreD/momarreDa

ممرض/ممرضه

nuts gōz

جوز

O

oasis wāHa

واحه

occupied (toilet, telephone)
maJghool

مشغول

o'clock* es-sāAa

الساعه

October oktōbar

أكتوبر

odd (strange) ghareeb

غريب

of* min

من

off (lights) ma'fool

مقفول

it's just off Tal'at Harb Street
taHweeda waHda min
shāriA TalAat Harb

تحويده واحده من شارع
طلعت حرب

we're off tomorrow iHna
Aanddinā agāza bokra

إحنا عندنا أجازه بكره

office (place of work) maktab

مكتب

officer (said to policeman) afanddim

أفندم

often dīman

دايماً

not often aHyānan

أحيانا

how often are the buses? ay
maād magee' el otobeesāt?

أيه ميعاد مجيئ
الأتوبيسات؟

oil (for car, for salad) zayt

زيت

ointment marham

مرهم

OK kwayis

كويس

are you OK? (to man) inta
kwayis?

إنت كويس؟

(to woman) inti kwayisa?

إنتى كويسه؟

is it OK with you? (to
man/woman) da kwayis
maAāk/maAākee?

دا كويس معاك/معاكى؟

is it OK to ...? momkin ...?

ممكن...؟

that's OK, thanks da
tamām, shokran

دا تمام، شكراً

I'm OK ana bekhayr

أنا بخير

I feel OK (said by man/woman)
ana kwayis/kwayisa

أنا كويس/كويسه

is this train OK for ...? el aTr
da monāsib le ...?

القطر دا مناسب لـ...؟

old (person) Aagooz

عجوز

(thing) adeem

قديم

dialogue

how old are you? (to man/
woman) Aandak/Aandik
kam sana?
I'm 25 ana Aandee kham-
sa weAeshreen sana
and you? (to man/woman)
winta/winti?

old-fashioned mōDa
adeema

موضه قديمه

old town (old part of town)

elmadeena eladeema

المدينه القديمه

in the old town fil madeena
eladeema

فى المدينه القديمه

olive oil zayt zatoon

زيت زيتون

olives zatoon

زيتون

black/green olives zatoon
eswid/akhDar

زيتون إسود/أخضر

Oman Aomãn

عمان

omelette omlit

أومليت

on* Aala

على

on the street Aala eT-Taree'

على الطريق

on the beach Aalal blãJ

على البلاج

is it on this road? howa
AaT-Taree' da?

هو على الطريق دا؟

on the plane Aala eT-Tiara

على الطياره

on Saturday yõm es-sabt

يوم السبت

on television fee
et-telayfizyõn

فى التليفزيون

I haven't got it on me mish
maAãya

مش معايا

this one's on me (drink) el
mashroob da Aala Hesãbee

المشروب دا على حسابي

the light wasn't on en-noor
kan maTfee

النور كان مطفى

what's on tonight? fee ay
en-naharda?

في إيه النهارده؟

once (one time) marra waHda

مره واحده

at once (immediately)
AalaTool delwa'tee

على طول دلوقتى

one* wãHid (m), waHda (f)

واحد/واحده

the white one el'abyaD (m),
elbayDa (f)

الأبيض/البيضاء

one-way ticket tazkara
waHda

تذكره واحده

only bas

بس

only one wãHid bas

واحد بس

it's only 6 o'clock es-sãAa
sitta bas

الساعه سته بس

I've only just got here ana
lessa wāSil

أنا لسه واصل

on/off switch kobs en-noor

كبس النور

open (adj) maftooH

مفتوح

(verb) fataH

فتح

when do you open? (to
man/woman) betiftaH/
betiftaHee imta?

بتفتح/بتفتحى إمتى؟

I can't get it open mish ādir
aftaH-ha

مش قادر أفتحها

in the open air felkhala

فى الخلاء

opening times mawaAeed
elfatH

مواعيد الفتح

open ticket tazkara maftooHa

تذكره مفتوحه

opera obra

أوبرا

operation (medical) Aamalaya

عمليّة

operator (telephone: man/woman)
Aamil telefonāt/Aamlit
telefonāt

عامل تليفونات/
عاملة تليفونات

From any phone, public or
private, the number for
the inland operator is 10;
for the international operator it is
120.

opposite: the opposite direction enaHya et-tania

الناحيه الثانيه

the bar opposite elbār ellay
fee enaHya et-tania

البار اللى فى الناحيه
الثانيه

opposite my hotel oddām
elfondo' betāAee

قدام الفندق بتاعى

or ow

أو

orange (fruit) borto'ān

برتقال

(colour) borto'ānee

برتقالى

fizzy orange AaSeer
borto'ān ghāzee

عصير برتقال غازى

orange juice AaSeer borto'an

عصير برتقال

order: can we order now? (in
restaurant) momkin noTlob
delwa'tee?

ممكن نطلب دلوقتى؟

I've already ordered, thanks

ana Talabt khalaS,
shokran

انا طلبت خلاص، شكراً

I didn't order this ana
maTalabtish da

انا مطلبتش ده

out of order AaTlān

عطلان

ordinary Aādee

عادى

other tanee

ثانى

the other one et-tānee

الثانى

the other day el yōm
et-tanee

اليوم الثانى

I'm waiting for the others
ana mistannee elbā'yeen

أنا مستنى الباقيين

do you have any others? (to
man/woman) Aandak/Aandik
ghayrha tanee?

عندَك/عندِك غيرها
ثانى؟

otherwise walla

وإلا

our* btaAna

بتاعنا

ours* btaAna

بتاعنا

out: he's out howa barra

هو بره

three kilometres out of town
talat kilomitrāt khārig
elbalad

ثلاث كيلومترات خارج
البلد

outside barra

بره

can we sit outside?
momkin no'Aod barra?

ممكن نقعد بره؟

oven forn

فرن

over: over here hena

هنا

over there henak

هناك

over 500 aktar min khoms-
maya

أكثر من خمسمائة

it's over intahit

إنتهت

overcharge: you've over-
charged me (to man) inta
daffaAtenee floos keteer

أنت دفعتنى فلوس كتير

(to woman) inti daffaAteenee
floos keteer

إنتى دفعتينى فلوس كتير

overnight (travel) Tool ellayl

طول الليل

owe: how much do I owe you? (to man/woman) ana Aalaya kam leek/leekee?

انا علىّ كام لك/لكى؟

own: my own ... ... btaAee/btaAtee (m/f)

بتاعى/بتاعتى...

are you on your own? (to man) inta lewaHdak?

إنت لوحدك؟

(to woman) inti lewaHdik?

إنتى لوحدكِ؟

I'm on my own ana lewaHdee

أنا لوحدى

owner (man/woman) mālik/malka

مالك/مالكه

oyster maHār

محار

P

pack (verb) Aabba

عبّأ

a pack of cigarettes Aelbit sagāyer

علبة سجاير

package (parcel) Tard

طرد

package holiday reHla

shamla

رحله شامله

packed lunch ghada moAab-ba'

غذاء معبأ

packet bāko

باكو

page (of book) SafHa

صفحه

could you page Mr ...? momkin tinādee elostāz ...?

ممكن تنادى الأستاذ...؟

pain wagaA

وجع

I have a pain here Aandee wagaA hena

عندى وجع هنا

painful mo'lim

مؤلم

painkillers mosakkin

مُسكن

painting Soora

صوره

pair: a pair of ... gōz ...

جوز

Pakistani bākistānee

باكستانى

palace aSr

قصر

pale (face) miSfer

مِصفر

(colour) fāteH

فاتح

pale blue azra' fāteH

أزرق فاتح

Palestine felesTeen

فلسطين

pan Halla

حَلّه

panties libās Hareemee

لِباس حريمى

pants (underwear: men's) libās

لِباس

(women's) libās Hareemee

لِباس حريمى

(US: trousers) banTaloon

بنطلون

pantyhose sharāb Haraymee Taweel

شراب حريمى طويل

paper wara'

ورق

(newspaper) gornāl

جرنال

a piece of paper Hettit wara'a

حتة ورقه

paper handkerchiefs manadeel wara'

مناديل ورق

papyrus wara' el bardee

ورق البردى

parcel Tard

طرد

pardon (me)? (didn't under-stand/hear) afanddim?

أفندم؟

parents ahl

أهل

park (noun) mow'af

موقف

(verb) rakan

ركن

can I park here? momkin arkin hena?

ممكن أركن هنا؟

parking lot mow'af Aarabayyāt

موقف عربيات

part (noun) goz'

جزء

partner (boyfriend) SāHib

صاحب

(girlfriend) SaHbah

صاحبة

party (group) magmooAa

مجموعة

(celebration) Hafla

حفلة

passenger (man/woman) rākib/rākba

راكب/راكبة

passport basbōr

باسبور

All visitors to Egypt must hold passports that are valid for at least six months beyond the proposed date of entry to the country.

Most Arab countries except Egypt and Jordan will deny entry to anyone whose passport shows evidence of a visit to Israel, so if you are travelling around the Middle East, be sure to visit Israel after you have been to Syria, Lebanon or wherever.

Once in Egypt you should always carry your passport with you: you'll need it to register at hotels, change money, collect mail and possibly to show at police checkpoints. It's a good idea to photocopy the pages recording your particulars, just in case you lose your passport.

past* : in the past min zamān

من زمان

just past the information office yadōbak baAd maktab elmaAloomāt

يا دوبك بعد مكتب المعلومات

path mamar

ممر

pattern batrōn

باترون

pavement raSeef

رصيف

on the pavement Aala

er-raSeef

على الرصيف

pay (verb) dafaA

دفع

can I pay, please? (to man/woman) momkin adfaA, low samaHt/samaHtee?

ممكن أدفع لو سمحت/ سمحتى؟

it's already paid for el Hisāb khāliS

الحساب خالص

dialogue

who's paying? meen HayedfaA?
I'll pay ana HadfaA
no, you paid last time, I'll pay (to man/woman) la', inta/inti dafaAt/dafaAtee elmarra ellay fātit, ana HadfaA elmarra dee

payphone telefōn Aomoomee

تليفون عمومى

peaceful silmee

سلمى

peach khōkh

خوخ

peanuts fool soodānee

فول سودانى

pear kommitra

كمثرى

peculiar (strange) ghareeb

غريب

peg (for washing) maJbak

مشبك

(for tent) watad

وتد

pen alam

قلم

pencil alam roSāS

قلم رصاص

penfriend (man/woman) Sādee'

morasla/Sādee'it morasla

صديق مراسله/صديقه

مراسله

penicillin bensileen

بنسلين

people nās

ناس

the other people in the hotel

en-nās et-tanyeen fil

fondo'

الناس الثانيين في

الفندق

too many people nās keteer

ناس كثير

pepper (spice) felfil eswid

فلفل إسود

per: per night fil layla

فى الليله

how much per day? bekam

fil layla?

بكام فى الليله؟

per cent nisba me'awaya

نسبه مئويه

perfect tamām

تمام

perfume reeHa

ريحه

perhaps gāyez

جايز

perhaps not momkin la'

ممكن لأ

period (of time) modda

مده

(menstruation) el Aāda

esh-shahraya

العاده الشهريه

permit (noun) taSreeH

تصريح

person shākhS

شخص

personal stereo kassit Soghī

yar

كاسيت صغير

petrol banzeen

بنزين

petrol can SafeeHet banzeen

صفيحة بنزين

petrol station maHaTTit

banzeen

محطة بنزين

Pe

155

pharmacy agzakhana

أجزاخانه

For minor health complaints a visit to a pharmacy is likely to be sufficient. Pharmacies are found in every town and Egyptian pharmacists are well trained and dispense a wide range of drugs, including many available only on prescription in Europe. They usually speak English.

Pharaoh farAōn

فرعون

phone (noun) telefōn

تليفون

(verb) ettaSal

إتصل

All towns and cities have at least one 24-hour telephone and telegraph office (maktab et-telfonāt/sentrāl) for calling long distance and abroad. Usually, you book the call through the exchange, giving the number to a clerk and paying in advance, either for a set amount of time or you make a deposit, settling the bill afterwards. Many telephone offices (and some airports and stations) now have orange direct-dial phones that take phonecards (sold on the premises), enabling you to avoid the system of booking long-distance and

international calls through the exchange.

Phonecard rates are slightly dearer than calls booked through the exchange, but you only pay for the time used; calls over six minutes during peak hours (8am–8pm local time) cost triple the normal rate. You can also make calls through a hotel with a trunk or direct international line (most places with three or more stars have them); this costs between 15-100 per cent above the normal rate. Always check the rate first. Regular phone boxes really only serve for local calls which cost 25pt (though some kiosks only accept the old 5pt coins). You can also make local calls on semi-public phones owned by shopkeepers or hoteliers, who charge 50-100pt. Only in Cairo will you find payphones for dialling abroad.

phone book daleel telefōnāt

دليل تليفونات

phone box kabeenit telefōn

كابينة تليفون

phonecard kart telefōn

كارت تليفون

phone number raQam telefōn

رقم تليفون

photo Soora

صوره

excuse me, could you take a photo of us? (to man/woman)

baAd iznak/iznik, momkin
teSSowarna/teSSowarina?

بعد إذنك/ إذنك،
ممكن تصورنا/تصورينا؟

Before taking a
photograph of someone,
ask their permission first,
especially in the more remote
regions where you can cause
genuine offence. Say: 'momkin
akhod soora?' (can I take a photo?).
You may also find that people stop
you from taking photos that show
Egypt in a 'poor' or 'backward' light.
On a more positive front, taking a
photograph of (and sending it to)
someone you've struck up a
friendship with, or exchanging
photographs, is often greatly
appreciated. Avoid photographing
anything militarily sensitive (bridges,
train stations, dams etc).

phrasebook daleel sayāHee

دليل سياحى

piano bayānoo

بيانو

piastre ersh

قرش

pickpocket (man/woman)
nashāl/nashāla

نشال/نشاله

pick up: will you be there to
pick me up? (to man)

momkin tekoon henak
Aalashan tewaSSalnee?

ممكن تكون هناك علشان
توصلنى؟

(to woman) momkin
tekoonee henak Aalashan
tewaSSalinee?

ممكن تكونى هناك
علشان توصلينى؟

picnic (noun) nozha

نزهه

picture soora

صوره

piece Hetta

حته

a piece of ... Hettit ...

حتة...

pigeon Hamāma

حمامه

pillow makhadda

مخده

pillow case kees makhadda

كيس مخده

pin (noun) dabboos

دبوس

pineapple ananās

أناناس

pineapple juice AaSeer
ananās

عصير أناناس

pink bambee

بمبى

pipe (for smoking) bebba

بيبه

(for water) masoora

ماسوره

pistachio fosto'

فستق

pity: it's a pity maAlesh

معلش

pizza beetza

بيتزا

place (noun) makān

مكان

at your place (to man/woman)
fee baytak/baytik

فى بيتك/بيتك

at his place fee bayto

فى بيته

plain (not patterned) sāda

ساده

plane Tīyāra

طياره

by plane beT-Tīyāra

بالطياره

plant nabāt

نبات

plasters blastar

بلاستر

plastic blastik

بلاستك

plastic bag shanTa
blastik

شنطه بلاستك

plate Taba'

طبق

platform raSeef

رصيف

which platform is it for
Tahrir station? raSeef
nimra kam lemidān et-
taHreer?

رصيف نمره كام لميدان
التحرير؟

play (verb) laAab

لَعب

(noun: in theatre) masraHaya

مسرحيه

pleasant mofriH

مفرح

please (to man/woman) low
samaHt/samaHtee

لو سمحت/سمحتى

yes, please īwa, low
samaHt/samaHtee

أيوه لو سمحت/سمحتى

could you please ...?
momkin ... low
samaHt/samaHtee?

ممكن...لو سمحت/
سمحتى؟

please don't ma ... low
samaHt/samaHtee

ما...لو سمحت/
سمحتى

pleased: pleased to meet you
Tesharrafna

تشرفنا

pleasure: my pleasure aī
khidma

أى خدمه

plenty: plenty of ... keteer
min ...

كثير من ...

there's plenty of time fee
wa't keteer

فى وقت كثير

that's plenty, thanks da
kifāya, shokran

دا كفايه ,شكراً

plug (electrical) feesha

فيشه

(in sink) saddādit HōD

سدادة الحوض

plumber sabbāk

سباك

pm*

poached egg bayD masloo'

بيض مسلوق

pocket gayb

جيب

point: there's no point
mafeesh fīda

مفيش فائده

poisonous mosammim

مسمم

police bolees

بوليس

call the police! eteSSil bil
bolees!

إتصل بالبوليس

 Egypt has various police
forces. The Municipal
Police have a monopoly on
law and order in smaller towns. Their
uniform (khaki in winter, tan or white
in summer) resembles that of the
Traffic Police, who wear striped
cuffs. Both get involved in accidents
and can render assistance in
emergencies. However, relatively few
officers speak anything but Arabic.
If you've got a problem or need to
report a crime, always go to the
Tourist Police. The ordinary ranks
wear the regular khaki uniform with
a Tourist Police armband; officers
wear black uniforms in winter and
white in summer. Found at tourist
sites, museums, airports, stations
and ports, they often speak a foreign
language (usually English).
The fourth force is the Canal Security
police (dressed in black and armed
with Kalashnikovs) who guard
embassies, banks and highways. To
guard vital utilities there are also
Electricity, Airport and River Police
forces; the last is responsible for
overseeing felucca journeys between
Aswan and Luxor.
The emergency phone number for
the police is 122.

policeman rāgil bolees

رجل بوليس

police station esm esh-
shorTa

قسم الشرطه

polite mo'addab

مؤدب

polluted millawis

ملوث

pomegranate rommān

رمان

pool (for swimming) Hammām
sibāHa

حمام سباحه

poor (not rich) fa'eer

فقير

(quality) mish kwayis

مش كويس

pop music moseeQa afrangee

موسيقى أفرنجى

(Western) moseeQa
gharbaya

موسيقى غربيه

pop singer (man/woman)
moghannee/moghanaya

مغنى/مغنيه

popular maHboob

محبوب

pork khanzeer

خنزير

port (for boats) meena

ميناء

porter (in hotel) shīyāl

شيال

Port Said bor saAeed

بور سعيد

posh (restaurant) fākhir
giddan

فاخر جدا

(people) foo'awee

فوق قوى

possible momkin

ممكن

is it possible to ...?
momkin ...?

ممكن...؟

as ... as possible bee ... ma
yomkim

بـ...ما يمكن

post (noun: mail) bosTa

بوسطه

(verb) baAat

بعث

could you post this for me?
momkin termee lee
eg-gawāb da fee el bosTa?

ممكن ترمى لى الجواب دا
فى البوسطه؟

postcard kart

كارت

postcode ramz bareedee

رمز بريدى

poster Soora

صوره

(advert) eAlān

إعلان

poste restante see post office

post office bosTa

بوسطه

Post offices are generally
open daily (except Fridays)
8am–2pm (Ramadan
9am–3pm), though central offices
may stay open until 8pm.
When sending mail from Egypt, it
speeds up the delivery if you get
someone to write the name of the
country in Arabic. As a rule, around
15 per cent of correspondence (in
either direction) never arrives; letters
containing photos or other items are
especially prone to go astray.
It's best to send letters from a major
city or hotel; blue mailboxes are for
overseas airmail, red ones for
domestic post. Airmail (bareed
gowee) stamps can be purchased at
post offices, hotel shops and
postcard stands, which may charge
slightly above the normal rate.
Registered mail can be sent from
any post office. Selected post offices
in the main cities also offer an
Express Mail Service (36hr to
Europe, 48hr to the US).
To send a parcel, take the goods
unwrapped to a major post office for
customs inspection, weighing and
wrapping.
Receiving letters poste restante is a
bit of a lottery, since post office

workers don't always file letters
under the surname. Ask for all your
initials to be checked (including M
for Mr, Ms, etc). To pick up mail you'll
need your passport.

potato baTāTis (f)

بطاطس

pottery (objects) khazaf

خزف

pound (money: Egyptian)
geneeh

جنيه

(British) estirleenee

إسترلينى

(weight) wazn

وزن

power cut el kaharaba
ma'Tōaa

الكهرباء مقطوعه

power point bareeza

بريزه

practise: I want to practise my
Arabic (said by man/woman)
Aayiz/Aīza a'owwee
elAarabee betāAee

عايز/عايزه أقوى العربى
بتاعى

prawns gambaree

جمبرى

prefer: I prefer ... ana
afaDDal ...

أنا أفضّل ...

pregnant Hāmil

حامل

prescription (for medicine)
roshetta

روشته

present (gift) hidaya

هديه

president (of country:
man/woman) ra'ees/ra'eesa

رئيس/رئيسه

pretty gameel

جميل

it's pretty expensive da
ghālee awee

دا غالي قوى

price taman

ثمن

prickly heat Hamw en-neel

حمو النيل

prime minister (man/woman)
ra'ees wozarā'/ra'eesit
wozarā'

رئيس وزراء/رئيسة وزراء

prince ameer

أمير

princess ameera

أميره

printed matter maTbooaāt

مطبوعات

private khāS

خاص

private bathroom Hammām

khāS

حمام خاص

probably gāyiz

جائز

problem moshkila

مشكله

no problem! mafeesh
moshkila!

مفيش مشكله!

program(me) barnāmig

برنامج

pronounce: how is this pronounced? izzay
tenTa'/tenTa'ee dee?

إزاى تنطق/تنطقى دى؟

properly (repaired, locked etc)
kwayis

كويس

protection factor (of suntan
lotion) marham Hemāya

مرهم حمايه

Protestant brotistantee

بروتستانتى

public holiday agāza rasmaya

أجازه رسميه

Egypt abounds in holidays
and festivals of all kinds,
both Muslim and
Christian, national and local.
Ramadan, the month when all
Muslims observe a total fast from
dawn to sunset, can pose big

problems for travellers because
transport services may be limited.
But the celebratory evenings are
good times to hear music and to
enjoy Egyptian hospitality.
If you are a non-Muslim you are not
expected to observe Ramadan, but it
is good to be sensitive about not
eating or drinking (and especially not
smoking) in public.
All Islamic holidays and festivals
follow the Islamic calendar. This is
lunar based, so dates vary each
year in relation to the Western
calendar.

The Islamic festivals are:
Ramadan
Eid al-Fitr
Eid al-Adha
Islamic New Year
Birthday of Prophet Muhammad

Fixed public holidays are as follows:

1 January	New Year's Day
25 April	Liberation Day
1 May	Labour Day
23 July	Revolution Day
6 October	Armed Forces Day
23 October	Suez Day
23 December	Victory Day

pull shad
شد
pullover boloovar
بلوفر
puncture (noun) khorm
خرم

purple banafsigee
بنفسجى
purse (for money) bok
بوك
(US: handbag) shanTit eed
شنطة يد
push za'
زق
pushchair Aarabayit Tefl
عربية طفل
put HaT
حط
where can I put ...? aHoT ...
fayn?
أحط....فين؟
could you put us up for
the night? momkin
nenām hena
ellaylādee?
ممكن ننام هنا الليلة دى؟
pyjamas bjāma
بيجامه
pyramid haram
هرم

Q

Qatar Qatar
قطر
quality nōA
نوع

163

quarter robA

ربع

quayside: on the quayside

Hafit elmarsa

حافة المرسى

queen malika

ملكه

question so'āl

سؤال

queue (noun) Taboor

طابور

quick sareeA

سريع

that was quick da sareeA
awee

دا سريع قوى

which is the quickest
way there? aī Taree'
elasraA?

إيه الطريق الأسرع؟

quickly bisorAa

بسرعه

quiet (place, hotel) hādee

هادى

quiet! hidoo'!

هدوء!

quite (fairly) ta'reeban

تقريباً

(very) giddan

جداً

that's quite right da ta'ree-

---

ban SaHeeH

دا تقريباً صحيح

quite a lot keteer awee

كثير قوى

R

rabies dā' elkalb

داء الكلب

Rabies is endemic in
Egypt, so avoid touching
any strange animal, wild
or domestic. Treatment must be
given between exposure to the
disease and the onset of symptoms;
once these appear, rabies is
invariably fatal. To err on the side of
caution, consider having a rabies jab
before going to Egypt. It will not
avoid the need for treatment
altogether, should you become
infected, but fewer injections will be
required.

race (for runners, cars) sebā'

سباق

radiator radyatayr

رادياتير

radio radyo

راديو

on the radio Aala er-radyo

على الراديو

rail: by rail bes-sikka el
Hadeed

بالسكه الحديد

railway es-sikka el Hadeed

السكه الحديد

rain (noun) naTara

مطره

in the rain fen-naTara

فى المطره

it's raining betnaTTar

بتمطر

raincoat balTo maTar

بالطو مطر

raisins zebeeb

زبيب

Ramadan RamaDān

رمضان

rape (noun) eghteSāb

إغتصاب

rare (uncommon) nādir

نادر

(steak) mish mistewee awee

مش مستوى قوى

rash (on skin) TafH

طفح

raspberry toot

توت

rat far

فار

rate (for changing money) seAr

سعر

rather: it's rather good shakla-

ha maA'ool

شكلها معقول

I'd rather ... ana afaDDal ...

أنا أفضل

razor makanit Hila'a

مكنة حلاقه

razor blades amwās Hila'a

أمواس حلاقه

read ara

قرأ

ready gāhiz

جاهز

are you ready? (to man) inta
mostaAid?

إنتَ مستعد؟

(to woman) inti
mostaAidda?

إنتى مستعده؟

I'm not ready yet (said by
man/woman) ana lessa mish
mostaAid/mostaAidda

أنا لسه مش مستعد/
مستعده

dialogue

when will it be ready?
Hatkoon gahza imta?
it should be ready in a
couple of days Hatkoon
gahza khilāl yōmayn

real Ha'ee-ee

حقيقى

really awee

قوى

I'm really sorry (said by man/woman) ana āsif/āsfa begad

أنا آسف/آسفه بجد

that's really great da SaHeeH shay' AaZeem

دا صحيح شئ عظيم

really? (doubt) SaHeeH?

صحيح؟

(polite interest) maA'ool?

معقول؟

rear lights el loomaD el warrānaya

اللمض الورانيه

rearview mirror mrāya war-rānaya

مرايه ورانيه

reasonable (prices etc) maA'ool

معقول

receipt waSl

وصل

recently min orīyib

من قريب

reception (in hotel) este'bāl

إستقبال

at reception Aand eleste'bāl

عند الإستقبال

reception desk maktab elesti'bāl

مكتب الإستقبال

receptionist (man/woman) mowaZZaf/mowaZZafit este'bāl

موظف/موظفة إستقبال

recognize etAarraf Aala

إتعرف على

recommend: could you recommend ...? (to man/woman) momkin te'ollee/te'olelee ...?

ممكن تقول لى / تقولى لى ...؟

record (music) isTwāna

إسطوانه

red aHmar

أحمر

Red Sea el baHr elaHmar

البحر الأحمر

red wine nebeet aHmar

نبيذ أحمر

refund (noun) targeeA

ترجيع

can I have a refund? momkin akhod feloosee tanee?

ممكن آخد فلوسى ثانى؟

region manTe'a

منطقه

registered: by registered mail

166

bareed mosaggal

بريد مسجل

registration number nimrit elAarabayya

نمرة العربيه

religion deen

دين

remains (of city etc) kharabāt

خرابات

remember: I don't remember mish fākir

مش فاكر

I remember ana fākir

أنا فاكر

do you remember? (to man) inta fākir?

إنت فاكر؟

(to woman) inti fakra?

إنتى فاكره؟

rent (noun: for apartment etc) eegār

إيجار

(verb: car etc) aggar

أجّر

to rent lil egār

للإيجار

dialogue

I'd like to rent a car (said by man/woman) ana Aayiz/Aīza a'aggar Aarabayya

for how long? lemoddit ad ay?

two days yomayn

this is our range dee mooAaddalatna

I'll take the ... Hākhod el...

is that with unlimited mileage? dee ellay maAalhāsh Hodood lessa-far?

it is īwa

can I see your licence, please? (to man) momkin ashoof rokhSitak, low samaHt?

(to woman) momkin ashoof rokhSitik, low samaHtee?

and your passport (to man/woman) we basbo-rak/basborik?

is insurance included? shāmil et-ta'meen?

yes, but you pay the first fifty pounds (to man) īwa, bas inta lāzim tedfaA khamseen geneeh fee el-'owil

(to woman) īwa, bas inti lāzim tedfaAee khamseen geneeh fee el-'owil

can you leave a deposit of

167

thirty pounds? (to man/woman) momkin teseeb/teseebee talateen geneeh Aarboon?

rented car Aarabayya mit'ag-gara

عربيه متأجره

repair (verb) SallaH

صلح

can you repair it? momkin tiSallaH da?

ممكن تصلح دا؟

repeat Aād

عاد

could you repeat that? momkin teAeed tanee?

ممكن تعيد ثاني؟

reservation Hagz

حجز

I'd like to make a reservation (said by man/woman) Aayiz/Aīza aHgiz

عايز/عايزه أحجز

dialogue

I have a reservation ana
Hagazt hena
yes sir, what name please?
HaDir yafanddem, taHt
esm meen?

reserve (verb) Hagaz

حجز

dialogue

can I reserve a table for
tonight? momkin aHgiz
Tarabayza lel-layla dee?
yes madam, for how many
people? HaDir ya
madām, lekam waHid?
for two letnayn
and for what time?
wessāAa kām?
for eight o'clock essāAa
tamaniya
and could I have your
name please? momkin
ākhod ismik, low samaH-
tee?

rest: I need a rest (said by man/woman) ana meHtāg/meHtāga istirāHa

أنا محتاج/محتاجة إستراحه

the rest of the group bā'ee el magmooAa

باقى المجموعه

restaurant maTAam

مطعم

Eating out falls into two camps. At a local level there are cafés and diners, and loads of street stalls, which sell one or two simple dishes. More formally and expensively, there are restaurants catering to middle-class Egyptians and tourists. Menus here offer a broader range of dishes, and sometimes specialise in foreign cuisine. Restaurants will also invariably add a service charge and taxes to your bill, which can increase the total by 10-12 per cent. You are also expected to tip.

The classic Egyptian restaurant or café meal is either a lamb kabab or kofta (spiced mince patties), accompanied or preceded by a couple of dips. The dips are usually houmous (made from chickpeas), TeHeena (tahini, paste made from sesame seeds) and baba ghan-noog (tahini with aubergine).

In a basic place, salad, fool medammis (brown beans) and bread could also be on offer and chicken (frākh) is a standard, both in cafés and as a takeaway food from spit-roast stands. Pigeon (Hamām) is common too, most often served with spicy wheat (freek) stuffing. In slightly fancier places you may also encounter pigeon in a Tāgin, stewed with onions, tomatoes and rice in an earthenware pot.

More expensive restaurants feature these same dishes, plus a few that are more elaborate. Some may precede main courses with a larger selection of dips, plus olives, stuffed vine leaves and so on. Soups too, are occasionaly featured, most famously molokhayya, which is made from stewing Jew's mallow in chicken stock. Two common main dishes are maHshee, comprising stuffed vegetables (tomatoes, aubergines etc), and Torlee, a mixed vegetable casserole with chunks of lamb, or occasionally beef.

Fish (samak) is featured on restaurant menus in Alexandria, Aswan, the Red Sea coast and Sinai. You may also find squid (sob-bayT), shrimps (gambaree) and octopus (ekhTaboot).

One confusion you'll often run up against is that pasta, rice, chips (French fries) and even crisps (potato chips) are interchangeable. Order rice and you'll get chips, and your querying of the matter will be regarded as inexplicable.

restaurant car Aarabayyit el akl

عربية الأكل

resthouse istirāHa

إستراحه

 Chiefly found in the Western Desert oases, government resthouses offer basic triple-bed rooms and cold showers at very reasonable prices. Guests may have to share with strangers unless they're willing to pay for beds to be kept unoccupied. Apart from tourists, resthouses are mostly used by truckers.

rest room tawalet
تواليت

retired: I'm retired ana Aalal maAāsh
أنا على المعاش

return: a return to Aswan tazkarit Aowda le Aswān
تذكرة عوده لأسوان

return ticket tazkarit Aowda
تذكرة عوده
see ticket

reverse gear marshidayr
مارشدير

revolting mo'rif
مقرف

rice roz
رز

rich (person) ghanee
غنى
(food) dasim
دسم

ridiculous mish maA'ool
مش معقول

right (correct) SaH
صح
(not left) yemeen
يمين

you were right (to man) inta kont Aala Ha'
إنت كنت على حق
(to woman) inti kontee Aala Ha'
إنتى كنتى على حق

that's right da SaH
دا صح

this can't be right da mish momkin yekoon SaH
دا مش ممكن يكون صح

right! SaH!
صح!

is this the right road for ...? da eT-Taree' eS-SaHeeH le ...?
دا الطريق الصحيح لـ ....؟

on the right Aalal yemeen
على اليمين

to the right lelyemeen
لليمين

turn right Howid yemeen
حود يمين

right-hand drive dereksayoon Aalal yemeen
دريكسيون على اليمين

ring (on finger) khātim
خاتم

I'll ring you (to man/woman) HāteSSil beek/beekee
حاتصل بيك/بيكى

ring back ettaSal baAdayn

إتّصل بعدين

ripe (fruit) mistaywee

مستوى

risky khaTar

خطر

river nahr

نهر

road Taree'

طريق

is this the road for ...? da Taree' le ...?

دا طريق ل ...؟

down the road fee ākhir esh-shāreA

فى آخر الشارع

road map khareeTit Toro'

خريطة طرق

rob: I've been robbed ana etsara't

أنا إتسرقت

rock Hagar

حجر

(music) moseeQa rok

موسيقى روك

on the rocks (with ice) bil talg

بالثلج

roll (bread) Aaysh fayno medowwar

عيش فينو مدوّر

Roman romānee

رومانى

roof (of house) SaT-H

سطح

(of car) sa'f

سقف

room ōDa

أوضة

in my room fee oDtee

فى أوضتى

dialogue

do you have any rooms?
(to man/woman) Aandak/
Aandik aī ewaD faDya?
for how many people?
lekām wāHid
for one/for two lewāHid/
letnayn
yes, we have rooms free
īwa, Aandina ewaD faDya
for how many nights will it
be? lekām layla?
just for one night layla
waHda
how much is it? bekām?
... with bathroom and ...
without bathroom ...
beHammām we ... min
ghayr Hammām
can I see a room with

bathroom? momkin ashoof ōDa be Hammām?

OK, I'll take it okay, Hākhod dee

room service khedma lil ewaD

خدمة للاوض

rope Habl

حبل

rosé (wine) wardee

وردى

roughly (approximately) ta'ree-ban

تقريبا

round: it's my round da dōree

دا دورى

round-trip ticket tazkarit Aowda

تذكرة عودة

route Taree'

طريق

what's the best route? ay aHsan Taree'?

إيه أحسن طريق؟

rubbish (waste) zebāla

زبالة

(poor quality goods) nōA mish kwayis

نوع مش كويّس

rubbish! (nonsense) da kalām fāDee!

دا كلام فاضى!

rucksack shanTit Dahr

شنطة ضهر

rude mish mo'addab

مش مؤدّب

ruins kharabāt

خرابات

rum ram

رم

rum and Coke® ram we kakoola®

رم وكاكولا

run (verb: person) geree

جرى

S

sad Hazeen

حزين

saddle (for bike) korsee

كرسى

(for horse) sirg

سرج

safe (not in danger) ameen

أمين

(not dangerous) amān

أمان

Sahara SaHara

صحرا

sail (noun) shirāA

شراع

sailboarding 'sailboarding'

سيلبوردنج

salad salāTa

سلاطة

salad dressing SalSa les-salāTa

صلصة للسلاطة

sale: for sale lil bayA

للبيع

salt malH

ملح

same: the same zī

زى

the same as this zī da

زى دا

the same again, please (said by man/woman) wāHid tānee, low samaHt/samaHtee

واحد ثانى، لو سمحت/ سمحتى

it's all the same to me koloo zī baADoo ben nesbālee

كلّه زى بعضه بالنسبة لى

sand ramla

رملة

sandals Sandal

صندل

sandstorm AāSifa ramlaya

عاصفة رمليّة

sandwich sandawitsh

ساندوتش

sanitary napkins/towels fewoT SeHHaya

فوط صحيّة

Saturday yōm es-sabt

يوم السبت

Saudi Arabia es-soAodaya

السعوديّة

sauce Tagin

طاجن

saucepan Halla

حلّة

saucer Taba' fongān

طبق فنجان

sausage sodo'

سجق

say āl

قال

how do you say ... in Arabic? izzay ti'ool ... bil Aarabee?

إزّاى تقول ... بالعربى؟

what did he say? howa āl ay?

هوّ قال إيه؟

she said ... hayya ālit ...

هيّ قالت ...

could you say that again? (to man/woman) momkin teAeed/teAeedee ellay oltu/oltee tanee?

ممكن تعيد/تعيدى
اللى قلته/قلتيه ثانى؟

scarf (for neck) talfeeAa

تلفيعة

(for head) asharb

أشارب

scenery manZar

منظر

schedule (US: timetable) gadwal el mowāAeed

جدول المواعيد

scheduled flight reHla yōmaya

رحلة يوميّة

school madrasa

مدرسة

scissors ma'aS

مقص

scorpion Aa'rab

عقرب

scorpions and snakes
The danger from scorpions and snakes is minimal as most species are nocturnal and generally avoid people, However, you shouldn't go barefoot, turn over any rocks or stick your hands into dark crevices anywhere off the beaten track. If stung, cold-pack the area and get to a doctor.
All snake bites should be washed immediately. Stay calm, as panicking

sends the venom through your bloodstream more quickly, and get immediate help.

scotch weskee

ويسكى

Scotch tape® solotabe

سولوتيب

Scotland eskotlanda

إسكتلندا

Scottish eskotlandee

إسكتلندى

I'm Scottish (said by man/woman) ana eskot-landee/eskotlandaya

أنا إسكتلندى/
إسكتلندية

scrambled eggs bayD ma'lee

بيض مقلى

scuba-diving 'scuba diving'

سكوبا دايفينج

sea baHr

بحر

by the sea gamb el baHr

جنب البحر

seafood wagabāt baHaraya

وجبات بحريّة

seafront wag-hit el baHr

واجهة البحر

on the seafront Aala wag-hit el baHr

على واجهة البحر

seasick: I feel seasick (said by man/woman) Hāsis/Hassa bidowarān

حاسس/حاسّة بدوران

I get seasick baygeelee dowarān

بيجيلى دوران

seaside: by the seaside gamb el blāJ

جنب البلاج

seat korsee

كرسى

is this seat taken? Had aAid hena?

حد قاعد هنا؟

second (adj) et-tānee

الثانى

(in time) sanya

ثانية

just a second! sanya waHda

ثانية واحدة

second-class (travel etc) dara-ga tania

درجة ثانية

second-hand mostaAmal

مستعمل

see shāf

شاف

can I see? momkin ashoof?

ممكن أشوف

have you seen ...? (to man/

woman) shoft/shoftee ...?

شفت/شفتى ...؟

I saw him this morning ana shoftoo eS-SobHaya

أنا شفته الصبحيّة

see you! netlā'a baAdayn!

نتلاقى بعدين!

I see (I understand) īwa

أيوه

self-service khedma zātaya

خدمة ذاتيّة

sell bāA

باع

do you sell ...? (to man/ woman) betbeeA/ betbeeAee ...?

بتبيع بتبيعى ...؟

send baAat

بعت

I want to send this to England (said by man/woman) ana Aayiz/Aīza abAat da lingilterra

أنا عايز/عايزة أبعت دا لإنجلترا

separate monfaSil

منفصل

separately (pay, travel) lewaHdee

لوحدى

September sebtamber

سبتمبر

serious (problem, illness) kha-
Teer

خطير

service charge (in restaurant)
rasm el khedma

رسم الخدمة

service station maHaTTit
banzeen

محطّة بنزين

set menu Qīmit TaAām
moHadadda

قائمة طعام محدّدة

several keteer

كثير

sew khīyaT

خيّاط

could you sew this back
on? (to man/woman)
momkin tekhīyaT/
tekhīyaTee da?

ممكن تخيّط/تخيّطى دا؟

sex gins

جنس

sexy moghray

مغرى

shade: in the shade feD-Dil

فى الضل

shallow (water) mish
ghoweeT

مش غويط

shame: what a shame! Haga

teksif!

حاجة تكسف!

shampoo (noun) shamboo

شامبو

share (verb: room, table etc)
assim

قسّم

sharp (knife) Hāmee

حامى

shaver makanit Hilā'a

مكنة حلاقة

shaving foam kraym Hilā'a

كريم حلاقة

shaving point bareeza li
makanit el Hilā'a

بريزة لمكينة الحلاقة

she* hayya

هيّ

is she here? hayya
hena?

هيّ هنا؟

sheep kharoof

خروف

sheet (for bed) mlāya

ملايا

shelf raff

رف

shell Sadafa

صدفة

shellfish Sadafa

صدفة

ship (big) safeena

سفينة

(small) markib

مركب

by ship bes-safeena

بالسفينة

shirt ameeS

قميص

shit! ellaAna!

اللعنة!

shock (noun) Sadma

صدمة

I got an electric shock from
the ... ana etkahrabt min ...

أنا إتكهربت من ...

shocking faZeeA

فظيعة

shoe fardit gazma

فردة جزمة

a pair of shoes gazma

جزمة

shoelaces robaT gazma

رباط جزمة

shoe polish warneesh

ورنيش

shoe repairer gazmagee

جزمجي

shop maHal

محل

(small, local) dokkān (f)

دكان

Shops generally open at
9.30 or 10am. Most shops
close at 10pm, though
some may be open until midnight or
even 24 hours a day. Many shops
close in the afternoon between
1.30–4 pm.

shopping: I'm going
shopping ana rīeH ashteree
Hagāt

أنا رايح أشترى حاجات

shop window vatreenit el
maHal

فاترينة المحل

shore shaT

شط

short oSīyar

قصيّر

shorts short

شورت

should: what should I do?
aAmil ay?

أعمل إيه؟

you should ... mafrooD
innak ...

مفروض إنّك ...

you shouldn't ... mish
mafrooD innak ...

مش مفروض إنّك...

he should be back
soon howa mafrooD
yekoon hena baAd

shwīya

مفروض يكون
هنا بعد شوية

shoulder kitf

كتف

shout (verb) zaA-Aa'

زعّق

show (in theatre) AarD
masraHee

عرض مسرحى

could you show me?
momkin tewarreenee?

ممكن تورّينى؟

shower (in bathroom) dosh

دش

(of rain) shita

شتا

with shower beddosh

بالدش

shrine DareeH

ضريح

shut (verb) afal

قفل

when do you shut? (to man/
woman) biti'fil/biti'filee
imta?

بتقفل/بتقفلى إمتى؟

when does it shut? baye'fil
imta?

بيقفل إمتى؟

they're shut a'fleen

قافلين

I've shut myself out el bab
et'efil wana barra

الباب إتقفل وانا برّه

shut up! ekhras!

إخرس!

shutter (in camera) monaZZim
fatHet el Aadasa

منظم فتحة العدسة

(on window) sheesh

شيش

sick (ill) Aīyān

عيّان

I'm going to be sick (vomit)
ana HaraggaA

أنا حارجّع

side gamb

جنب

the other side of the street
el gamb el tanee meshāriA

الجنب الثانى من الشارع

side street shāriA gānaybee

شارع جانبى

sidewalk raSeef

رصيف

on the sidewalk Aala
er-raSeef

على الرصيف

sight: the sights of ... manāZ-
er el ...

مناظر ال...

sightseeing: we're going
sightseeing rīHeen fee

gowla sayāHaya

رايحين فى جولة سياحيّة

sightseeing tour gowla sayā
Haya

جولة سياحيّة

sign (roadsign etc) ishāra

إشارة

silk Hareer

حرير

silly ahbal/habla (m/f)

أهبل/هبلة

silver (noun) faDDa

فضّة

similar zī

زى

simple (easy) sahl

سهل

since: since last week min el
esbooA ellay fāt

من الأسبوع اللى فات

since I got here min sāAit
ma waSalt hena

من ساعة ما وصلت هنا

sing ghanna

غنّى

singer (man/woman) moghan-
nee/moghanaya

مغنّى/مغنيّة

single: a single to ... tazkara
le ...

تذكرة ل...

I'm single (said by man/woman)

ana Aāzib/Aazba

أنا عازب/عازبة

single bed sireer faraDānee

سرير فرضانى

single room ōDa le wāHid

أوضة لواحد

single ticket tazkara waHda
واحدة

واحدة

sink (in kitchen) HōD

حوض

sister okht

أخت

sister-in-law neseeba

نسيبة

sit: can I sit here? momkin
aAod hena?

ممكن أقعد هنا؟

is anyone sitting here? fee
Had āAed hena?

فى حد قاعد هنا؟

sit down aAad

قعد

sit down! o'Aod!

قُعد!

size Hagm

حجم

(clothing) ma'āss

مقاس

skin gild

جلد

skin-diving ghōS

غوص

skinny rofīyaA awee

رُفيّع قوى

skirt gonilla

جونلّة

sky sama

سما

skyscraper naT-Het seHāb

ناطحة سحاب

sleep (verb) nām

نام

did you sleep well? (to man/
woman) nimt/nimtee
kwayis?

نمت/نمتى كويّس؟

sleeper (whole train) atr en-
nōm

قطر النوم

sleeping bag 'sleeping bag'

سليبنباج

sleeping car Aarabayyit
nōm

عربيّة نوم

sleeve komm

كم

slide (photographic) 'slide'

سلايد

slow baTee'

بطئ

slow down! (driving) haddee
es-sorAa!

هدّى السرعة!

slowly berrāHa

بالراحة

very slowly baTee'
awee

بطئ قوى

small Soghīyar

صغيّر

smell: it smells (smells bad)
reHet-ha weHsha

ريحتها وحشة

smile (verb) ebtasam

إبتسم

smoke (noun) dokhān

دخّان

do you mind if I smoke?
momkin adakhan?

ممكن أدخّن؟

I don't smoke
mabadakhansh

مابدّخنش

do you smoke? (to man/
woman) betdakhan/
betdakhanee?

بتدّخن/بتدخنى؟

snack akla khafeefa

أكلة خفيفة

snake teAbān

تعبان

sneeze (noun) yeATas

يعطس

snorkel 'snorkel'

سنوركل

snorkelling ghōS

غوص

so: it's so good momtāz giddan

مُمتاز جداً

it's so expensive da ghālee
awee

دا غالى قوى

not so much mish awee

مش قوى

not so bad mish weHesh
awee

مش وحش قوى

so am I, so do I ana kaman

أنا كمان

so-so yaAnee

يعنى

soaking solution (for contact
lenses) maHlool let-
tanDeef

محلول للتنضيف

soap Saboon

صابون

soap powder masHoo' ghaseel

مسحوق غسيل

sock fardit sharāb

فردة شراب

socket (electrical) bareeza

بريزة

soda (water) 'soda'

صودا

sofa kanaba

كنبة

soft (material etc) nāAim

ناعم

soft-boiled egg bayD bresh-
toh

بيض بريشته

soft drink mashroob ghayr
koHollee

غير كوحولّى

soft drinks
Every main street has a
couple of stand-up juice
bars, recognisable by their
displays of fruit. Normally you order
and pay at the cash desk before
exchanging a token for your drink
at the counter; it's usual to leave a
tip.
Street vendors also sell iced, strong,
sweet lemonade (Aaseer lamoon),
bitter-sweet liquorice water and
deliciously refreshing tamarind (tamr
hind-dee).
Western-style soft drinks, including
Coca Cola and 7-Up (called Seven)
are available everywhere. You have
to pay a deposit on the bottle to take
one away.

soft lenses Aadasāt laSQa

عدسات لاصقة

sole (of shoe) naAl

نعل

(of foot) baTn er-rigl

بطن الرجل

could you put new soles on
these? momkin terakkib
naAl gedeed le dool?

ممكن تركّب نعل
جديد لدول؟

some: can I have some?
momkin ākhod shwīya?

ممكن آخذ شويّة؟

can I have some water?
momkin shwīyit mīya?

ممكن شويّة ميّة؟

somebody, someone Had

حد

something Haga

حاجة

something to eat Haga
tettākil

حاجة تتاكل

sometimes aHyānan

أحيانا

somewhere fee Hitta
moAayana

فى حتّة معيّنة

son ibn

إبن

song oghnaya

أغنية

son-in-law neseeb

نسيب

soon Hālan

حالاً

I'll be back soon HargaA
besoraA

حارجع بسرعة

as soon as possible
be'asraA ma yomkin

بأسرع ما يمكن

sore: it's sore betewgaA

بتوجع

sore throat wagaA fee ez-zōr

وجع فى الزور

sorry: I'm sorry (said by
man/woman) ana āsif/āsfa

أنا آسف/أسفة

sorry? (didn't understand/hear)
afanddim?

أفندم؟

sort: what sort of ...? aī nōA
min ...?

أى نوع من...؟

soup shorba

شوربة

sour (taste) HāmiD

حامض

south ganoob

جنوب

in the south fil ganoob

فى الجنوب

South Africa ganoob afreQya

جنوب أفريقيا

South African: I'm South
African (said by man/woman)
ana ganoob afreeQee/
afreQaya
أنا جنوب أفريقى/أفريقيّة
southeast el ganoob
es-shar'ee
الجنوب الشرقى
southwest el ganoob el gharbee
الجنوب الغربى
souvenir tizkār
تذكار
Spain asbania
أسبانيا
Spanish asbānee
أسبانى
spare tyre Aagala estebn
عجلة إستبن
speak: do you speak English?
(to man/woman) betikkallim/
betikkallimee ingleezee?
بتتكلّم/بتتكلّمى
إنجليزى؟
I don't speak ... ana
mabakkallimsh ...
أنا مابتكلّمش...
can I speak to ...? momkin
akkallim ...?
ممكن أتكلّم...؟

dialogue

can I speak to Magdi?
momkin akallim magdi?
who's calling? meen
maAāya?
it's Patricia 'Patricia'
I'm sorry, he's not in, can I
take a message? (said by
man/woman) ana āsif/āsfa,
howa mish mowgood,
teHebbee teseebee resāla?
no thanks, I'll call back
later la' shokran, ana Hat-
teSil baAdayn
please tell him I called
momkin te'ollo ennay
ittaSalt

spectacles naDDāra
نظّارة
spend Saraf
صرف
sphinx abol hōl
أبو الهول
spider Aankaboot
عنكبوت

spirits
For serious drinking,
Egyptians get stuck into
spirits. The favoured tipple is brandy,
known by the slang name of jaz

Sp

183

(literally bottle), which comes under three labels: aHmar (the cheapest), maAatta' (the best) and vin (the most common). zebeeb is similar to Greek ouzo, but drunk neat. Avoid Egyptian-made gin and whisky, whose labels are designed to resemble famous Western brands. Imported spirits are sold at duty-free shops in the main resorts for modest sums.

spoon maAla'a
معلقة

sport rayāDa
رياضة

sprain: I've sprained my ...
ana lawayt ...
أنا لويت...

spring (season) er-rabeeA
الربيع
in the spring fer-rabeeA
فى الربيع

square (in town) medān
ميدان

squid sobbayT
سبيط

stairs salālim (f)
سلالم

stale mish TāZa
مش طازة

stamp (noun) TābeA
طابع

dialogue

> a stamp for England, please (to man/woman)
> TābeA lingiltera, low samaHt/samaHtee
> what are you sending? (to man) Aayiz tebAat ay?
> (to woman) Aīza tebAatee ay?
> this postcard el kart da
> see post office

standby Qīmit el entiZār
قائمة الإنتظار

star nigma
نجم

start (noun) el bedāya
البداية
(verb) bada'
بدأ
when does it start? bayeb-da' imta?
بيبدأ إمتى؟
the car won't start el Aarabayya mabiddorsh
العربيّة مابتدورش

starter (food) fateH lil shahaya
فاتح للشهيّة

station (train) maHaTTit es-sekka el Hadeed
محطّة السكّة الحديد

(bus) mow'af otobees

موقف أوتوبيس

statue temsāl

تمثال

stay: where are you staying?

(to man) inta nazil fayn?

إنت نازل فين؟

(to woman) inti nazla
fayn?

إنتى نازلة فاين؟

I'm staying at ... (said by
man/woman) ana nazil/nazla
fee ...

أنا نازل/نازلة فى...

I'd like to stay another two
nights (said by man/woman)
Aayiz/Aīza aAod layltayn
tanyeen

عايز/عايزة أقعد
ليلتين ثانيين

steak felay

فيليه

steal sara'

سرق

my bag has been stolen
shanTītee etsara'it

شنطتى إتسرقت

steep (hill) metdaHdar

متدحدر

step: on the steps Aala
essalālim

على السلالم

sterling estirlaynee

إسترلينى

steward (on plane) moDeef

مضيف

stewardess moDeefa

مضيفة

still: I'm still here ana lessa
hena

أنا لسّة هنا

is he still there? howa lessa
henāk?

هوّ لسّة هناك؟

keep still! esbat maHallak!

إثبت محلك!

sting: I've been stung ana
et'araST

أنا إتسرقت

stockings sharāb Haraymee
Taweel

شراب حريمى طويل

stomach meAda

معدة

stomachache maghaS

مغص

stone (rock) Hagar

حجر

stop (verb) wa'af

وقف

please, stop here (to taxi driver
etc) o'af hena, low samaHt

أقف هنا، لو سمحت

do you stop near ...? bito'af

orīyib min ...?

بتوقف قريّب من ....؟

stop it! baTTal da!

بطّل دا!

stopover 'transit'

ترانزيت

storm AāSifa

عاصفة

straight (whisky etc) 'straight'

ستريت

it's straight ahead AalaTool

على طول

straightaway Towālee

طوّالى

strange (odd) ghareeb

غريب

stranger (man/woman) gha-
reeb/ghareeba

غريب/غريبة

strap (on watch) ostayk

أستيك

(on dress, suitcase) Hezām

حزام

strawberry farowla

فراولة

stream magra

مجرى

street shāriA

شارع

on the street feshāriA

فى الشارع

streetmap khareeTit Toro'

خريطة طرق

string khayT

خيط

strong shedeed

شديد

(taste) Hāmee

حامى

(drink) morakkaz

مركّز

stuck maznoo'

مزنوق

it's stuck etzana'it

إتزنقت

student (male/female) Tālib/
Tāliba

طالب/طالبة

stupid ghabee

غبى

Sudan essodān

السودان

suddenly fag'a

فجأة

suede shamwā

شموا

Suez es-sways

السويس

Suez Canal Qanāt es-sways

قنال السويس

sugar sokkar

سكّر

suit (noun) badla

بدلة

  it doesn't suit me (jacket etc)

  ma bitnasibneesh

  ماتناسبنيش

  it suits you (to man/woman)

  Helwa Aalayk/Aalaykee

  حلوة عليك/عليكى

suitcase shanTit safar

شنطة سفر

summer Sayf

صيف

  in the summer feS-Sayf

  فى الصيف

sun shams (f)

شمس

  in the sun fesh-shams

  فى الشمس

  out of the sun feDDil

  فى الظل

sunbathe Hammām shams

حمّام شمس

sunblock (cream) kraym DeD esh-shams

كريم ضد الشمس

sunburn lafHet shams

لفحة شمس

sunburnt maHroo' min esh-shams

محروق من الشمس

Sunday yōm el Had

يوم الحد

sunglasses naDDāra shamsaya

نظّارة شمسيّة

sun lounger korsay lil blāJ

كرسى للبلاج

sunny: it's sunny moshmisa

مشمسة

sunset ghroob esh-shams

غروب الشمس

sunshade tanda

تندة

sunshine shoAāA esh-shams

شعاع الشمس

sunstroke Darbit shams

ضربة شمس

suntan samār min esh-shams

سمار من الشمس

suntan lotion marham lesh-shams

مرهم للشمس

suntanned ismar min esh-shams

إسمر من الشمس

suntan oil zayt lesh-shams

زيت للشمس

super lazeez

لذيذ

supermarket 'supermarket'

سوبرماركت

supper Aashā

عشا

supplement (extra charge) rasm

iDāfee

رسم إضافى

sure: are you sure? (to man)

inta mota'akid?

إنت متأكّد؟

(to woman) inti

mota'akida?

إنتى متأكّدة؟

sure! okay!

أوكى!

surname esm el Aayla

إسم العيلة

swearword sheteema

شتيمة

sweater swaytar

سويتر

sweatshirt fanilla

فانلّة

Sweden es-swayd

السويد

Swedish swaydee

سويدى

sweet Helw

حلو

sweets Halawayāt

حلويّات

swim (verb) Aām

عام

I'm going for a swim (said by man/woman) ana rīH/rīHa

aAoom

أنا رايح/رايحة أعوم

let's go for a swim yalla

nerooH neAoom

يللا نروح نعوم

swimming costume mayoo

Haraymee

مايوه حريمى

swimming pool Hammām

sibāHa

حّمام سباحة

swimming trunks mayoo

rigālee

مايوه رجالى

switch (noun) kobs

كوبس

switch off Taf-fa

طفّى

switch on wallaA

ولّع

swollen werim

ورم

Syria sorya

سوريا

T

table tarabayza

طرابيزة

a table for two tarabayza

litneen

طرابيزة لثنين

tablecloth mafrash tarabayza

مفرش طرابيزة

table tennis bing bong

بنج بونج

tailor tarzee

ترزى

take akhad

أخذ

can you take me to the ...? (to man/woman) momkin takhodnee/takhdenee lil ...?

ممكن تاخذني /تاخذيني لل ....؟

do you take credit cards? (to man/woman) betākhod/ betakhdee 'credit card'?

بتاخذ/بتاخذى كريدت كارد؟

fine, I'll take it Tayib, Hakhdoo

طيّب حاخذه

can I take this? (leaflet etc) momkin ākhod da?

ممكن آخذ دا؟

how long does it take? betākhod ad ay wa't?

بتاخذ قد إيه وقت؟

it takes three hours

betākhod talat saAāt

بتاخذ تلات ساعات

is this seat taken? fee Had āAid hena?

فى حدّ قاعد هنا؟

talcum powder bodrit talk

بودرة تلك

talk (verb) etkallim

إتكلّم

tall (person) Taweel

طويل

(building) Aālee

عالى

tampons 'Tampax'®

تامباكس

tan (noun) samār min esh-shams

سمار من الشمس

to get a tan esmar

إسمر

tap Hanafaya

حنفيّة

taste (noun) TaAm

طعم

can I taste it? momkin adoo'oo?

ممكن ادوقه؟

taxi taksee

تاكسى

service taxi taksee khidma

تاكسى خدمة

will you get me a taxi? (to man/woman) momkin tegiblee/tegibelee taksee?

ممكن تجيبلي / تجيبيلي تاكسي؟

where can I find a taxi? fayn momkin alā'ee taksee?

فين ممكن ألاقى تاكسى؟

dialogue

to the airport/to the ... Hotel, please lil maTār/lefondo' el ..., low samaHt

how much will it be? Haykoon bekām?

fifteen pounds bekhamastashar geneeh

that's fine right here, thanks hena kwayis, shokran

Collective service taxis are one of the best features of Egyptian transport. They operate on a wide variety of routes, are generally quicker than buses and trains, and fares are very reasonable.
The taxis are usually big Peugeot saloons carrying seven passengers or minibuses seating a dozen people. Most business is along specific

routes, with more or less non-stop departures throughout the day on the main ones, while cross-desert traffic is restricted to early morning and late afternoon. As soon as the right number of people are assembled, the taxi sets off.
On established routes service taxis keep to fixed fares for each passenger. Alternatively, you can charter a whole taxi for yourself or a group – useful for day excursions, or on odd routes. You will have to bargain hard to get a fair price.
Equally ubiquitous are four-seater taxis (black and white in Cairo, black and yellow in Alexandria) which often pick up extra passengers heading in the same direction. As meters are rarely used (or work), the trick is to know the fare and to pay on arrival, rather than ask or haggle at the beginning. Above all, don't confuse these cabs with larger special taxis (usually Peugeot 504s or Mercedes) which cost three times more and prey on tourists.
You will also come across carettas – horse-drawn buggies, also known as hantoor. These are primarily tourist transport, and you'll be accosted by drivers in Alexandria, a few parts of Cairo and most of all in Luxor and Aswan. Fares are high by local taxi standards and, despite supposed tariffs set by the local councils, are in practice entirely negotiable. In a few small towns, mostly in Middle Egypt, carettas remain part of the local city

transport. Ask locals the price of
fares before climbing on board.

taxi-driver sowā' taksee

سوّاق تاكسى

taxi rank mow'af taksayāt

موقف تاكسيّات

tea (drink) shī

شاى

tea for one/two, please (to
man/woman) wāHid/itnayn
shī, low samaHt/samaHtee

واحد /إثنين شاى،
لو سمحت/سمحتى

Tea is Egypt's national
beverage and it is
generally made by boiling
the leaves, and served black and
sugared to taste –though posher
cafés use teabags and may supply
milk (ask for shī bel-laban if you
want milk). A glass of mint tea (shī
ben neAnāA) is refreshing when the
weather is hot. You may also enjoy
herbal teas like fenugreek (Helba),
aniseed (yansoon) or cinnamon
(erfa).
A drink characteristic of Egypt is
karkaday, a deep red infusion of
hibiscus flowers. Most popular in
Luxor and Aswan, it is equally
refreshing drunk hot or cold.
Elsewhere they tend to use
dehydrated extract instead of real
hibiscus, so it doesn't taste as good.

teabags kayās shī

كياس شاى

teach: could you teach me?
(to man/woman) momkin
teAllimnee/
teAallimenee?

ممكن تعلّمنى/تعلّمينى؟

teacher (man/woman)
modariss/modarissa

مدرّس/مدرّسة

team faree'

فريق

tearoom Hogrit shī

حجرة شاى

teaspoon maAla'it shī

معلقة شاى

tea towel fooTit shī

فوطة شاى

teenager (male/female)
morāhiQ/morahQa

مراهق/مراهقة

telephone telefoon

تليفون

see **phone**

television teleefizyōn

تليفزيون

tell: could you tell him ...? (to
man/woman) momkin to'ol
loo/laha ...?

ممكن تقول له/لها ...؟

temperature (weather) dargit

el Harāra

درجة الحرارة

(fever) Homma

حُمّى

temple (religious) maAbad

معبد

tent khayma

خيمة

term (at university, school) faSl

فصل

terminal mow'af

موقف

terminus (rail) mow'af

موقف

terrible faZeeA

فظيع

terrific momtāz

ممتاز

than* min

من

smaller than aSghar min

أصغر من

thank: thanks, thank you

shokran

شكراً

thank you very much

shokran giddan

شكراً جدّاً

thanks for the lift shokran

Aala eltowSeela

شكراً على التوصيلة

no thanks la' motshakkir

لآ متشكر

dialogue

thanks shokran

that's OK, don't mention it

Aafwan, mafeesh mashāk-il

that: that boy el walad

da

الولد دا

that girl el bint dee

البنت دى

that one da/dee (m/f)

دا/دى

I hope that ... atmanna

keda ...

أتمنّى كده

that's nice da gameel

دا جميل

is that ...? da/dee ...?

دا/دى؟...

that's it (that's right) SaH

صح

the* el

ال

theatre masraH

مسرح

their* btaAhom

بتاعهم

theirs* btaAhom

بتاعهم

them* homma

همّا

  for them leehom

ليهم

  with them maAāhom

معاهم

  to them leehom

ليهم

  who? – them meen? – homma

مين؟ – همّا

then (at that time) baAdayn

بعدين

  (after that) we baAdayn

وبعدين

there henāk

هناك

  over there henāk

هناك

  up there foo' henāk

فوق هناك

  is/are there ...? fee ...?

فى ....؟

  there is/are ... fee ...

فى ...

  there you are (giving something) itfaDal

إتفضّل

Thermos® flask tormos

ترمس

these* dōl

دول

they* homma

همّا

thick Tekheen

تخين

  (stupid) ghabee

غبى

thief (man/woman) Harāmee/ Haramaya

حرامى/حراميّة

thigh fakhd

فخد

thin rofīyaA

رفيّع

thing Hāga

حاجة

  my things Hagātee

حاجاتى

think fakkar

فكّر

  I think so Aala maZon

على ما ظن

  I don't think so maAtaQedsh

ماعتقدش

  I'll think about it Hafakkar fee elmowDooA

حافكّر فى الموضوع

third-class daraga talta

درجة ثالثة

thirsty: I'm thirsty ana
AaTshān
أنا عطشان

this: this boy el walad da
الولد دا

this girl el bint dee
البنت دى

this one da/dee (m/f)
دا / دى

this is my wife dee mrātee
دى مراتى

is this ...? da/dee ...?
دا / دى ...؟

those* dōl
دول

thread (noun) khayT
خيط

throat zōr
زور

throat pastilles bastilya
خلال

through khilāl
باستيليا

does it go through ...? (train,
bus) bayAaddee Aala ...?
بيعدّى على ...؟

throw (verb) rama
رمى

throw away (verb) ramā
رمى

thumb eS-SobaA el kebeer
الصبع الكبير

thunderstorm AāSifa raAdaya
عاصفة رعديّة

Thursday yōm el khamees
يوم الخميس

ticket tazkara
تذكرة

dialogue

a return to Aswan tazkarit
Aowdah le aswān

coming back when?
weHatergaA imta?

today/next Tuesday
ennaharda/yōm el talāt
el gī

**that will be two hundred
pounds** da Haykōn
bemaytayn geneeh

ticket office (bus, rail) maktab
tazākir
مكتب تذاكر

tie (necktie) garafatta
جرافتّة

tight (clothes etc) dīya'
ضيّق

it's too tight da dīya' awee
دا ضيّق قوى

tights sharāb Haraymee
Taweel
شراب حريمى طويل

time* wa't

وقت

what's the time? es-sāAa
kām?

الساعة كم؟

this time el marrādee

المرّة دى

last time el marra el-lee
fātit

المرّة اللى فاتت

next time el marra eg-gīya

الجايّة

three times talāt marāt

ثلاث مرّات

Time is a more elastic concept than Westerners are used to. In practice, 'five minutes' often means an hour or more, 'later' (baAdayn), the next day; and 'tomorrow' (bokra) an indefinite wait for something that may never happen. Remember that Western abruptness strikes Egyptians as rude; never begrudge the time it takes to say 'peace be upon you' (essalāmo Alaykom) or to return a greeting.

timetable gadwal el
mowāAeed

جدول المواعيد

tin (can) Aelba

علبة

tinfoil wara' solofān

ورق سولوفان

tin-opener fattāHit Aelab

فتّاحة علب

tiny Soghīyar awee

صغيّر قوى

tip (to waiter etc) ba'sheesh

بقشيش

As a presumed-rich foreigner (khawāga), you will be expected to be liberal with ba'sheesh. The most common form this takes is tipping: a small reward for a small service, which can encompass anyone from a waiter or lift operator to someone who unlocks a tomb or museum room. A small sum is expected – between £E2 and £E5. In restaurants, you tip 10–12 per cent in expensive places, giving a higher percentage where the sums involved are trifling. In juice bars and diners, customers simply put 50-100pt on a plate by the exit.

A second type of ba'sheesh is more expensive: rewarding the bending of rules. Examples might include letting you into an archeological site after hours, finding you a sleeper on a train when the carriages are 'full', and so on. This should not be confused with bribery, which is a more serious business with its own etiquette and risks best not entered into.

The last kind of ba'sheesh is alms giving. The disabled are traditional recipients of such gifts; children, however, are a different case, pressing their demands only on tourists.

tire (US) kowetsh

كاوتش

tired taAbān

تعبان

I'm tired (said by man/woman)
ana taAbān/taAbāna

أنا تعبان/تعبانة

tissues kleniks

كلينكس

to: to Cairo/London lil Qāhi-ra/'London'

للقاهرة/لندن

to Egypt/England le masr/ingiltera

لمصر/إنجلترا

to the post office le maktab elbosTa

لمكتب البوسطة

toast (bread) 'toast'

توست

today en-naharda

النهارده

toe SobaA rigl

صبع رجل

together maAa baAD

مع بعض

we're together (in shop etc)
eHna maAa baAD

إحنا مع بعض

toilet tawalet

تواليت

where is the toilet? fayn et-tawalet?

فين التواليت؟

I have to go to the toilet ana lāzim arooH let-tawalet

أنا لازم أروح للتواليت

toilet paper wara' tawalet

ورق تواليت

tomato TamāTem

طماطم

(in Cairo) ooTa

قوطة

tomato juice Aaseer TamaTem

عصير طماطم

tomb ma'bara

مقبرة

tomorrow bokra

بكرة

tomorrow morning bokra eS-SobH

بكرة الصبح

the day after tomorrow baAd bokra

بعد بكرة

tongue lisān

لسان

tonic (water) mīya
maAdanaya
ميّة معدنيّة

tonight ellaylādee
الليلة دى

too (excessively) awee
قوى
(also) kamān
كمان

too hot Har awee
حر قوى

too much keteer awee
كثير قوى

me too wana kamān
وانا كمان

tooth sinna
سنّة

toothache wagaA senān
وجع سنان

toothbrush forshit senān
فرشة سنان

toothpaste maAgoon senān
معجون سنان

top: on top of ... foo' el ...
فوق ال ...

at the top of the ... Aalal ...
على ال ...

top floor ed-dōr el fo'ānee
الدور الفوقانى

torch baTTaraya
بطّاريّة

total (noun) magmooA
مجموع

tour (noun) gowla
جولة

is there a tour of ...? fee
gowla le ...?
فى جولة ل ...؟

tour guide (man) morshid
sayāHee
مرشد سياحى
(woman) morshida sayāHaya
مرشدة سياحيّة

tourist (man/woman)
sayeH/sayHa
سايح/سايحة

tourist information office
maktab es-sayāHa
مكتب السياحة

 In Egypt, you'll get a variable service from local tourist offices. The most knowledgable and helpful ones are in Cairo, Aswan, Luxor, Alexandria, and the oases of Siwa and Dakhla. Elsewhere, most provincial offices are good for a dated brochure, if nothing else.
In towns and cities, travel agencies can advise on (and book) transport, accommodation and excursions. Receptionists at hotels can also be a source of information, and maybe practical assistance. In Luxor, Hurghada and some of the Western

Desert oases, most guesthouses double as information exchanges and all-round 'fixers', as do campsites and backpackers' hotels in Sinai.

tour operator maktab sayāHa

مكتب سياحة

towards tegāh

تجاه

towel fooTa

فوطة

town madeena

مدينة

in town fee wesT el balad

فى وسط البلد

just out of town fee DawāHee el madeena

فى ضواحى المدينة

town centre wesT elbalad

وسط البلد

toy leAba

لعبة

track (US: platform) raSeef

رصيف

traditional aSlee

أصلى

traffic moroor (f)

مرور

traffic jam zaHmit moroor

زحمة مرور

traffic lights isharāt el moroor

إشارات المرور

train aTr

قطر

by train bil aTr

بالقطر

Covering a limited network of routes, trains are best used for long hauls between the major cities, when air-conditioned services offer a more comfortable alternative to buses and taxis. For shorter journeys however, trains are slower and less reliable. Air-conditioned trains nearly always have two classes of carriage. The most comfortable option is first class (daraga oola) which has waiter service, reclining armchairs and no standing in the aisles. Unfortunately for those trying to sleep, they also screen videos until midnight. Air-conditioned second class superior (daraga tania momtāza) is less plush and more crowded, but at two thirds of the price of first class it's a real bargain.

Seats are reservable up to seven days in advance. There is occasional double booking but a little ba'sheesh to the conductor usually sorts out any problem. One common difficulty is that return-trip bookings can't be arranged at the point of origin, so if you're travelling back to Cairo or Aswan/Luxor (or vice versa), it's best to book your return seat the day you arrive. Most travel agencies sell first-class tickets for a small commission, which saves you having to queue.

dialogue

> is this the train for Luxor?
> howa da aTr lo'Sor?
> sure akeed
> no, you want that platform there (to man) la', Aayiz er-raSeef ellay henāk
> (to woman) la', inti Aīza er-raSeef ellay henāk

trainers (shoes) gazma kowetsh
جزمة كاوتش

train station maHaTTit aTr
محطّة قطر

tram tormī
ترماي

translate targim
ترجم

could you translate that? (to man/woman) momkin tetargim/tetargimee da?
ممكن تترجم/تترجمى دا؟

translator (man/woman) motargim/motargima
مترجم/مترجمة

trash zebāla
زبالة

travel safar
سفر

we're travelling around eHna benetgowil
إحنا بنتجوّل

travel agent's wikālit safar
وكالة سفر

traveller's cheque sheek sayāHee
شيك سياحى

 Carry the bulk of your money in a well-known brand of traveller's cheque, with credit cards and/or Eurocheques for backup. American Express, Barclays, Citibank and Bank of America traveller's cheques are accepted by most banks and exchange offices. Any other brand will prove more trouble than it's worth. Eurocheques backed by a Eurocard can be cashed at most branches of the Banque Misr.

tray Sanaya
صينيّة

tree shagara
شجرة

trim: just a trim, please (to man/woman) taHdeed bass,

low samaHt/samaHtee

تحديد بس لو
سمحتى/سمحتي

trip (excursion) reHla

رحلة

I'd like to go on a trip to ...
(said by man/woman) ana
Aayiz/Aĭza aTĮaA reHla
lee ...

أنا عايز/عايزة أطلع
رحلة ل ...

trolley 'trolley'

ترولى

trouble (noun) mashākil

مشاكل

I'm having trouble with ...
ana Aandee mashākil
maAa ...

أنا عندى مشاكل مع ...

trousers banTaloon

بنطلون

true Ha'ee'ee

حقيقى

that's not true da mish SaH

دا مش صح

trunk (US: of car) shanTa

شنطة

try (verb) Hāwil

حاول

can I try it? (food) momkin
adoo'oo?

ممكن أدوقه؟

try on garrab Aala

جرّب على

can I try it on? momkin
agarrabo Aalaya?

ممكن أجرّبه علىّ؟

T-shirt fanilla noS kom

فانلّة نص كم

Tuesday yōm et-talāt

يوم الثلاث

Tunisia toonis

تونس

tunnel nafa'

نفق

Turkey torkaya

تركيا

Turkish torkee

تركى

Turkish coffee ahwa torkee

قهوة تركى

Turkish delight malban

ملبن

turn: turn right Howid
yemeen

حوّد يمين

turn left Howid shimāl

حوّد شمال

turn off (TV etc) afal

قفل

where do I turn off? fayn
a'fil el ...?

فين أقفل ال ....؟

turn on (TV etc) wallaA

ولّع

turning (in road) taHweed

التحويده

twice marritayn

مرّتين

twice as much eD-DeAf

الضعف

twin beds sireerayn

سريرين

twin room ōDa litnayn

أوضة لتنين

twist: I've twisted my ankle

ana lowayt kaAbee

أنا لويت كعبى

type (noun) nōA

نوع

another type of ... nōA

tanee min ...

نوع ثانى من ...

typhoid tīfood

تيفود

typical aSlee

أصلى

tyre kowetsh

كاوتش

U

ugly weHesh awee

وحش قوى

UK elmamlaka elmottaHida

المملكة المتّحدة

umbrella shamsaya

شمسيّة

uncle (father's brother) Aamm

عم

(mother's brother) khāl

خال

under (in position) taHt

تحت

(less than) a'all min

أقل من

underdone (meat) nīya

نيّة

underground (railway) nafa'

نفق

underpants libās

لباس

understand: I understand ana

fāhim

أنا فاهم

I don't understand mish

fāhim

مش فاهم

do you understand? (to man)

inta fāhim?

إنت فاهم؟

(to woman) inti fahma?

إنتى فاهمة؟

unemployed AaTil

عاطل

United States amreeka

أمريكا

university gamAa

جامعة

unleaded petrol banzeen ghayr monaQQa

بنزين غير منقّى

unlimited mileage masāfa ghayr maHdooda

مسافة غير محدودة

unlock fataH

فتح

unpack faDDa

فضّى

until leHad

لحد

unusual shāz

شاذ

up foo'

فوق

up there foo'

فوق

he's not up yet (not out of bed) howa lessa maS-Heesh

هوّ لسّة ماصحيش

what's up? (what's wrong?) fee ay?

فى إيه؟

Upper Egypt wagh eblee

وجه قبلى

(colloquial) eS-SeAeed

الصعيد

upset stomach wagaA baTn

وجع بطن

upside down ma'loob

مقلوب

upstairs foo'

فوق

urgent mistaAgil

مستعجل

us* lena

لينا

with us maAana

معانا

for us lena

لينا

USA elwelāyāt el mottaHada el amreekaya

الولايات المتحدة الأمريكيّة

use (verb) estaAmil

إستعمل

may I use ...? momkin astaAmil ...?

ممكن أستعمل ...؟

useful mofeed

مفيد

usual Aādee

عادى

V

vacancy: do you have any vacancies? (hotel: to man/woman) fee Aandak/Aandik aī ewaD faDiya?

فى عندك/عندِك أىّ أوض فاضية؟

vacation (from university) agāza

أجازة

on vacation fee agāza

فى أجازة

vacuum cleaner moknesa bil kahraba

مكنسة بالكهرباء

valid (ticket etc) SalHa

صالحة

how long is it valid for? SalHa le'ad ay?

صالحة لقد إيه؟

valley wadee

وادى

Valley of the Kings wadee el mlook

وادى الملوك

valuable (adj) sameen

ثمين

can I leave my valuables here? momkin aseeb momtal-akātee hena?

ممكن أسِيب ممتلكاتى هنا؟

value (noun) eema

قيمة

van Aarabayyit na'l

عربيّة نقل

vary: it varies betikhtelif

بتختلف

vase vāZa

فازة

vegetables khoDār

خضر

vegetarian (noun: man/woman) nabātee/nabātaya

نباتى/نباتيّة

The concept of vegetarianism is totally incomprehensible to most Egyptians, and you'll be hard pushed to exclude meat from your diet. If you do get across that you 'don't eat meat', you're likely to be offered chicken or fish as a substitute.

very awee

قوى

very little for me Haga baSeeTa Aalashānee

حاجة بسيطة علشانى

I like it very much ana baHebbo/baHebbaha

203

keteer awee (m/f)

أنا بحبّه/بحبّها كتير قوى

via Aan Taree'

طريق

video 'video'

فيديو

video recorder gihāz tasgeel 'video'

جهاز تسجيل فيديو

view manZar

منظر

village Qarya

قرية

vinegar khal

خل

viper fībar

فيير

visa veeza

فيزة

Almost all Europeans, North Americans and Australasians must obtain tourist visas for Egypt. Regular tourist visas are available from Egyptian consulates abroad, or on the spot at Cairo, Luxor and Hurghada airports. Though you might have to wait a bit, the process is generally painless and cheaper than getting a visa through a consulate. Both the single-visit and multiple-entry types of visa entitle you to stay in Egypt for one month, though the latter allows you to go in and out of the country three times within this period.

Tourists who overstay their (regular) visa are allowed a fifteen day period of grace in which to renew it. After this they're fined unless they can present a letter of apology from their embassy (which may in itself cost something). Visitors anticipating an extended stay may apply for a tourist residence visa, valid for up to six months at a time.

visa extension tamdeed veeza

تمديد فيزا

visit (verb) zār

زار

I'd like to visit ... (said by man/woman) ana Aayiz/Aīza azoor ...

أنا عايز/عايزة أزور

vodka 'vodka'

فودكا

voice SōT

صوت

voltage volt

فولت

see electricity

vomit raggaA

رجّع

waist wesT

وسط

wait estanna

إستنّى

wait for me estannānee

إستنّانى

don't wait for me matistana-
neesh

ماتستنانيش

can I wait until my wife gets
here? momkin astanna
leHad ma tegee mrātee?

ممكن أستنّى لحد ما
تيجى مراتى؟

can you do it while I wait?
(to man/woman) momkin
teAmiloo/teAmilha wana
hena?

ممكن تعمله/تعملها
وأنا هنا؟

could you wait here for me?
momkin testannānee hena?

ممكن تستنّانى هنا؟

waiter garsōn

جرسون

waiter! low samaHt!

لو سمحت!

waitress garsōna

جرسونة!

waitress! low samaHtee!

جرسونة! لو سمحتى!

wake: can you wake me up at
5.30? momkin teSaHHee-
nee es-sāAa khamsa
wenoS?

ممكن تصحّينى الساعة
٥.٣٠؟

Wales 'Wales'

ويلز

walk: is it a long walk? hayya
masāfa Taweela?

هيّ مسافة طويلة؟

it's only a short walk da
mish beAeed

دا مش بعيد

I'll walk ana Hamshee

أنا حامشى

I'm going for a walk ana
khārig atmasha

أنا خارج أتمشّى

wall HayTa

حيطة

wallet maHfaZa

محفظة

want Aāz

عاز

I want a ... (said by man/
woman) ana Aayiz/Aāiza ...

أنا عايز/عايزة ...

I don't want any ... ana

mish Aayiz/Aīza aī ...

أنا مش عايز
/عايزة أى ...

I want to go home ana
Aayiz/Aīza arowaH

أنا عايز/عايزة أروّح

I don't want to ana mish
Aayiz/Aīza

أنا مش عايز/عايزة

he wants to ... howa
Aayiz ...

هو عايز ...

what do you want? (to
man/woman) Aayiz/Aīza
ay?

عايز/عايزة إيه؟

war Harb

حرب

ward (in hospital) Aambbar

عنبر

warm dāfee

دافى

was*: he was howa kān

هوّ كان

she was hayya kānit

هيّ كانت

it was kān/kānit ... (m/f)

كان/كانت

wash (verb) ghasal

غسل

can you wash these? (to
man/woman) momkin tegh-

sil/teghsillee dōl?

ممكن تغسل/تغسلى دول؟

washhand basin HōD

حوض

washing (clothes) ghaseel

غسيل

washing machine ghassāla

غسّالة

washing powder mas-Hoo'
ghaseel

مسحوق غسيل

washing-up: do the
washing-up yeghsil
elmowaAeen

يغسل

washing-up liquid sā'il leghasl
elmowaAeen

سائل لغسل المواعين

wasp dabboor

دبّور

watch (wristwatch) sāAa

ساعة

will you watch my things for
me? (to man) momkin
tākhod bālak min Hagā
tee?

ممكن تخذ بالك من
حاجاتى؟

(to woman) momkin takhdee
bālik min Hagātee?

ممكن تاخذى بالك من
حاجاتى؟

water mīya

ميّة

may I have some water?

momkin shwīyit mīya?

ممكن شويّة ميّة؟

The tap water in Egyptian towns and cities is mostly safe to drink, but heavily chlorinated. In rural areas, Sinai campsites and desert resthouses there's a fair risk of contaminated water. Consequently most tourists stick to bottled mineral water, which is widely available. However, excessive fear of tap water is unjustified. Once you have adjusted, it's usually OK to drink it without further purification. What you should avoid is any contact with stagnant water that might harbour bilharzia. Irrigation canals and the slower stretches of the River Nile are notoriously infested with these minute worms. Don't drink or swim there, walk barefoot in the mud or even on grass that's wet with Nile water. But it's OK to bathe in the saline pools of the desert oases.
see **mineral water**

watermelon baTTeekh

بطّيخ

waterproof (adj) Did el mīya

ضد الميّة

waterskiing 'waterskiing'

ووتر سكيينج

wave (in sea) mōga

موجة

way: it's this way fil ettegāh da

فى الإتجاه دا

it's that way fil ettegāh da

فى الإتجاه دا

is it a long way to ...? howa eTTaree' beAeed le ...?

هوّ الطريق بعيد ل ...؟

no way! abadan!

أبداً!

dialogue

could you tell me the way to ...? (to man/woman)
momkin te'ollee/
te'olelee eTTaree' le ...?
go straight on until you reach the traffic lights
imshee Aala Tool leHad matlā'ee esharāt elmroor
turn left Howid/Howidee shmāl
take the first on the right owil Taree' Aala eedak/eedik el yemeen

we* eHna

إحنا

weak (person) DaAeef

ضعيف

(drink) khafeef

خفيف

weather gow

جوّ

wedding Haflit gowāz

حفلة جواز

wedding ring khātim eg-
gowāz

خاتم الجواز

Wednesday yōm el arbaA

يوم الأربع

week esbooA

إسبوع

a week (from) today baAd
esbooA min ennaharda

بعد أسبوع من النهارده

a week (from) tomorrow
baAd esbooA min bokra

بعد أسبوع من بكرة

weekend ākhir elesbooA

آخر الأسبوع

at the weekend yōm
eg-gomAa

يوم الجمعة

weight wazn

وزن

weird ghareeb

غريب

welcome: you're welcome
(don't mention it) Aafwan

عفوا

well: I don't feel well (said by
man/woman) ana taAbān/
taAbana shwīya

أنا تعبان/تعبانة شوية

she's not well hayya taA-
bana shwīya

هي تعبانة شوية

you speak English very
well (to man) inta
bititkallim/ingleezee
kwayis awee

إنت بتتكلّم إنجليزى
كويّس قوى

(to woman) inti
bititkallimee ingleezee
kwayis awee

إنتى بتتكلّمى إنجليزى
كويّس قوى

well done! Aafārim Aalayk!

عفارم عليك

this one as well wedee
kamān

ودى كمان

well well! (surprise) mish
maA'ool!

مش معقول!

dialogue

how are you? (to man/
woman) izzayak/izzayik?
إيه؟

very well, thanks (said by
man/woman) kwayis/kway-
isa, shokran

and you? (to man/woman)
winta/winti?

well-done (meat) maTbookha
kwayis
مطبوخة كويس

Welsh welzee
ويلزى

I'm Welsh (said by man/woman)
ana welzee/welzaya
أنا ويلزى/ويلزيّة

were*: we were konna
كنّا

you were kont
كنت

they were kāno
كانوا

west gharb
غرب

in the west fil gharb
فى الغرب

Western (from Europe, US)
afrangee
أفرنجى

wet mablool
مبلول

what? ay?
إيه؟

what's that? ay da?
إيه دا؟

what should I do? a'Amil
ay?
أعمل إيه؟

what a view! manZar
gameel!
منظر جميل!

what bus do I take? ākhod
aī otobees?
آخذ الأوتوبيس؟

wheel Aagala
عجلة

wheelchair korsee lil Aagaza
كرسى للعجزة

when? imta?
إمتى؟

when we get back lamma
nergaA
لما نرجع

when's the train/the ferry?
imta el aTr/el 'launch'?
إمتى ييجى
القطر/اللنش؟

where? fayn?
فين؟

I don't know where it is

mish Aārif hiya fayn

مش عارف هيّ فين

dialogue

where is the Greek
Museum? fayn elmat-Haf
elyonānee?
it's over there howa henak
could you show me where
it is on the map? momkin
tewarrehoolee Aala el
khareeTa?
it's just here howa hena
beZ-ZabT

which: which bus? aī oto-
bees?

أيّ أوتوبيس؟

dialogue

which one? aī wāHid?
that one da
this one? dowwa?
no, that one la', da

while: while I'm here wana
hena

ونا هنا

whisky weskee

ويسكى

white abyaD

أبيض

white wine nebeet abyaD

نبيت أبيض

who? meen?

مين؟

who is it? meen?

مين؟

the man who ... er-rāgil el-
lee ...

الراجل اللى ...

whole: the whole week el
isbooA kolloo

الأسبوع كلّه

the whole lot kollohom

كلّهم

whose: whose is this? da
bitaA meen?

دا بتاع مين؟

why? lay?

ليه؟

why not? la' lay?

لا ليه؟

wide AareeD

عريض

wife: my wife mrātee

مراتى

will* : will you do it for me?
(to man/woman) momkin
teAmelhoolee/teAmeli-

hoolee?

ممكن تعملهولي/
تعمليهولى؟

wind (noun) reeH (f)

ريح

window shebbāk

شبّاك

near the window gamb esh-shebāk

جنب الشبّاك

in the window (of shop) fil vatreena

فى الفاترينة

window seat korsee gamb esh-shebbāk

كرسى جنب الشبّاك

windsurfing 'windsurfing'

وندسرفنج

wine nebeet

نبيز

can we have some more wine? momkin nebeet tanee?

ممكن نبيز تانى؟

A half-dozen or so Egyptian wines are produced at Giancolis, near Alexandria. The most commonly found are Omar Khayyam (a dry red), Cru des Ptolémées (a dry white) and Rubis d'Egypt (a rosé).

wine list Qīmit en-nebeet

قائمة نبيز

winter sheta

شتا

in the winter fesh-sheta

فى الشتا

with maAa

مع

I'm staying with ... ana a-īd maAa ...

أنا قاعد مع ...

without min ghayr

من غير

witness (man/woman) shāhid/shahda

شاهد/شاهدة

will you be a witness for me? (to man/woman) momkin tesh-hadlee/tesh-hadi lee?

ممكن تشهد/تشهدى لى؟

woman sit

ست

women
Many women visitors do a range of things that no respectable Egyptian woman would consider: dressing 'immodestly', showing shoulders and cleavage, sharing rooms with men to whom they are not married, drinking alcohol in bars or restaurants, smoking, even travelling alone on public transport, without a relative as

an escort. Though some Egyptians
know enough about Western ways to
realize that this does not signify a
prostitute (as it would for an
Egyptian woman), most are ready to
think the worst. There are a few
steps you can take to improve your
image (see dress page 84).
On public transport, try to sit with
other women – who may often invite
you to do so. On the Cairo Metro and
trams in Alexandria there are
carriages reserved for women. If
you're travelling with a man, wearing
a wedding ring confers
respectability, and asserting that
you're married is better than
admitting to be 'just friends'. As
anywhere, looking confident and
knowing where you're going is a
major help in avoiding hassle.
Problems – most commonly hissing
or groping – tend to come in
downtown Cairo and in the public
beach resorts (except Sinai's Aqaba
coast or Red Sea holiday villages
which are more or less the only
places where you'll feel happy about
sunbathing).
Some women find that verbal hassle
is best ignored, while others may
prefer to use an Egyptian brush-off
like 'khalās!' (that's it!). If you get
groped the best response is to yell
'sebnee le waHdee!' (leave me
alone!) which will shame any
assailant in public, and may attract
help.

wonderful rā'eA
رائع
won't* : it won't start
mabaydorsh
مابيدورش
wood (material) khashab
خشب
wool Soof
صوف
word kelma
كلمة
work (noun) shoghl
شغل
(verb) shagh-ghal
شغّال
it's not working mish
shaghghāl
مش شغّال
worry: I'm worried ana al'ān
أنا قلقان
worse: it's worse da aswa'
دا أسوأ
worst el aswa'
الأسوأ
would: would you give this
to ...? momkin teddee da
lee ...?
ممكن تدّى دا ل ...؟
wrap: could you wrap it up?
(to man/woman) momkin tel-
effoo/teleffeeh?
ممكن تلفّه/تلفّيه؟

wrapping paper wara' lil laf

ورق للفّ

wrist resgh

رسغ

write katab

كتب

could you write it down? (to man/woman) momkin tektiboo/tektibeeh?

ممكن تكتبه/تكتبيه؟

writing paper wara' lil ketāba

ورق للكتابة

wrong: it's the wrong key da mish elmoftāH eSaHeeH

دا مش المفتاح الصحيح

this is the wrong train da mish el aTr eSaHeeH

دا مش القطر الصحيح

the bill's wrong el fatoora ghalaT

الفاتورة غلط

sorry, wrong number (said by man/woman) āsif/āsfa, el nimra ghalaT

آسف/أسفة، النمرة غلط

sorry, wrong room āsif/āsfa, el ōDa ghalaT

آسف/أسفة، الأوضة غلط

there's something wrong with ... fee Aayb fee ...

في عيب في...

what's wrong? fee Haga

ghalaT?

في حاجة غلط؟

Y

yacht yakht

يخت

yard (measurement) yarda

ياردة

year sana

سنة

yellow aSfar

أصفر

Yemen el yaman

اليمن

yes īwa

أيوه

yesterday embāreH

إمبارح

yesterday morning embāreH eS-SobH

إمبارح الصبح

the day before yesterday owel embāreH

أوّل إمبارح

yet leHad delwa'tee

لحد دلوقتي

dialogue

is it here yet? hayya mow-gooda delwa'tee?
no, not yet la', lessa
you'll have to wait a little longer yet lāzim testanna shwīya tanyeen

yoghurt zabādee
زبادى

you* (to man/woman) inta/inti
إنت/إنتى
(to more than one person) intoo
إنتو

this is for you (to man/woman)
da Aalashanak/Aalashanik
دا علشانَك/علشانِك

with you (to man/woman)
maAāk/maAākee
معاك/معاكى

 If you are addressing a woman or an elderly man, avoid 'inta' or 'inti' (you), as it may be considered disrespectful. If you are speaking either to an older person, someone of the opposite sex, or to a person for the first time, use words such as 'afanddim' (sir/madam), 'Habretak' (you: formal said to a man) and 'Habretek' (you: formal, said to a woman).

young shāb
شاب

your* (m/f object, male owner)
btāAak/btaAtak
بتاعك/بتاعتك
(m/f object, female owner)
btāAik/btaAtik
بتاعك/بتاعتك

your camera (to man/woman)
kamiretak/kamiretik
كاميرتك/كاميرتك

yours* (m/f object, male owner) da
btāAak/dee btaAtak
دا بتاعك/دى بتاعتك
(m/f object, female owner) da
btāAik/dee btaAtik
دا بتاعك/دى بتاعتك

youth hostel bayt shabāb
بيت شباب

 Egypt's youth hostels are cheap but their drawbacks are considerable. A day-time lock-out and night-time curfew are universal practice; so too is segregating the sexes and (usually) foreigners and Egyptians. The better hostels are in Cairo, Sharm el-Sheikh and Ismailiya.
see **hotel** and **resthouse**

Z

zero Sifr

صفر

zip sosta

سوستة

could you put a new zip on?
(to man/woman) momkin
terakkib/terakkibee sosta
gedeeda?

ممكن تركّب/تركّبى
سوستة جديدة؟

zip code ramz bareedee

رمز بريدى

zoo gonaynit el Hīyowanāt

جنينة الحيوانات

Arabic

→

English

Colloquialisms

The following are words you might well hear. You shouldn't be tempted to use any of the stronger ones unless you are sure of your audience.

abadan! no way!
āllah wa akbar! God almighty!
āllah yenowar! well done!
ekhras! shut up!
ekhs Alayk! shame on you!
ellaAna! damn!
fa'r! shit!
ghebee! fool!, idiot!
hala hala! well, well!, well I never
Hasib! look out!
intaAama? are you blind?
khallee balak take care
mish teHasib? can't you watch what you're doing?
momtāz excellent
ra'iA great
salām? is that right?
Toz? so what?
ya salām! my goodness! (lit: oh peace!)

The alphabetical order in this section is:

a, ā, A, b, d, D, e, f, g, h, H, i, ī, j, J, k, l, m, n, o, ō, Q, r, s, S, t, T, w, y, z, Z

a

a'all less
a'all min under, less than
aAad sit down
aAma blind
ab father
abadan never; ever
abAad further
abl before
abol hōl sphinx
aboo father of
abyaD white
ad ay? how many?
adeem old; ancient
afal close; shut; lock; turn off
afanddim sir; madam
  afanddim? pardon (me)?, sorry?
afaS basket
a'fleen they're shut
afrangee Western (from Europe, US)
agāza holiday, vacation
agāza rasmaya public holiday
aggar rent, hire
aghla more expensive
aghosTos August
agnabaya (f) foreigner
agnabee (m) foreign; foreigner

agzakhana chemist's, pharmacy
ahbal silly
ahl parents
ahlan hello; welcome
ahlan bik/biki hello; welcome (to man/woman)
ahlan bikom hello; welcome (to more than one person)
ahlan wa sahlan welcome
ahwa coffee; café, coffee house
aHmar red
aHsan better; best
aHyānan sometimes, not often
aī what; which
aī Had anybody
aī Hāga anything
  aī Hāga tania? anything else?
aī khidma my pleasure
akh brother
akhad take, accept; collect; have
akhbār (f) news
akhd el HaQā'ib baggage claim
akhDar green
akheer last
akheeran eventually
akkid confirm
akl food
aktar more
  aktar bekteer a lot more
  aktar min more than, over
alam pen
alam gāf ballpoint pen
alam roSāS pencil

219

alAa fortress, citadel; castle
alb heart
alf thousand
alfayn two thousand
almānee German
aloo hello
amar moon
amān safe (not dangerous)
ameen safe (not in danger); honest
amees shirt
amreeka United States, America
amrekānee American
ana I; me
ara read
arbaAa four
arbaAtāshar fourteen
arbiAeen forty
arD (f) floor; ground
arkhas less expensive
arsa bite
arsit Hashara insect bite
asansayr lift, elevator
asār archeology; monument
asāsee essential
asbānee Spanish
ash'ar blond
asharb scarf (for head)
ashoof? can I see?
asmar dark (hair)
assim share
aswa' worse
  el aswa' worst
asfar yellow
aslee traditional; typical
asr palace
atal kill
atmanna keda I hope so; I

hope that
aTaA cut (verb)
aTfāl children
aTr train
aTr en-nōm sleeper
aTrash deaf
awee too; really, very
ay? what?
ay ... ow ... either ... or ...
azra' blue

ā

ābil meet
āfil closed
ākheer latest
ākhir bottom
ākhir elesbooA weekend
āl say
āllah Allah, God
ānisa Miss
āsif/āsfa sorry; excuse me (said by man/woman)

A

Aabr across
Aadee ordinary
Aadwa infection
AaDDa bite (by animal)
AaDm bone
Aafsh zāyid excess baggage
Aafwan you're welcome, don't mention it
Aagala bicycle; wheel
Aagooz/Aagooza old (person); senior citizen (man/woman)

Aala on

Aalal on; at the top

Aalashanha for her

Aalashanna for us

Aalashān because

Aalashānoo for him

AalaTool frequent; straight ahead

AalaTool delwa'tee at once, immediately

Aamal do

Aam gedeed saAeed! Happy New Year!

Aamm uncle (father's brother)

Aamma aunt (father's sister)

Aan about

Aand at

Aandak/Aandik ...? have you got any ...? (to man/woman)

Aan Taree' via

Aa'rab scorpion

Aarabayya car

Aarabayya beHSān horse-drawn buggy

Aarabayya HanToor horse-drawn buggy

Aarabayya mit'aggara rented car

Aarabayyit aTr carriage

Aarabayyit bidoon tadkheen nonsmoking compartment

Aarabayyit el akl buffet car

Aarabayyit na'l van

Aarabayyit nōm sleeping car

Aarabayyit shonaT luggage trolley

Aarabee Arab

Aarboon deposit

AarD fair (adj)

AarD masraHee show (in theatre)

AareeD wide

Aarraf introduce

Aasha dinner, evening meal; supper

Aashara ten

Aashar talāf ten thousand

Aash-shaT ashore

Aaskar camp

AaSree modern

AaTal break down

AaTlān out of order

AaTshān thirsty

Aayāda clinic

Aayiz: ana Aayiz I want (said by man)

Aayiz ay? what do you want? (to man)

Aayla family

Aayn (f) eye

Aaysh bread

Aazba single (woman)

AaZeem great, excellent

Aād repeat

Aādee normal, usual, ordinary

Aālam world

Aālamee international

Aālee high; loud; tall

Aām general (adj); swim

Aāmil/Aāmla ay? how do you do? (to man/woman)

Aāraf know

Aāsifa storm

Aāsifa raAdaya thunderstorm

Aāsifa ramlaya sandstorm

AāTil unemployed

Aāzib single (man)

Aeed milād birthday

Aeed milād el meseeH
  Christmas
Aeed milād saAeed! merry
  Christmas!; happy birthday!
Aeed sham el neseem Easter
Aelba can; small tin; pack
Aelbit sagāyer a pack of
  cigarettes
Aemil make
Aezooma invitation (for meal)
Ainwān address
Aishreen twenty
Aīyān ill, sick
Aīza: ana Aīza I want (said by
  woman)
  Aīza ay? what do you
  want? (to woman)
Aoboor cruise; crossing (by sea)
Ao'd necklace
Aolow height (mountain)
Aomla coin
Aomr life; age

b

ba'āl delicatessen; grocer's
baAat send; post, mail
baAd after
baAdak/baAdik after you (to
  man/woman)
baAdayn afterwards, later
  (on); then
baAd bokra the day after
  tomorrow
baAd eD-Dohr afternoon
bab door
baba dad
bada' start, begin

badal instead
badawee Bedouin
badree early
baHebbo/baHebbaha I like it
  (m/f object)
baHr sea
  el baHr elaHmar Red Sea
  el baHr el metowaSSiT
  Mediterranean
balad country, nation
baladee national
bambee pink
banafsigee purple
bango marijuana
banseeyōn boarding house,
  guesthouse
banTaloon trousers, pants
banyo bath
banzeen petrol
bar' lightning
baraka blessing
bard cold (noun)
bardān cold (adj)
bareed mail
bareed gowee airmail
bareed mosaggal by
  registered mail
barra outdoors; outside
barTamān jar
bas just, only
ba'sheesh tip, gratuity; bribe;
  alms
bas hena just here
bas keda nothing else
batrōn pattern
baTee' slow
baTn er-rigl sole (of foot)
baTTal da! stop it!
baTTanaya blanket

baTTar**aya** battery; torch, flashlight

bawwāba gate

bayDa egg

bayn among; between

bayt house; home

bayt shabāb youth hostel

bayyāA garayid newsagent's

bāa sell

bāko packet

bāligh/balgha adult (man/woman)

be'asraA ma yomkin as soon as possible

beAeed far; in the distance

bebalāsh free (no charge)

bebba pipe (for smoking)

beddosh with shower

beDāAa Horra duty-free (goods)

bekam? how much is it?

bekhayr OK, fine

bekteer a lot

belHa' fairly

benafsee by myself

berrāHa slowly

bes-safeena by ship

bes-sikka el Hadeed by rail

betelloo beef; veal

betHeb: inta betHeb ...? do you like ...? (to man)

betHebee: inti betHebbee ...? do you like ...? (to woman)

betnaTTar it's raining

beT-Tīyāra by plane

beZZabT! exactly!

bil: bil Aarabayy**a** by car

  bil Aarabee in Arabic

  bil inglee**zee** in English

bil bareed eg-gowee by airmail

bil layl in the evening; at night

bint girl; daughter

bint akh niece (brother's daughter)

bint Aamm cousin (on father's side: uncle's daughter)

bint Aamma cousin (on father's side: aunt's daughter)

bint khala cousin (on mother's side: aunt's daughter)

bint khāl cousin (on mother's side: uncle's daughter)

bint okht niece (sister's daughter)

birka lake

bisabab e-... because of ...

bisorAa quickly

biTa'it SoAood boarding pass

blāJ beach

blooza blouse

bo' mouth

boHayrit nāSSer Lake Nasser

bok purse (for money)

bokra tomorrow

bokra eS-SobH tomorrow morning

bonnay brown

bosTa post office; post, mail

boS Aala look at

bowwāb doorman

btaA: da btaA meen? whose is this?

btaAha her; hers

btaAhom theirs; their

btaAitkoo your; yours (m object, to more than one person)

btaAna ours; our

btaAtee my; mine (f object)
btaAtkoo your; yours (f object, to more than one person)
btāAee my; mine (m object)
btāAak/btaAtak your; yours (m/f object, male owner)
btāAik/btaAtik your; yours (m/f object, female owner)
btāAo his (m/f object)

d

da this; that; this one; that one; it is; this/that is (m object)
da ...? is this/that ...?; is it ...?
daAa invite
da Aalashanak/Aalashanik this is for you (to man/woman)
daAwa invitation
dada baby-sitter, child-minder
dafaA pay
dahab gold
dakhal go in
daleel telefōnāt phone book; directory enquiries
dameem ugly
damm blood
da'n (f) chin; beard
daraga oolā first-class
daraga talta third-class
daraga tania economy class, second-class
daraga tania momtāza second-class superior
daras learn

dars lesson
dayr monastery
dayr 'ebTee Coptic monastery
dā' elkalb rabies
dāfee warm
dākhelee indoors
dee (f) this; that; this one; that one; this/that is; it is
dee ...? is this/is that ...?; is it ...?
de'ee'a minute
de'ee'a waHda just a minute
deen religion
delwa'tee now
dibbāna fly
dīman often; always
dokhān smoke
dokkān (f) shop (small, local)
dolāb cupboard
dort el mīya toilet, rest room
dosh shower (in bathroom)
dowa (m) medicine; drug
dowlee national
dowrit el mīya toilet, rest room
dowsha noise
dōl those/these
dōr floor, storey
drāA arm

D

Dahr back (of body)
Dahr el markib deck
DaHya suburb
Dakhm enormous

Darbit shams sunstroke, heatstroke
DareeH shrine
Darooree necessary
Dayf/Dayfa guest (man/woman)
DāyiA missing
Dānee lamb (meat)
Did against
Dohr noon

e

ebree' jug
ebTee Coptic
ed-da give
ed-dōr el arDee ground floor, (US) first floor
ed-dōr el awwal first floor, (US) second floor
ed-dōr el fo'ānee top floor
ed-dōr et-taHtānee downstairs
eD-DeAf twice as much
eD-Dohr midday; at midday
eD-Dohraya this afternoon
eed hand; handle
eegār rent
eema value
efl lock
eggazā'ir Algeria
eHna we
eHwid shimāl turn left
ekhtafa disappear
ekhtelāf difference
el the
el Aafw don't mention it
el Hamdoo lillāh I'm fine (lit: praise be to Allah)

ellay baAd next
ellaylādee tonight; this evening
elmadeena eladeema old town
elmamlaka elmottaHida UK
elmenew menu
elwagba elra'eesaya main course
embāreH yesterday
embāreH eS-SobH yesterday morning
emshee warāya follow me
en-naharda today
en-naharda eS-SobH this morning
enSāb injured
er-rabAa (f) fourth
er-rabeeA spring
er-rābiA (m) fourth
esbooA week
el esbooA eggī next week
esm name; first name
esmak/esmik ay? what's your name? (to man/woman)
esmee ... my name is ...
esm el Aayla surname
esm esh-shorTa police station
essalāmo Alaykom hello (lit: peace be upon you)
essana eggedeeda New Year
es-sāAa o'clock
es-sāAa kām? what's the time?
es-sikka el Hadeed railway
estaAmil use
estanna wait
este'bāl reception
estirleenee pound (British)

eswid black
eS-SaHara' esh-shar'aya Eastern Desert
eS-SeAeed Upper Egypt
eS-SobH in the morning
eS-SobH badree early in the morning
etAarraf Aala recognize
etfaDDal/etfaDDalee here you are (to man/woman)
etgaraH injured
etkallim talk
ettafa'na it's a deal
et-talta (f) third
et-tania (f) second
et-tālit (m) third
et-tānee second (adj); the other one
ettaSal phone, call
ettaSal baAdayn ring back
ettigāh direction
eTlāQan not in the least
eT-Taree' er-ra'eesee main road
eT-Taree' es-sareeA motorway, freeway, highway
ezāz glass (material)
ezāza bottle

f

faDDa silver
fa'eer poor (not rich)
fag'a suddenly
fagr dawn
fahim: ana fahim I understand
fakahānee greengrocer's (fruit shop)
fakhm luxurious
fakkar think
fallāHeen: el fallāHeen country, countryside
falooka Egyptian sailboat
fanilla noS kom T-shirt
fann art
far rat; mouse
faransa France
faransāwee French
farAōn Pharaoh
fardit gazma shoe
fardit sharāb sock
faree' team
faSl term (at university, school)
fataH unlock; open
fateH lil shahaya starter, appetizer
fatoora bill
faTāTree pastry shop
fawākih fruit
fayn? where?
   fayn da/dee? where is it?
faZeeA terrible, awful
fāDee empty
feD-Dil in the shade
feD-Dohr at noon
feD-Dohraya in the afternoon
fee ... in; at; on
   fee ... there is/are ...
   fee el wesT in the centre
fee ay? what's up?, what's the matter?
fee Aandak/Aandik ...? do you have ...?
fee Aayb faulty
fee SeHHetak! cheers!
felesTeen Palestine

fen-nos in the middle
feTār breakfast
fibrīer February
fil in; at; on
  fil 'ākher at the back
  fil mo'addima at the front
fil khareg abroad
fil layla per night
fiaDān flood
fībar viper
floos (f) money
fondo' hotel
foo' up; up there; upstairs; above
  foo' el ... on top of ...
  foo' henāk up there
fooTa towel; serviette, napkin
fooTit Hammām bath towel
forn oven; bakery
forsha brush
forSa saAeeda nice to meet you
fostān dress
frākh chicken

g

ga come in
gabal mountain
gadwal el mowāAeed timetable, schedule
gamal camel
gamārek Customs
gamAa university
gamb side; next to; near
  gamb el baHr by the sea
gameel pretty, lovely, beautiful; exciting; nice;

mild
ganāza funeral
ganoob south
  fil ganoob in the south
  el ganoob el gharbee southwest
  el ganoob es-shar'ee southeast
garafatta tie, necktie
garrab Aala try on
garrāH asnān dentist
garsōn waiter
garsōna waitress
gayb pocket
gazma shoes
gazmagee shoe repairer
gazzār butcher's
gāb get, fetch; bring
gāhiz ready
gāmiA mosque
gāmid hard
gāyiz perhaps; probably
gedeed new
geneeh Egyptian pound
geree run
gezeera island
ghabee thick, stupid; idiot
ghadā lunch
ghalaT confusion, mix-up; wrong, incorrect
  el nimra ghalaT wrong number
ghalTa mistake
ghanee rich (person)
ghanna sing
gharāma fine (punishment)
gharb west
  fil gharb in the west
ghareeb/ghareeba strange,

weird, peculiar; stranger (man/woman)
ghasal wash
ghaseel washing, laundry
ghassāla washing machine
ghaTa lid; cap
ghayr Aādee extraordinary
ghāba forest
ghālee expensive
ghoraf rooms
ghorfa room
ghoweeT deep
ghōs snorkelling; skin-diving
ghroob esh-shams sunset
gid grandfather
gidda grandmother
giddan very, extremely
gild skin; leather
gins sex
ginsaya nationality
gism body
gomAa: el gomAa Friday
gomrok custom
gonayna garden
gonaynit el Hīowanāt zoo
gonilla skirt
gooA hungry
gornāl newspaper
gornālgee newsagent's
gow dull (weather)
gowa inside
gowabāt letters
gowāb letter
gowla tour
gowla mowwagaha guided tour
gowla sayāHaya sightseeing tour
goz' part

gōz husband; double; a pair of; a couple of

h

habla (f) silly
hansh hip
haram pyramid
hayya she; her; it
hādee quiet
hedaya gift
hedoom clothes
hena here; over here
  hena ... here is/are ...
  hena taHt down here
henāk there; over there
hidaya present, gift
hidoo'! quiet!
homma they; them
howa he; him; it; air

H

Hab like; love
Habba Habba gradually
Habl ghaseel clothes line
Had somebody, someone
Hadsa accident
HaDretak/HaDretik you (formal: to man/woman)
Ha'ee'ee real; true; genuine
Hafeed grandson
Hafeeda granddaughter
Hafit elmarsa on the quayside
Hafla party (celebration)
Haflit gowāz wedding
Haga something

Hagar stone, rock

Hagaz reserve, book

Hagm size

Hagz reservation

Hala'a circle

Halawanee cake shop, patisserie

Hama father-in-law

Hamāt mother-in-law

HammaD develop

Ham-mām bathroom

Ham-māmāt toilets, rest room

Ham-mām dākhil el ghorfa en-suite bathroom

Ham-mām er-rigāl men's room, gents (toilet)

Ham-mām khāS private bathroom

Ham-mām shams sunbathe

Ham-mām sibāHa (swimming) pool

Ham-mām sibāHa lel aTfāl children's pool

Hanafaya tap; fountain (for drinking)

HanToor horse-drawn buggy; donkey-drawn cart

Hara' burn

Harāmee/Haramaya thief (man/woman)

Harāra heat

Harb war

Haree'a fire

Hareer silk

HareeS careful

Harrān hot

Haseerit blāJ beach mat

Hashara insect

Hasheesh grass

HaSal happen

HatDallim it's getting dark

Hateshrab/Hateshrabee ay? what'll you have? (to man/woman)

HaT put

HayTa wall

Hazeen sad

HaZ luck

HaZ saAeed! good luck!

Hādis sir'a burglary

Hādsa crash

Hāga thing

Hāga tania something else

Hālan soon; immediately

Hāmee strong (taste); hot, spicy; sharp (knife)

HāmiD sour

Hāmil pregnant

Hāra lane

Hāsib charge

Hāsib! look out!

Hātee kebab house

Hāwil try

Hebbee friendly

Hedood border

Hel'ān earrings

Helm dream

Helw sweet, dessert; nice

Hetta bit, piece

Hetta tania somewhere else

Hettit ... a bit/piece of ...

Hidāshar eleven

Hizām belt; strap

Hīawān animal

Hob love

HōD bathtub; washhand basin; sink

Hogrit fondo' hotel room

Hogrit nōm bedroom
Hogrit shī tearoom
Homār donkey
Hosān horse
Howālee about, approximately
Howid turn

i

ibn son
ibn akh nephew (brother's son)
ibn Aamm cousin (on father's side, uncle's son)
ibn Aamma cousin (on father's side, aunt's son)
ibn khāla cousin (on mother's side, aunt's son)
ibn khāl cousin (on mother's side, uncle's son)
ibn okht nephew (sister's son)
ibreel April
ikhtār choose
iktashaf find out
ilāha goddess
imta? when?
ingiltera Britain; England
ingleezee British; English
inshā'allāh hopefully; God willing
inta/inti you (to man/woman)
inta!/inti! hey!
intoo you (to more than one person)
iqāma kamla full board
irsh piastre
isAāf ambulance

isAāf awwalee first aid
isboaayn fortnight
ishtara buy
iskinderaya Alexandria
ismaA listen
istaAgil hurry
istirāHa resthouse
iswera bracelet
itfaDal/itfaDalee come in; help yourself; here you are (to man/woman)
itHarrak move
itmanna hope
itnayn both; couple (two people)
itnāshar twelve
'iTaA cut (noun)
izzay how
izzayak/izzayik? how are you?; how do you do? (to man/woman)

ī

īwa yes

j

jeb jeep

J

Jelātee ice cream

k

kaAb ankle; heel
kabeena cabin
kabeenit telefōn phone box
kabreet matches
kahraba electricity
kalb dog
kallif cost
kamān too, also
  kamān shwīya in a minute
kamirit tasgeel camcorder
kanaba sofa, couch
kareem kind, generous
karsa disaster
kart card; business card;
  postcard
kartōn carton
kart sheekāt cheque card
kart telefōn phonecard
kasar break
kashaf check
kaslān lazy
kassit Soghīyar personal
  stereo
katab write
kays cash desk
kān he was; it was
kānit she was; it was
kāno they were
kās glass
kāzeno bar and tea room,
  usually along the Nile
kebeer large, big
kees carrier bag
kees makhadda pillow case
kelma word
kelomitr kilometre

keteer a lot, lots; many;
  several; much
  keteer awee too much, too
  many; quite a lot
  keteer min ... lots/plenty
  of ...
khabeer experienced
khad cheek (on face); take,
  accept
khadoom helpful
khafeef light (not heavy); weak
khalaS finish
khalāS already
  khalāS Hashtreeha it's a deal
khaleeg bay
khallee bālak! be careful!
khamastāshar fifteen
khamsa five
  el khamsa (f) fifth
khamseen fifty
kharabāt ruins; remains
kharaz beads
khareef autumn, (US) fall
khareeTa map
kharoof sheep
kharrab damage
kharrabt damaged
khashab wood (material)
khaT line
khaTar dangerous
khaTeeb/khaTeeba
  fiancé/fiancée
khaTeer serious
khawāga foreigner
khayma tent
khayT string; thread
khazaf ceramics; pottery
khāl uncle (mother's brother)
khāla aunt (mother's sister)

khāmis: el khāmis (m) fifth
khāS private
khātim ring
khāTeb engaged (to be married: man)
khedma lel ewaD room service
khedma zātaya self-service
khesir lose
khilāl through
khoDaree greengrocer's (vegetable shop)
khoDār vegetables
khomsomaya five hundred
khorm hole; puncture
khoroog exit
khoSooSan especially
kifāya enough
kitāb book
kobbāya glass; mug
kobree bridge
kobs switch
kol each, every; eat
kol Hāga everything
kol Hetta everywhere
kolohom the whole lot; all of them; altogether
koloo all of it
kol wāHid everyone
konna we were
kont you were
kornaysh corniche, coastal road
korsee chair; seat; saddle (for bike)
korsee blāJ deckchair
kosharee snack bar selling 'kosharee', an Egyptian rice speciality

kotshayna game
kowetsh tyre, (US) tire
kōra ball
kōrit Qadam football
kwayis good; OK, all right; fine; nice; properly
 inta kwayis? are you OK? (to man)
 inti kwayisa? are you OK? (to woman)

I

la' no
 la'! don't!
 la' lay? why not?
 la' motshakkir no thanks
 la' shokran no thanks
 la' TabAan certainly not; of course not
laAab play
laban milk
lafHet shams sunburn
lagha cancel
lahab fire (blaze)
laHma meat
lamba lamp; lightbulb
la ... wala ... neither ... nor ...
lay? why?
layl night
laylit imbbāreH last night
laylit rās es-sana New Year's Eve
lazeez delicious
lākin but
lāzim: ana lāzim ... I must ...
le to; into
leehom for them

leh to him
leha to her
lehom to them
leHad until
leHad delwa'tee yet
lena us; for us
lesh-shamāl to the north
lesh-shimāl to the left
lewaHdee separately
lil to the
lil bayA for sale
lil egār to rent; for hire
lil khareg abroad
lil yemeen to the right
lisān tongue
logha language
logha Aarabayya Arabic
lokanda small hotel
lo'sor Luxor
low if
low samaHt/samaHtee please; excuse me (to man/woman)
lōn colour

m

ma'āss size (clothing)
maAa with
maAa baAD together
maAada except
maAak kabreet? do you have a light? (for cigarette)
ma Aamaltish didn't
maAana with us
maAandeesh: maAandeesh khālis I don't have any
maAassalāma goodbye
maAād appointment

maAāh with him
maAāha with her
maAāhom with them
maAāk/maAākee with you (to man/woman)
maAbad temple (religious)
maAdan metal
maAla'a spoon
maAla'it shī teaspoon
maAlaysh it doesn't matter; it's a pity
maAlomāt information
maA'ool reasonable
maA'ool? really?
maAraD trade fair; exhibition
maArafsh I don't know
maAtaQedsh I don't think so
mabaHebboosh I don't like it
mabakkallimsh ... I don't speak ...
ma'bara tomb
mablool wet
mabna building
mabrook! congratulations!
mabsooT happy
ma'dartish ... I couldn't ...; I can't ...
madām lady; Mrs
madeena town; city
madfan cemetery (historic, Islamic)
madkhal entrance; lobby
madrasa school
mafDelshee Haga there's none left
mafeesh none; there isn't any
    mafeesh ... ba'ee there's no ... left

233

mafeesh Had no-one, nobody

mafeesh Hāga nothing

mafeesh Haga tania nothing else

mafeesh moshkila! no problem!

ma'fool off

mafrooD innak ... you should ...

maftooH open

magalla magazine

magaree express (train)

magāl field

maghāra cave

maghrib: el maghrib Morocco

maghsala laundry (place)

magmooA total

magmooAa party, group

magnoon crazy

magra stream

mahfoof crazy

mahragān festival

maHal shop

maHal AaSeer juice bar

maHal be'āla food shop/store

maHal hadāya gift shop

maHallee local

maHal toHaf antique shop

maHaTTa destination

maHaTTit aTr train station

maHaTTit banzeen petrol station, gas station

maHaTTit es-sekka el Hadeed railway station

maHaTTit otobees bus station; bus stop

maHboob popular

maHfaza wallet

maHroo' min esh-shams sunburnt

maJbak peg (for washing)

maJghool busy; engaged, occupied

makana machine

makān place

makhadda pillow; cushion

makhbaz cake shop

makhTooba engaged (to be married: woman)

maksoor broken

maktab office

maktaba bookshop, bookstore; library

maktab amanāt left luggage (office)

maktab bareed post office

maktab elbareed (elra'eesee) main post office

maktab elesti'bāl reception desk

maktab es-sayāHa tourist information office

maktab et-telfonāt 24-hour telephone office

maktab sentrāl 24-hour telephone office

maktab Sarf bureau de change

maktab tazakir ticket office

makwa iron

makwagee person who takes in laundry

mala fill up; fill in

malAab playground

malH salt

malha laylee nightclub

malyān full

mamar path
manakheer nose
manshoor leaflet; brochure
manTe'a district, area, region
manZar view; scenery
mar go through
maraD illness; disease
marham lotion; ointment
marHaban lil ... welcome to ...
markib boat; ship
markib Sayd fishing boat
markib Soghīyar dinghy
marra once
  el marra eg-gīya next time
  el marra el-lee fātit last time
  marra tania again
  marra waHda once
marrādee: el marrādee this
  time
marritayn twice
marwaHa fan
masak hold; catch
masā' el khayr, masā' en-noor
  good evening; good night
masāfa distance
masākin eT-Talaba student
  hostel
mashā leave
mashākil trouble
mashbak ghaseel clothes peg
mash-hoor famous
mashroob non-alcoholic
  drink
mas-Hoo' ghaseel washing
  powder, soap powder
masraH theatre
masraHaya play (in theatre)
maSr Egypt
maSree Egyptian

maSr el adeema Old Cairo
maSr el farAoonaya Ancient
  Egypt
mat-Haf museum
matmannāsh I hope not
maTār airport
maTAam restaurant
maTbakh kitchen
maTlaA hill
maya hundred
ma'zana minaret
maznoo' stuck
mazraAa farm
mazzeeka music
maZbooT accurate
mālik/malka owner
  (man/woman)
māris March
mās diamond
māt die
māyo May
meAaddaya ferry
meAda stomach
meAza goat
medān square (in town)
meen? who?
meena harbour; port
mesa evening
meseeHee Christian
mestaAgil express (mail)
metarrab dusty
meTala' divorced
millawis polluted
milowwin colour
min than; of; from
  min isbooA a week ago
min abl already
minayn: inta/inti minayn?
  where are you from? (to

man/woman)

min **fa**Dlak excuse me

min **ghayr** without

min ghayr koHol non-
alcoholic

mish not

  mish **awee** not so much

  mish delwa'tee not just
now

mish fāhim I don't
understand

mish kwayis bad; poor; badly

mish lāzim it's not necessary

mish maA'ool ridiculous;
surprising

mish mo'addab rude

mish modhish amazing,
surprising

mistaAgil urgent

mitayn two hundred

mitgowiz married

mit'kh-khar late

mīya water

mīya maAdanaya mineral
water

mīya min elHanafaya tap
water

mīyit dead

mīyit shorb drinking water

mlāya sheet (for bed)

mo'addab polite

mo'addam in advance

mo'assir impressive

mobāshir direct

modariss/modarissa teacher
(man/woman)

modda period (of time)

modeer/modeera manager
(man/woman)

modhish fantastic, incredible

moDeef/moDeefa steward;
stewardess

mofaDDal favourite

mofeed useful

mofriH pleasant

moftāH key

moghray sexy

mohim important

mokalma khārigaya long-
distance call

mokhaddarāt drugs (narcotics)

mokhtalif different

molā'im convenient

mo'lim painful

momil boring

momkin possible

  momkin ...? may I ...?;
please could you ...?; is it
OK to ...?

  momkin inta/inti ...? can you
...? (to man/woman)

momtāz excellent

momteA enjoyable;
interesting

momyā mummy (in tomb)

monfaSil separate; apart from

moolid fair

morakkaz strong (drink)

morAeb horrible

moreeH comfortable

mo'rif dreadful, revolting,
disgusting

  mo'rif aktar much worse

morshid (sayāHee)/morshida
(sayāHayya) tour guide
(man/woman)

mosaAda help

mosallee funny, amusing

mosammim poisonous

mosaTTaH flat (adj)

moseeQa music

moseeQa afrangee pop music (Western)

moseeQa gharbaya pop music (Egyptian)

moseeQa SeAeedee folk music (in Upper Egypt)

moseeQa shaAbaya folk music

moseer exciting

moshkila problem

mostaAid ready

mostaAmal second-hand

mosta'bal future

mostaHeel impossible

mostanad document

mostashfa hospital

moSir: ana moSir I insist

motowaSSiT medium, medium-sized

motshakkir: la' motshakkir no thanks

mow'af park; rail terminus

mow'af Aarabayyāt car park, parking lot

mow'af otobees bus station

mow'af taksayāt taxi rank

mowāfi' accept; agree

mowQiA elmoAaskar campsite

mozayyaf false

mozAig annoying

mōAzam mostly

mōAzam el wa't most of the time

mōDa adeema old-fashioned, unfashionable

mōt death

mrātak your wife

mrātee my wife

mrāt ibn daughter-in-law

n

naAam yes
 naAam? pardon (me)?, sorry?

naAl sole (of shoe)

nabāt plant

nabātee/nabātaya vegetarian (man/woman)

nadah call

naDDāra glasses, spectacles, (US) eyeglasses

naDDāra shamsaya sunglasses

nafa' underground, (US) subway; tunnel

nafoora fountain

nahr river

nahr en-neel Nile

naHt carving

nak-ha delicacy

nakhla palm tree

namoosa mosquito

namoozag form (document)

nasa forget

nasayt I forget, I've forgotten

nasheeT lively

nashra brochure

naTara rain

nazal get off; get out; go down

nāAim soft

nādee coffee and gaming house

nādir rare; hardly ever

237

nām sleep
nār (f) fire
nās people
nāshif dry (adj)
nebeet wine
neDeef clean
nehāya end
neHās aSfar brass
neseeb son-in-law; brother-in-law
neseeba daughter-in-law; sister-in-law
netlā'a baAdayn! see you later!
nimra number, figure
nimrit el kōd dialling code
nisma breeze
nī not cooked, raw
nokta joke
noor light
noS half
    fee noS el-balad in town
noS ellayl midnight
    fee noS ellayl in the middle of the night
noS eoāma half board
noS et-taman half-price
noS sāAa half an hour
noS tazkara half fare
nozha picnic
nōA quality; type
nōm wefTār bed and breakfast

O
■

oddām in front
oghnaya song
ogra fare

okht sister
oktobar October
olā (f) first
omāsh material, cloth
omm mother of
ordon: el ordon Jordan
orīyib recent
    min orīyib recently
    orīyib awee nearby
orobba Europe
orobbee European
osra malakaya dynasty
ostāz Mr
osīyar short
otobees bus
otobees el maTār airport bus
otobees safar long-distance bus
oTn cotton
oTTa cat
ow or
owalan at first
owil embāriH the day before yesterday
owwil (m) first

Ō
■

ōDa room
ōDa lewāHid single room
ōDa litnayn twin room; double room
ōDit es-sofra dining room

Q

Qahira: el Qahira Cairo
Qanāl canal
Qanāl es-sways Suez Canal
Qar-rar decide
Qarya village
Qānoon law
Qism department
Qīma menu
Qods: el Qods Jerusalem
QonSolaya consulate

r

ra'aba neck
ra'aS dance
ra'āSa belly-dancer
raAee gemāl camel driver
rabb god
ra'eesee main, central
raff shelf; bunk
ragaA go back; get back;
  come back, return; give
  back
raggaA vomit
rakab get on
rakan park
ramla sand
ramz bareedee postcode, zip
  code
raQam number
raQam er-riHla flight number
raQam telefōn phone number
rasm drawing; charge
rasm eddokhool admission
  charge

rasmee formal
rasm iDāfee supplement
ra'S dance
raSeef platform, (US) track;
  pavement, sidewalk; jetty
ra'S shaAbee folk dancing
ra'S shar'ee belly-dance;
  belly-dancing
rattib arrange, fix
raTeb damp; cool
rayāDa sport
rā'eA wonderful
rāgil man
rāgil bolees policeman
rāH go; go back
rākib/rākba passenger
  (man/woman)
rās (f) head
reef countryside, country
reeH (f) wind
reggāla men
reHla journey; excursion, trip
reHla beg-gemāl camel trip
reHla dākhilaya domestic
  flight
reHla gowaya flight
reHla oSīyara excursion
reHla saAeeda! have a good
  journey!
reHla shamla package holiday
reHla yōmaya scheduled
  flight; day trip
rekheeS cheap, inexpensive;
  low
resāla message
ri'atayn lungs
rigl (f) leg; foot
rikoob el khayl horse riding
robA quarter

robAomaya four hundred
rofīyaA thin
rokba knee
rokhSa licence
rokhSit sewā'a driving licence
rokoob eg-gimāl camel ride
romādee grey
roshetta prescription

S
—

sa'Aa chilled
saAeeda greetings
saAet HayT clock
sabaAtāshar seventeen
sabat basket
sabAa seven
sabAeen seventy
sa'f ceiling
safar travel; departure; journey
safar bel gimāl camel trek
safāra embassy
safeena ship (large)
sahl simple, easy
sakan live; accommodation
sakheef silly
sakrān drunk
salālim (f) stairs
sama sky
samak fish
sameen valuable
sana year
sanya second (in time)
sara' steal
saradeeb catacombs
sareeA quick, fast

satāyer blinds; curtains
sayeH tourist (man)
sā' drive
sāAa hour; wristwatch
sāAid help
sāda plain
sāHil coast
sāyib loose
seAr rate
seAr et-taHweel exchange rate
sha'a flat, apartment
shaAr hair
shabakit namosaya mosquito net
shabboora mist; fog
shad pull
shafāyef lips
shafsha' jug
shagara tree
shagh-ghal work
shahr month
shaHāt beggar
shamāl north
shamāl gharb northwest
shamāl shar' northeast
shamAa candle
shams (f) sun
shamsaya umbrella
shamsayit blāJ beach umbrella
shamwā suede
shanab moustache
shanTa bag; hand luggage; briefcase
shanTit Dahr rucksack
shanTit eed handbag, (US) purse
shanTit safar suitcase

shanTit wesT money belt

shar' east

   fee esh-shar' in the east

sharāb drink

shar'ee eastern

shaT shore

shaT el baHr coast

shāb young

shāf see

shākhS person

shāl carry

shāriA street

shāriA gānaybee side street

shāTer clever

shāz unusual

shebbāk window

shebbāk tazākir box office

shebsee® crisps

shedeed strong

sheek cheque, (US) check

sheek sayāHee traveller's
   cheque

sheesh shutter (on window)

sheta winter

   fesh-sheta in the winter

shimāl left

shirāA sail

shirka company (business)

shita shower (of rain)

shī tea (drink)

shīyāl porter (in hotel)

shoAāA esh-shams sunshine

shoft/shoftee ...? have you
   seen ...? (to man/woman)

shoghl work ; job; business

shokran thanks, thank you

   **shokran gazeelan, shokran
   giddan** thank you very
   much

la', shokran no, thanks

shonaT luggage, baggage

shōka fork

shwīya (a) few; a bit

shwīya shwīya gradually

sibā' gimāl camel racing

sigār cigar

sigāra cigarette

siggāda carpet

sikka alley

sikkeena knife

silmee peaceful

simeA hear

sinna tooth

sireer bed; couchette; berth

sireerayn twin beds

sireer faraDānee single bed

sireer litnayn double bed

sirg saddle (for horse)

sit woman

sitta six

sittāshar sixteen

sitteen sixty

sittoomaya six hundred

sīHa tourist (woman)

so'āl question

sobAomaya seven hundred

sokhn hot

sokkar sugar

soo' market, bazaar

soor fence

sorya Syria

sosta zip

sowā' driver (man)

sowā'a driver (woman)

sowā' taksee taxi-driver

stella® lager

S

SaAb hard, difficult
Sab**ā**H el khayr, Sab**ā**H en-**noo**r good morning
Sab**oo**n soap
Sa**da**fa shellfish; shell
Sa**fee**Ha can; large tin
Sa**fee**Hit ... a can of ...
Sa**f**Ha page
Sa**H** right, correct
Sa**Ha**ra desert; Sahara
Sa**H**ā get up
Sa**H**ba friend; girlfriend; owner
Sa**Hee**H? really?
Sa**l**Ha valid
Sa**l**laH mend, repair
Sa**l**ōn compartment (on train)
Sa**na**ya tray
San**doo'** box
San**doo'** el **bos**Ta letterbox, mailbox
Sa**raf** spend; cash; change
Sa**rf** change
Sa**T-H** roof
Sa**Tr** line
Sa**yd sa**mak fishing
Sa**yf** summer
feS-Sayf in the summer
S**ā**Hib friend; boyfriend; owner
S**ā**la lounge; foyer
S**ā**lit el akl dining room
S**ā**lit es-safar departure lounge
Se**dr** chest
Se**HHee** healthy

S**ifr** zero
So**ba**A finger
So**ba**A **rig**l toe
So**b**H morning
So**d**āA headache
So**ghī**yar small, little
S**oof** wool
S**oo**ra poster; painting; photo; picture

t

ta**A**bān tired
ta'**geer** Aa**ra**bayy**āt** car rental
ta**H**seen improve
ta**Ht** below; down; under
ta**H**weed turning
tak**see khi**dma service taxi
tak**yeef (ho**wa) air-conditioning
ta**la**teen thirty
talat tal**āf** three thousand
tala**tt**āshar thirteen
ta**l**āta three
ta'**leed** fake; imitation
tal**fee**Aa scarf
ta**lg** ice
tal**lā**ga fridge
ta**man** price; charge
tama**neen** eighty
ta**ma**nia eight
taman**tā**shar eighteen
ta**mām** perfect; completely
ta**n**da sunshade
ta**nee** more; another; other
ta**Qā**ToA **To**ro' junction; crossroads, intersection
tara**bay**za table

ta'reeban almost, nearly; quite; approximately

tawalet ladies' (toilets), ladies' room

tawalet rigālee gents (toilet), men's room

tazkara ticket; single ticket

tazkara maftooHa open ticket

tazkara waHda single ticket

tazkarit Aowda return ticket, round-trip ticket

teAbān snake

teAbān kobra cobra

tebeA follow

tegāh towards

tekheen fat

temsāl statue

ti'eel heavy

timsāH alligator

tisaAtāshar nineteen

tisAa nine

tisAeen ninety

tisAomaya nine hundred

tisbaH/tisbaHee Aala khayr good night (to man/woman)

tizkār souvenir

toHaf antiquities

toHfa antique

toltomaya three hundred

tomnomaya eight hundred

torāb dust

tormī tram

towSeel delivery (of mail)

tsharrafna nice to meet you

T

Ta'aya hat

TaAm taste; flavour

Taba' plate; dish, bowl

Tabakh cook

TabAan certainly, of course; definitely

   la' TabAan certainly not; of course not

TabeeAee natural

Taboor queue

Taf-fa switch off

Tafīya ashtray

TalaA go up

Talab ask

TamaA greedy

Tar fly

Tard package, parcel

Taree' road; avenue; route

Tawāri' emergency

Taweel long; tall

Tayr bird

TābeA stamp

Tālib/Tāliba student (male/female)

Tāza fresh

TeAem nice

Teen mud

Teez back part; bottom (of person)

Tefl child

Tekheen thick

Tīyāra plane, airplane

Tīyib OK

Tool height; length

Tool ellayl overnight

Tool el yōm all day

Tor'a corridor
Torab cemetery
Toro' map
Towālee straightaway

W

wa and
wa'af stop
wadee valley
wadee el mlook Valley of the Kings
wadee en-neel Nile Valley
wagaA hurt; pain; ache
wagba meal
wag-ha front
wagh eblee Upper Egypt
wag-hit el baHr seafront
waHda (f) one
waHda waHda gradually
waHeed alone
wala ana nor do I
wala Haga none
wala wāHid/waHda nobody
walad boy
walla otherwise
wallaA turn on, switch on
wallāAa, wallāAet sagāyer lighter
wana? and me?, what about me?
wara behind
wara' leaf; paper; banknote
wara' el bardee papyrus
wara' Ha'iT mural
wara' tawalet toilet paper
warda flower
warshit Aarabayyāt garage (for repairs)

wasākha dirt
waSal come; arrive, get in
waSl receipt
waSla connection
waSSal deliver
wa't time
wa't Taweel a long time
wazn weight
wāDiH clear
wāHa oasis
wāHid (m) one
wāTee low
we Alaykom es-salām reply to 'es-salāmoo Alaykom' (lit: and peace be upon you too)
we baAdayn then, after that
weddee friendly
weHesh bad; ugly; not nice; badly
   mish weHesh awee not so bad
weHesh awee ugly
wesikh filthy
wesT waist; centre
wesT el balad town centre; city centre
weSool arrival
widān ear
wikālit safar travel agent's
winta/winti? how about you? (to man/woman)
wish face

y

yaAnee so-so
yahoodee Jewish

yalla ... let's ...
  yalla besorAa! hurry up!
  yalla nimshee! let's go!
yanāyer January
yarHamkom allāh! bless you!
ye'khar delay
yemeen right (not left)
yeshmal include
yesmaH let (allow)
yetAash-sha have dinner
yimkin maybe; it depends
yolyo July
yonān: el yonān Greece
yonānee Greek
yonyo June
yowmayan daily
yōm day
  el yōm ellee ablo the day before
  el yōm ellee baAdo the day after
  el yōm et-tanee the other day
  yōm eg-gomAa at the weekend
yōm el arbaA Wednesday
yōm el Had Sunday
yōm el itnayn Monday
yōm el khamees Thursday
yōm es-sabt Saturday
yōm et-talāt Tuesday

Z
—

za' push
zaAlān angry
zaHma crowded
zakee intelligent

zamān a long time ago
zamb fault
zayt oil
zāhee bright (light etc)
zār visit
zibāla bin; dustbin, trashcan; rubbish, trash
zī the same; similar
zo'a' cul-de-sac
zokām cold (illness)
zōga wife
zōr throat

Z
—

Zarf envelope
Zābit bolees police officer

Arabic

→

English
Signs and
Notices

Contents

General Signs

خطر **khaTar** danger

خطر ممنوع اللمس **khaTar mamnooA ellams** dangerous, do not touch

... ممنوع **mamnooA ...** ... forbidden

إستعلامات **isteAlamāt** information

المفقودات **el mafQoodāt** lost property, lost and found

منطقة عسكريّة ممنوع الإقتراب أو التصوير **manTe'a Aaskarayya mamnooA el eQtirāb wat-taSweer** military zone, keep clear, no photography

ممنوع الإستحمام **mamnooA el estiHmām** no bathing

ممنوع التخييم **mamnooA et-takhyeem** no camping

ممنوع الدخول **mamnooA ed-dekhool** no entry, no admittance

ممنوع التصوير **mamnooA et-taSweer** no photographs

ممنوع التدخين **mamnooA et-tadkheen** no smoking

ممنوع السباحة **mamnooA es-sibāHa** no swimming

ممنوع المرور **mamnooA el moroor** no trespassing

Abbreviations

سم centimetres

جم grams

س hours

كجم kilograms

كم kilometres

ل litres

م metres

ملجم milligrams

ملل millitres

دق minutes

ق piastres

ج Egyptian pounds

Airport, Planes

مطار **maTār** airport

أوتوبيس المطار **otobees el maTār** airport bus

وصول **wesool** arrivals

249

مغادرة moghādara departures

رحلات دوليّة reHalāt
dowlayya international
departures

رحلات داخليّة reHalāt
dākhilayya domestic
departures

صالة الوصول sālit el wesool
arrivals hall

صالة السفر sālit es-safar
departure lounge

محطّة الوصول maHaTTit el
wesool destination

الرحلة تأخرت er-reHla
ta'akharit delayed

رقم الرحلة raQam er-reHla
flight number

تفتيش الحقائب tafteesh el
HaQā'ib baggage check

أخذ الحقائب akhd el HaQā'ib
baggage claim

التسجيل والدخول et-
tasgeel wed-dokhool
check-in

بوّابة bawwāba gate

إستعلامات isteAlamāt
information

Banks, Money

بنك 'bank' bank

بنك إسكندريّة 'bank'
iskinderaya Bank of
Alexandria

بنك القاهرة 'bank' el Qahira
Cairo Bank

بنك مصر 'bank' masr Masr
Bank

البنك الأهلى المصرى el
'bank' el ahlee el masree
National Bank of Egypt

الخزينة el khazeena cashier

قسم العملة الأجنبيّة qism el
Aomla el agnabaya foreign
exchange

ثمن الشرا taman esh-sherā'
buying rate

ثمن البيع taman elbayA selling
rate

نسبة التحويل nesbit et-
taHweel exchange rate

جنيه مصرى geneeh masree
Egyptian pound

قرش irsh piastre

جنيه إسترلينى geneeh

esterleenee pound sterling

دولار أمريكى dolār amreekee US dollar

دولار كندى dolār kanadee Canadian dollar

دولار أسترالى dolār ostrālee Australian dollar

كريدت كارد 'credit card' credit card

بنقبل الكريدت كارد bne'bal el 'credit cards' we accept credit cards

مابنقبلش الكريدت كارد ma bne'balsh el 'credit cards' credit cards not accepted

شيك سياحى sheek sayāHee traveller's cheque

Bus, Tram and Metro Travel

أوتوبيس otobees bus

مينى باص menibos minibus

موقف أوتوبيس mow'af otobees bus station

محطة أوتوبيس maHaTTit otobees bus stop

محطة maHaTTa terminal

رصيف raSeef ... bay no. ..., lane no. ...

وصول wesool arrivals

مغادرة moghādara departures

مخصّص لكبار السن mokhaSSaS le kebār es-sin reserved for the elderly

مكيّف mokayaf air-conditioned

تكييف takyeef air-conditioning

كشك تذاكر koshk tazākir ticket kiosk

رقم الكرسى raQam el korsee seat number

ترام 'tram' tram

تورماى toromāī tram

محطة ترام maHaTTit 'tram' tram stop

مترو metroo underground, (US) subway

Countries

الجزائر el gazayir Algeria

أمريكا amreeka America

أستراليا ostrālia Australia

251

كندا 'Canada' Canada

مصر maSr Egypt

إنجلترا ingiltera England

فرنسا faransa France

ألمانيا almāniya Germany

العراق el Arā' Iraq

إسرائيل isrā'eel Israel

الأردن el ordon Jordan

لبنان libnān Lebanon

ليبيا libya Libya

عمان Aomān Oman

فلسطين falasTeen Palestine

قطر Qatar Qatar

السعوديّة es-soAodayya
Saudi Arabia

السودان es-soodān Sudan

سوريا sorya Syria

تونس toonis Tunisia

تركيا torkaya Turkey

Customs

جمارك gamārik Customs

للأجانب فقط lil agānib faQaT
non-Egyptian passport
holders only

للمصريين فقط lil maSrayeen
faQaT Egyptian passport

holders only

فى حدود المسموح fee
Hodood el masmooH
nothing to declare

زيادة عن المسموح zayāda
Aan el masmooH something
to declare

جوازات gawazāt passports

مكتب النقد الأجنبى
maktab en-naQd el agnabee
currency declaration office

سوق حرّة soo' Horra duty-
free

Egyptian History

برج القاهرة borg el Qahira
Cairo Tower

القلعة el alAa Citadel

المماليك el mamaleek City of
the Dead (Tombs of the
Mamelukes)

كيلوباترا kelobatra Cleopatra

الدير البحرى ed-dayr el
baHree Hatshepsut's temple

إيزيس izees Isis

نفرتارى Nefertari Nefertari

نفرتيتى Nefertiti Nefertiti

الأهرام **el ahrām** The Pyramids

رمسيس **ramsees** Rameses

أبو الهول **aboo el hōl** The Sphinx

معبد أبو سمبل **maAbad aboo simbil** Temple of Abu Simbel

مدينة هابو **madeenit haboo** Temples of Rameses

وادى الملوك **wadee el mlook** Valley of the Kings

وادى الملكات **wadee el malekāt** Valley of the Queens

Emergencies

إسعاف **isAāf** ambulance

مطافئ **maTāfee** fire brigade

بوليس **bolees** police

مديرية أمن **moderayit amn** police headquarters

قسم ... **ism ...** ... Police Station

بوليس المطار **bolees el maTār** Airport Police

شرطة السكة الحديد **shorTit es-sikka el Hadeed** Railway Police

البوليس النهرى **el bolees en-nahree** River Police

شرطة السياحة **shorTit es-sayāHa** Tourist Police

بوليس المرور **bolees el mroor** Traffic Police

محطة إسعاف **maHaTTit isAāf** first-aid post

Forms

عنوان **Ainwān** address

العنوان فى مصر **el Ainwān fee maSr** address in Egypt

التاريخ **et-tareekh** date

تاريخ الميلاد **tareekh el milād** date of birth

تاريخ الصدور **tareekh essodoor** date of issue

مدّة الإقامة **moddit el iqāma** duration of stay

الإسم بالكامل **el esm bil kāmil** full name

الجنسيّة **el ginsaya** nationality

الوظيفة **el waZeefa** occupation

رقم الباسبور **raQam el**

253

basbōr passport number

محل الميلاد maHal el milād
place of birth

جهة الصدور gehit el eSdār
place of issue

الديانة el dayāna religion

التوقيع el towQeeA signature

رقم الفيزا raQam el veeza
visa number

رقم التأشيرة raQam el
ta'sheera visa number

Geographical Terms

حدود Hedood border

قناة Qanāl canal

دلتا delta delta

صحرا saHara desert

مركز markaz district

شرق shar' east

محافظة moHafza
adminstrative district

خليج khaleeg gulf

جزيرة gezeera island

بركة birka lake

جبل gabal mountain

شمال shimāl north

واحة wāHa oasis

راس ras point, head

مديريّة moderayya province

نهر nahr river

ملاحة mallāHa salt lake

جنوب ganoob south

عين Aayn spring

وادى wadee valley

غرب gharb west

Health

عيادة Aayāda clinic

دكتور/دكتورة doktōr/
doktōra doctor (m/f)

جرّاح/جرّاحة أسنان garrāH/
garrāHit asnān dentist (m/f)

مستشفى mostashfa hospital

قسم العيادة الخارجيّة Qism
el Aīyāda el khārigayya
outpatients' clinic

أجزاخانة agzakhāna
pharmacy, chemist's

صيدليّة sīdalayya pharmacy,
chemist's

Hiring, Renting

للإيجار lil egār for hire, to rent

عجل للإيجار Aagal lil eegār bicycles for hire

تأجير عربيّات ta'geer Aarabayyāt car rental

Hotels

فندق fondo' hotel

لوكاندة lokanda small hotel

بنسيون banseeyōn boarding house

بيت شباب bayt shabāb youth hostel

مساكن الطلبة masākin eT-Talaba hostel

إستراحة istirāHa resthouse

إوض فاضية ewaD faDiya rooms to let

أوضة ōDa room

أوضة بالتكييف ōDa bil takyeef room with air-conditioning

أوضة لشنين ōDa litnayn double room/twin room

أوضة لشنين ōDa litnayn double room

أوضة لواحد ōDa le wāhid single room

دورة الميّه dort el mīya toilet, rest room

تكييف takyeef air-conditioned; air-conditioning

حمّام Ham-mām bathroom

حمّام داخل الغرفة Ham-mām dākhil el ghorfa en-suite bathroom

حمّام خاص Hammām khās private bathroom

دوش dosh shower

حوض سباحة HōD sebāHa swimming pool

Notices on Doors

مفتوح maftooH open

مغلق moghlaq closed

دخول dekhool entrance

خروج khoroog exit

مخرج makhrag exit

باب الطوارئ bab eT-Tawāri' emergency exit

255

إسحب esHab pull

إدفع edfaA push

العطلة الأسبوعية el AoTla el isbooAayya closing days

من ... إلى ... min ... ila ... from ... to ...

مواعيد العمل mowAaeed el Aamal opening hours

ممنوع الدخول mamnooA ed-dikhool no entry

خاص khās private

Place Names

العبّاسية el Aabbāsayya Abbasiya

أبو سمبل aboo simbil Abu Simbel

إسكندريّة iskinderaya Alexandria

أسيوط asyooT Assyut

أسوان aswān Aswan

باب زويلة bab zwayla Bab Zuwaila

القاهرة el Qahira Cairo

دهب dahab Dahab

الفيّوم el fayyoom El Faiyum

الخارجة el kharga El Khargs

الموسكى el mooskee El Muski

السيّدة زينب es-sayyida zaynab El Saiyida Zeinab

إسنا esna Esna

الجيزة el geeza Giza

حلوان Helwān Helwan

الإسماعيليّة el ismaAelayya Ismailia

الكرنك el karnak Karnak

خان الخليلى khān el khaleelee Khan el Khalili

الأقصر loo'sor Luxor

المنيل el manyal Manial

مرسى مطروح marsa maTrooH Marsa Matra

المقطم el me'aTTam Mokattam

الجرنة الجديدة el gorna e-gedeeda New Gurna

مصر القديمة maSr el adeema Old Cairo

الجرنة القديمة el gorna el adeema Old Gurna

بورسعيد bor saAeed Port Said

سقّارة sa'-āra Sakkara

شرم الشيخ sharm esh-shaykh Sharm el Sheikh

سينا seena Sinai

سيوة seewa Siwa

السويس es-sways Suez

وادى حلفا wadee Halfa Wadi Halfa

Post Office

مكتب بريد maktab bareed post office

مكتب البوسطة الرئيسى maktab elbosTa elra'eesee main post office

خطابات khiTābāt letters, mail

بريد جوّى bareed gowee airmail

مستعجل mistaAgil express

عادى Aadee ordinary

خطابات داخليّة khiTābāt dakhilayya inland mail

خطابات خارجيّة khiTābāt khārigayya overseas mail

بيع الطوابع bayA eT-TawābeA stamps

Religion

اللّه allāh Allah

اللّه أكبر allāhoo akbar Allah is almighty

بسم اللّه الرحمن الرحيم besmillāh er-raHmān er-raHeem in the name of Allah most kind most merciful

الصبر جميل eS-Sabr gameel patience is beautiful

لا إله إلاّ اللّه la ilāh illa allāh there is no God but Allah

قبلة ibla facing Mecca

جماعة الإخوان المسلمين gamāAit el ekhwān el moslimeen The Muslim Brotherhood

محمّد moHammad Muhammad

القرآن el Qor'ān The Quran

رمضان ramaDān Ramadan

ذكر zikr religious ritual

جامع gāmiA mosque

جامع الأزهر gāmiA el az-har Al-Azhar mosque

257

مسجد الحسين **mazgid el Hosayn** Al-Hussein Mosque

جامع إبن طولون **gāmiA ibn Tolōn** Ibn Tulun Mosque

المتحف الإسلامى **el mat-Haf el eslāmee** Islamic Museum

جامع محمّد على **gāmiA moHammad Aalee** Muhammad Ali Mosque

جامع السلطان حسن **gāmiA es-soolTān Hasan** Sultan Hasan Mosque

Restaurants, Cafés, Bars

مطعم **maTAam** restaurant

حاتى **Hātee** kebab house

قهوة **ahwa** traditional coffee house, tearoom

نادى **nādee** coffee and gaming house

فطاطرى **faTāTree** pastry shop

حلوانى **Halawanee** patisserie

كافيتيريا **'cafeteria'** snack bar

كشرى **kosharee** snack bar

selling 'kosharee', an Egyptian rice speciality

بار **'bar'** bar

كازينو **kāzeno** bar and tea room, usually along the Nile

محل عصير **maHal AaSeer** juice bar

Streets and Roads

سكّة **sikka** alley

كورنيش **kornaysh** corniche, coastal road

زقاق **zo'ā'** cul-de-sac

عطفة **AaTfa** lane

حارة **Hāra** lane, alley

طريق **Taree'** road

ميدان **medān** square

شارع **shāriA** street

Timetables

جدول المواعيد **gadwal el mowaAeed** timetable, schedule

ميعاد الوصول **meAād el weSool** arrival time

258

وقت القيام wa't el Qayām
departure time

ميعاد القيام meAād el
Qayām departure time

درجة daraga class

نوع القطر nōA el aTr class of
train

إكسبريس 'express' express
train

سياحى sayāHee fast train
with limited stops

مجرى magaree fast train with
limited stops

درجة أولى daraga oola first
class

درجة تانية daraga tania
second class

جهة الوصول ... gehat el
weSool ... terminates at ...

رقم القطر raQam el aTr train
number

Toilets

للرجال lil rigāl gents' toilets,
mens' rest rooms

للسيّدات lil sīyedāt ladies'
toilets, ladies' rest rooms

دورة الميّة dowrit el mīya
toilet, rest room

دورات الميّة dawrāt el mīya
toilets, rest rooms

حمّامات عامّة Hammāmāt
Aamma public toilets

Tourist Information

حجز تذاكر طيران وبواخر
Hagz tazākir Tīyarān we
bawākhir advance booking
for air and sea travel

تأجير سيّارات وأوتوبيسات
ta'geer slyarāt we otobeesāt
car and bus rental service

رحلات يوميّة reHalat
yowmayya day trips

حجز فنادق Hagz fanādi'
hotel reservations

رحلات نيليّة reHalāt
neelayya Nile Cruises

رحلات سياحيّة reHalāt
sayaHayya package tours

259

Train Travel

محطّة قطر maHaTTit aTr
railway station

حجز تذاكر ... Hagz tazākir
... advance booking for ...

إستراحة istirāHa buffet

بوفيه bofayeeh buffet

محطّة مصر maHaTTit maSr
Cairo Main Railway Station

هيئة سكك حديد مصر hī'it
sekkak Hadeed maSr Egypt
Railways

درجة أولى daraga oola first
class

معلومات maAloomāt
information

أمانات amanāt left luggage,
baggage checkroom

رصيف ... raSeef ...
platform no. ..., track no. ...

درجة ثانية daraga tania
second class

درجة ثانية ممتازة daraga
tania momtāza second class
superior

درجة ثالثة daraga talta third

class

شبّاك تذاكر shebbāk tazākir
ticket office

تذاكر tazākir tickets

Menu Reader: Food

Essential Terms

bread Aaysh عيش

cup fongān فنجان

dessert Helw حلو

excuse me (to get attention) min faDlak من فضلك

fish (noun) samak سمك

fork shōka شوكة

glass (tumbler) kobbāya كوبّاية

  (wine glass) kās كاس

knife sikkeena سكينة

meat laHma لحمه

menu elmenew المنيو

pepper (spice) felfil eswid فلفل إسود

plate Taba' طبق

salt malH ملح

soup shorba شوربة

spoon maAla'a معلقة

starter (food) fateH lil shahayya فاتح للشهيّة

table tarabayza طرابيزة

excuse me! (to man) low samaHt! لو سمحت!

excuse me! (to woman) low samaHtee! جرسونة! لو سمحتى!

Basics

زبدة zebda butter

سمنة samna clarified butter

قشطة ishTa cream

دقيق di'ee' flour

عسل نحل Aasal naHl honey

مربّى miraba jam

لبن laban milk

عسل إسود Aasal eswid molasses

زيت zayt oil

زيت زيتون zayt zatoon olive oil

سكر sookkar sugar

خل khall vinegar

زبادى zabādee yoghurt

Bread

عيش Aaysh bread

عيش فينو Aaysh feeno baguette

صميت simeet bread rings covered with sesame seeds

فينو مدوّر feeno medowar bread rolls

ساندوتش 'sandwich' sandwich

عيش شامى Aaysh shāmee white pitta bread

عيش بلدى Aaysh baladee wholemeal pitta bread

Cheese

جبنة gibna cheese

جبنة فلاحى gibna fallāHee cottage cheese

جبنة رومى gibna roomee hard, yellow, mature cheese

جبنة قديمة gibna adeema mature 'gibna fallāHee'

جبنة تلاجة gibna talaga mild white cheese

جبنة مطبوخة gibna maTbookha processed cheese wedges

جبنة بيضة gibna bayDa salty white cheese, similar to feta

263

Condiments, Herbs, Spices

ينسون yansoon anise

فلفل أسود filfil eswid black pepper

حبهان Habahān cardamom

شطة shaTTa chilli

قرفة erfa cinnamon

قرنفل oronfil cloves

كزبرة kozbara coriander

كمون kamoon cumin

حلبة Helba fenugreek

كزبرة خضرة kozbara khaDra fresh coriander

زنجبيل zangabeel ginger

نعناع neAnāA mint

بهارات boharāt mixed spice

جوزة الطيب gōzit eTTeeb nutmeg

بقدونس ba'doonis parsley

زعتر zaAter oregano

فلفل أحمر filfil aHmar paprika

زعفران zaAfaran saffron

ملح malH salt

سمسم simsim sesame seeds

تمر هندى tamr hindee tamarind

كركم korkom turmeric

Cooking Methods

فى الفرن fel forn baked

مسلوق masloo' boiled

ديب فراى 'deep fry' deep-fried

مقلى ma'lee fried

مشوى mashwee grilled

بالزيت bi zayt in oil

مسبّك mesabek simmered

بالبخار bil bokhar steamed

محشى maHshee stuffed (usually with minced meat and/or rice, herbs and pine nuts)

Desserts, Cakes and Biscuits (Cookies)

حلويات Halawayāt sweets, desserts

كيكة keeka cake

بسكوت baskōt biscuits,

cookies

بقلاوة **be'lāwa** baklava – layers of flaky filo pastry and nuts, soaked in syrup

جلاش **goolāsh** baklava

كحك **kaнk** biscuits made with flour and butter and covered in icing sugar

خشاف **khoshaf** dried fruit soaked in milk or syrup (eaten during Ramadan)

زلابية **zalabya** fritters soaked in syrup

سلطة فواكه **salaтit fowākih** fruit salad

أم على **oom Aali** hot pudding made from filo pastry soaked in milk with raisins, sugar, coconut, nuts and cinnamon

أيس كريم **'ice cream'** ice cream

جيلاتى **Jelāti** ice cream

بليلة **bleela** milk pudding with nuts, raisins and wheat

مهلبية **mahalabaya** milk

pudding with rice, cornflour and rosewater, topped with pistachios

بالوظة **balōza** pudding made from cornflour, ground rice and sugar

مشمشية **meshmeshia** pudding made from cooked dried apricots and cornflour

أرز باللبن **roz bil laban** rice pudding

بسبوسة **basboosa** semolina cake with nuts, soaked in syrup

كنافة **konāfa** sticky noodle-like pastry with nuts and syrup

قطايف **aтayef** thick pancake filled with nuts and coconut and soaked in syrup

فطير **feтeer** type of pancake made from layers of flaky pastry with sweet or savoury fillings

Eggs and Egg Dishes

بيض bayD eggs

أطباق البيض aTbā' el bayD
egg dishes

عجّة Aega baked omelette
with onions, parsley and
flour

بيض مسلوق bayD masloo'
boiled eggs

بيض مقلى bayD ma'lee
fried eggs

أومليت 'omelette' omelette

بيض بكبدة فراخ bayD bi
kibdit frākh scrambled eggs
with chopped chicken
liver

شكشوكة shakshooka
scrambled eggs with
minced beef

بيض ببسطرمة bayD bi
basTerma scrambled eggs
with spicy cold meat

Fish and Fish Dishes

سمك samak fish

طاجن سمك Tāgin samak
baked fish with rice or
cracked wheat

كابوريا kaboriā crab

قراميط arameeT eel

ثعابين taAabeen eel

ترانشات taranshāt fillets

سمك مقلى samak ma'lee
fish fried in oil

سمك مشوى samak mashwi
grilled fish

إستاكوزا stakosa lobsters

بورى boree mullet

إخطبوط ekhTaboot octopus

طاجن جمبرى Tāgin
gambaree potted shrimps

جمبرى gambaree prawns;
shrimps

رز بالجمبرى roz bi
gambaree prawns and rice

فسيخ feseekh salted fish

سردين 'sardine' sardines

رنجة ringa smoked herring

كلمارى kalamari squid

سبيط **so**bayt squid

مرجان **mor**gan type of flat fish

بلطى **bol**Tee type of freshwater fish similar to bream

Fruit

فواكه fo**wā**kih fruit

تفاح to**ffāH** apples

مشمش **mish**mish apricots

موز **mōz** bananas

قشطة **esh**Ta custard apple

بلح **ba**laH dates

تين teen figs

تين شوكى teen **shō**ki Indian fig

عنب Aenab large, sweet grapes

عنب بناتى Aenab ba**nā**tee small, seedless grapes

جوافة ga**wā**fa guava

ليمون la**moon** lemons; limes

منجة **man**ga mango

شمام sha**mmām** melon

توت toot mulberries

برتقال بصرة borto'**ān** bi**so**ra navel oranges

برتقال borto'**ān** oranges

خوخ khōkh peaches

كمثرى **ko**mitra pears

أناناس ana**nās** pineapple

برقوق bar'**oo'** plums

رمان ro**mmān** pomegranates

سفندى safandee satsumas

فراولة fa**row**la strawberries

بطيخ ba**Teekh** watermelon

Meat and Meat Dishes

لحمة **laH**ma meat

لحمة بقرى **laH**ma ba'aree beef

مخ mokh brains

لحمة بقرى كندوز **laH**ma kan**dooz** braised beef

فراخ frākh chicken; grilled or stewed chicken, served with vegetables

شكشوكة shaksho**oka** chopped meat and tomato sauce with an egg on top

كباب **kabab** chunks of meat, usually lamb, grilled with onions and tomatoes

بط **baT** duck

وز **wizz** goose

حمام مشوى **Hamām mashwi** grilled pigeon

نص فرخة مشوية **noS farkha mashwaya** half a grilled chicken

كلاوى **kalāwi** kidney

لحمة ضانى **laHma Dānee** lamb; mutton

كبدة **kibda** liver

كفتة **kofta** minced meat flavoured with spices and onions, grilled on a skewer

شيش كباب وكفتة **sheesh kabab wi kofta** minced meat flavoured with spices and onions, grilled on a skewer

طرلى **Torlee** mixed vegetable casserole with chunks of lamb or beef

حمام **Hamām** pigeon

طاجن حمام **Tāgin Hamām** pigeon stewed with onions, tomatoes and rice in an earthenware pot (a Tāgin)

أرانب **arānib** rabbit

سجق **sogo'** sausages

لحم فيليه **laHma felay** sirloin steak

شاورما **showerma** slices of spit-roast lamb, served in pitta bread

كوارع **kawareA** sheep's trotters

لحمة قوزى **laHma oozee** spring lamb

رياش **rayash** T-bone steak

حمام محشى **Hamām maHshee** stuffed pigeon

ديك رومى **deek roomee** turkey

لحمة بتللو **laHma btelloo** veal

إسكالوب بتللو 'escalope' **bi telloo** veal escalope

Menu Terms

منيو 'menu' menu

لستة **lista** menu

مشروبات **mashrobat** drinks

أطباق البيض **aTbā'el bayD**
egg dishes

مشويات **mashwayat** grills

أطباق شرقية **aTbā' shar'aya**
oriental dishes

نشويات **nashowayat** rice,
pasta and potatoes

أنواع الشوربة **anwaA**
e-shorba soups

حلويات **Halawayat** sweets,
desserts

مقبلات **moqabbilāt** starter

مشهيات **moshahyāt** side
dishes

Nuts, Seeds etc

لوز **lōz** almonds

جوزهند **gōz hind** coconut

بندق **bondo'** hazelnuts

فول سودانى **fool soodanee**
peanuts

فزدق **fozdo'** pistachio nuts

حمص **Hommos** roasted
chickpeas, sugar-coated or
dried and salted

لب **lib** roasted seeds

(melon, sunflower etc)

عين جمل **Aayn gamal** walnuts

Pulses, Grains and Pasta

لوبيا **lobia** black-eyed
beans

فول مدمس **fool midamis**
brown Egyptian beans,
similar to broad/fava beans

فول **fool** brown Egyptian
beans, usually served with
oil and lemon, sometimes
also with onions, meat,
eggs or tomato sauce

حمص **Hommos** chickpeas;
houmous

فريك **freek** cracked wheat,
bulgur wheat

فلافل **falāfel** deep-fried
balls of spicy brown bean
purée

طعمية **TaAmaya** deep-fried
balls of spicy brown bean
purée

عدس بجبة **Aads bigebba**
green lentils

فاصوليا fa**So**lia haricot beans

عدس **A**ads lentils

عدس أصفر **A**ads **a**sfar red lentils

مكرونة makar**ō**na macaroni

مكرونة بالبشامل makar**ō**na bel bashamil pasta baked in bechamel sauce, similar to lasagne

أرز roz rice

كشرى ko**sh**aree rice, lentils, noodles and onions with a spicy tomato sauce

أرز بشعرية roz be she**A**raya rice with noodles

مكرونة عيدان makar**ō**na **A**īdan spaghetti

شعرية sha**A**raya vermicelli

Soups

شوربة sh**o**rba soup

أنواع الشوربة anw**ā**A e-sh**o**rba soups

شوربة فراخ sh**o**rbit fr**ā**kh chicken soup

شوربة عدس sh**o**rbit **A**ads lentil soup

شوربة لحمة sh**o**rbit la**H**ma meat soup

ملوخية molokh**a**ya soup made from Jew's mallow (similar to spinach) with meat or chicken broth and garlic

فتة fa**tt**a soup made from meat stock with bread, rice and tomato, sometimes with fried garlic and vinegar

شوربة طماطم sh**o**rbit **T**ama**T**em tomato soup

شوربة خضار sh**o**rbit kho**D**ār vegetable soup

Starters (Appetizers), Snacks, Side Dishes and Salads

بابا غنوج baba ghan-n**oo**g aubergine/eggplant purée with sesame-seed paste

حمص **H**omm**o**s chickpeas; houmous

تبولة **taboola** cracked wheat and tomato salad with onion and parsley

سلاطة زبادى **salaTit zabādi** cucumber and yogurt salad

طعمية **TaAmaya** deep-fried balls of spicy bean purée

فول مدمس **fool midamis** Egyptian brown bean purée

سلاطة خضرة **salāTa khaDra** green salad

بدنجان مخلل **bidingān mikhallil** marinated aubergine/eggplant

سلاطة شرقى **salāTa shar'ee** mixed vegetable and onion salad

طرشى **Torshi** pickles

سلاطة **salāTa** salad

طحينة **TeHeena** sesame-seed paste mixed with spices, garlic and lemon, eaten with pitta bread

سلاطة بيضة **salāTa bayDa** spiced yoghurt with herbs

سلاطططماطم **salaTit TamāTim** tomato salad

جبنة بيضة بالطماطم **gibna bayDa bi TamāTim** white cheese and tomato salad

ورق عنب **wara' Aenab** vine leaves stuffed with minced meat and/or rice, herbs and pine nuts and flavoured with lemon juice

Vegetable Dishes

بدنجان محشى **bidingān maHshee** stuffed aubergine/eggplant

كرنب محشى **koromb maHshee** stuffed cabbage

كوسة محشية **kosa maHshaya** stuffed courgettes/zucchinis

فلفل محشى **filfil maHshee** stuffed peppers

بطاطس محشية **baTāTis maHshaya** stuffed potatoes

طاجن خضار **Tāgin khoDār** vegetables baked with tomatoes

Vegetables

خضار **khoĐār** vegetables

خرشوف **kharshoof** artichokes

بدنجان **bidingān** aubergines, eggplants

فول حراتى **fool Herātee** broad beans

كرنب **koromb** cabbage

جزر **gazar** carrots

قرنبيط **arnabeeт** cauliflower

فلفل حامى **filfil Hāmee** chillies

كوسة **kosa** courgettes, zucchinis

قتة **atta** cucumber (large)

خيار **khiyār** cucumber (small)

ثوم **tōm** garlic

فاصوليا **faSolia** green beans

فلفل أخضر **filfil akhĐar** green peppers

فلفل أحمر **filfil aHmar** paprika; red peppers

خس **khass** lettuce

بامية **bamya** okra

بصل **baSal** onions

بسلة **bisilla** peas

بطاطس **baтāтis** potatoes

سبانخ **sabānekh** spinach beet

بصل أخضر **baSal akhĐar** spring onions, scallions

ذرة **dora** sweet corn, maize

بطاطا **baтāтā** sweet potatoes

طماطم **тamāтim** tomatoes

لفت **lift** turnips

ورق عنب **wara' Aenab** vine leaves

جرجير **gargir** watercress

فجل **figl** white radish

Menu
Reader:
Drink

Essential Terms

beer beera بيرة

bottle ezāza قزازة

  a bottle of beer ezāzit beera قزازة بيرة

coffee ahwa قهوة

cup fongān فنجان

glass (tumbler) kobbāya كوبّاية

  (wine glass) kās كاس

milk laban لبن

mineral water mīya maAdanaya ماء معدنيه

orange juice AaSeer borto'an عصير برتقال

red wine nebeet aHmar نبيذ أحمر

soft drink mashroob ghayr koHollee غير كوحولّى

sugar sokkar سكر

tea (drink) shī شاى

water mīya ميّة

white wine nebeet abyaD نبيت أبيض

wine nebeet نبيت

a cup of ..., please (to man/woman) fongān ..., low
samaHt/samaHtee فنجان. . . ، لو
سمحت/سمحتى

another beer, please (to man/woman) momkin beera tania, low
samaHt/samaHtee? ممكن بيرة ثانية لو
سمحت/سمحتي؟

Alcoholic Drinks

زبيب **zebeeb** an aniseed-
flavoured spirit, similar to
Greek ouzo

جاز **jaz** bottle; brandy

عمر الخيام **omar khīam** a
dry red wine

كرو دى بطليموس 'Cru des
Ptolémées' a dry white
wine

بيرة **beera** beer

ستيلا **beera stella®** lager

نبيذ أحمر **nebeet aHmar** red
wine

وردى **wardee** rosé wine

روبس دى إجبت **roobis**
'd'Egypt' a rosé wine

أحمر **aHmar®** a type of
brandy

معتق **meAatta'®** a type of
brandy

فين **vin®** a type of brandy

نبيذ أبيض **nebeet abyaD**
white wine

نبيذ **nebeet** wine

Coffee, Tea etc

قهوة **ahwa** coffee, Turkish
coffee

قهوة كابوتشينو **ahwa**
'cappuccino' cappuccino

قهوة محوجة **ahwa**
meHowega coffee spiced
with cardamom seeds

قهوة باللبن **ahwa bel laban**
coffee with milk

قهوة سادة **ahwa sāda**
coffee without sugar

قهوة إسبريسو **ahwa**
'espresso' espresso

قهوة مضبوطة **ahwa**
mazbooTa medium-sweet
coffee

قهوة فرنساوى **ahwa**
fransawi Nescafé; filter
coffee

قهوة عالريحة **ahwa Aar-**
reeHa slightly sweetened
coffee

قهوة زيادة **ahwa zayāda**
very sweet coffee

شاى **shī** tea

شاى باللبن shī bel laban
tea with milk

ينسون yansoon aniseed tea

قرفة erfa cinnamon tea

حلبة Нelba fenugreek tea

كركديه karkaday hibiscus
flower tea

شاى متلج shī metaleg iced
tea

شاى بالنعناع shī ben
neAnāA mint tea

سادة sāda without sugar

كاكاو kakow hot chocolate

سحلب saнlab hot drink
made from ground rice
and cornflour with milk,
sugar and nuts

Friut Juices and Other Soft Drinks

عصير موز AaSeer mōz
banana milk shake

عصير جزر AaSeer gazar
carrot juice

كاكولا kakoola® Coca
Cola®

سبورت كولا 'Sport Cola®'
(brand of) cola

خروب kharroob cold carob-
flavoured drink

عصير فواكه AaSeer
fowākih fruit juice

عصير جريب فروت AaSeer
graybfroot grapefruit juice

عصير جوافة AaSeer gowafa
guava juice

عصير لمون AaSeer lamoon
lemonade (made with real
lemon juice)

عرقسوس Aer'soos
liquorice water

عصير منجة AaSeer manga
mango juice

لبن laban milk

مية معدنية mīya
maAadanaya mineral water

بركة baraka® mineral water

سيوة Siwa® mineral water

كوكتيل 'cocktail' mixed
fruit juices

كندا دراى 'Canada dry'®
fizzy drink in a variety of
flavours

تيم **teem** ® orange drink

عصير برتقال **AaSeer borto'ān** orange juice

، سفن أب **7 Up'**® 7-Up®

عصير فراولة **AaSeer farowla** strawberry juice

عصير قصب **AaSeer 'asab** sugar cane juice

بيبسي **'Pepsi'**® Pepsi®

صودا **sōda** soda water

مشروب بيرل **mashroob birl** spring water

عناب **Aennab** tamarind and hibiscus drink

تمر هندى **tamr hindee** tamarind juice with water

مية **mīya** water